AT A TENDER AGE

AT A TENDER AGE

▪ Violent Youth ▪
and Juvenile Justice

RITA KRAMER

HENRY HOLT AND COMPANY
New York

Published by Henry Holt and Company, Inc.,
115 West 18th Street, New York, New York, 10011.
Published in Canada by Fitzhenry & Whiteside Limited,
195 Allstate Parkway, Markham, Ontario L3R 4T8.

Library of Congress Cataloging-in-Publication Data
Kramer, Rita.
At a tender age.
Bibliography: p.
Includes index.
1. Juvenile justice, Administration of—United
States—Case studies. 2. Juvenile delinquency—
United States—Case studies. 3. Violent crimes—
United States—Case studies. I. Title.
HV9104.K68 1988   364.3'6'0973   87–25202
ISBN: 0-8050-0419-X

First Edition

Designed by Curly-Q Designs
Printed in the United States of America
1 3 5 7 9 10 8 6 4 2

ISBN 0-8050-0419-X

CONTENTS

v

vi · Contents

ACKNOWLEDGMENTS

This book grew out of a suggestion made by my friend, the historian Diane Ravitch, who always gives me a push toward my next project, and who, in the summer of 1983, introduced me to Diane Kemelman, the administrative assistant corporation counsel of the City of New York, who in turn introduced me to Family Court. The two Dianes thought I would find what went on there interesting and, for the next three years, I did.

Many people were enormously helpful to me in the researching and writing of this book. Some of them—I think of Peter Reinharz and Philip Dobbs in particular—are identified in its pages. Peter sometimes seemed to be administering a law school with a class of one. He was a brilliant and enthusiastic teacher, and any errors that have crept into the text are the fault of the pupil, not the professor. Among those whose names do not appear in the book but whose help was invaluable were Suzanne K. Colt, then borough chief of the Manhattan Family Court division and now deputy division chief of the Office of the Corporation Counsel in Family Court for all five boroughs of New York City, who always found time to answer my questions about the law and the way it is applied in Family Court, and Stephen J. Bogacz, borough chief of the Queens Family Court division of the Corporation Counsel, who took me under his wing so I could observe the workings of the system.

I want to thank my agent, Michael Congdon, who saw this project through from the proposal stage and never faltered in his efforts on its behalf, and my skilled and tenacious editor, Marian Wood, who astonished me by really editing this book, challenging facts, demanding evidence, and suggesting better ways to put things in an age when many editors limit their activities to merely acquiring the books they publish.

All of these people—and the others who appear in these pages—made contributions to what is best about this book. Whatever its shortcomings, they are my responsibility, as are its conclusions.

There remains only to mention the one person without whom I could not have undertaken, persisted in, or finally shaped this book, my husband of almost four decades, Yale Kramer. Friend, critic, computer consultant, reader, editor, and patient listener, he made it all worthwhile. This book is dedicated to him.

AT A TENDER AGE

INTRODUCTION

When an individual actually enters upon a criminal career, let us try to catch him at a tender age, and subject him to rational social discipline . . .

> —Charles H. Cooley, " 'Nature v. Nurture' in the Making of Social Careers," *Proceedings of the National Conference of Charities and Corrections*, 1896

At twelve years of age, Billy L.* stands five feet eight and weighs 128 pounds. In the early morning hours of a Friday late in August 1984, Billy and two companions, sixteen-year-old Frankie W. and thirteen-year-old Jimmy P., came on a bag lady asleep on a bench in Central Park. According to Frankie's later account, Billy hit her on the head with a piece of pipe, saying, "Give me some pussy," and told the others to hold her legs. They took turns holding her down and repeatedly raping and sodomizing her. Later they reported dispassionately that she kept crying out, "Oh, God, please help me," and that afterward they beat her with their fists and kicked her on the body and face, and that then Billy found a stick in the bushes with which he hit her, stopping only when a light scared them off and the boys ran out of the park. The

*The cases in this book are real. Only the names have been changed.

1

woman's blood was on Billy's hands and clothing when the three were apprehended by police officers. They were taken in for questioning, and the two youngest were eventually tried in New York's Family Court; there, Billy was found to have committed an act "which if committed by an adult [a person over the age of sixteen] would constitute the crime of attempted rape in the first degree" and was given the maximum penalty provided for any act—even murder—committed by a person twelve years of age or younger: placement for a period of up to eighteen months. There is no legal minimum penalty.

While at the upstate facility, rather like an austere boys' camp, at which he was serving his eighteen months, Billy L. was brought back to Manhattan to be arraigned on an armed robbery charge. The robbery had occurred the previous April. Had that case been heard earlier, rather than having been scheduled on the court calendar some months after the time of his arrest, Billy might not have been in Central Park in August.

That same August, Tony S. turned fifteen. A handsome boy with long dark eyelashes and a pouty mouth, he had a short school attendance record, a medium-sized drug habit, a flashy wardrobe, and a reputation as a "chicken"—a young homosexual hustler—on the Lower East Side. He also had six previous appearances in Family Court, on charges from petty to grand larceny, when he was arrested for a robbery—a chain snatch—a few days after his birthday. Because the judge considered the identification by the victim and a witness to be insufficient since it was based partly on the clothes the thief was wearing at the time, the case was adjourned in contemplation of dismissal, meaning that if Tony kept out of trouble for six months, it would be dismissed finally and the records sealed.

Nine days later, Tony was arrested on First Avenue in the

Sixties, where he had grabbed a shoulder bag from a young woman coming home from a party. It was late and dark and there were not many people on the street, but when the victim's husband dropped his jacket and briefcase and started to chase after the thief, her cries caught the attention of a passerby who joined the chase from the other direction and Tony was caught between the two pursuers. The victim remembers that Tony glared at her defiantly and said, "Go on, bitch, call the cops. They can't do anything to me, I'm not sixteen yet."

On a steamy afternoon later that month, the police were staked out near the entrance to the subway station at Forty-sixth Street and Sixth Avenue. An old man had been killed there a few days earlier, pushed down the stairs in an attempted mugging. Tyrone B. had been hanging around the entrance eyeing the passersby when, around three o'clock, he saw an eighty-four-year-old woman and grabbed at her handbag. The strap was over her arm and as she clutched it to her chest, he grabbed at the bag, slamming her to the ground, cracking her head and smashing her hip. She was unable to give up the bag and he was pulling her along the sidewalk, slamming her on the ground and into the side of a building, when the police rushed him. The woman died in the hospital ten days later, and Tyrone B. was charged with manslaughter. Tyrone could not be charged with felony murder (murder occurring in the commission of a crime) because he was twelve years old and, under New York's Family Court Act, a person of his age cannot be convicted of a crime, but can only be "found to have committed an act which if committed by an adult would constitute the crime" of, say, robbery or assault. Since technically he could not be found to have committed a crime, he could not be found to have committed a murder in the commission of a crime.

Tyrone was sent to a youth facility about a hundred miles

north of New York City and was eligible for home visits after six months. After seventeen months of his eighteen-month term, he was transferred to a foster home in the city as part of a re-entry program designed to facilitate the return of the child to the community. A few weeks later, on a subway platform in lower Manhattan, he grabbed a woman's handbag. He gave her a push with his free hand and she lost her balance. She would have fallen onto the tracks except that he was still pulling at her bag and the strap was still around her shoulder, so he inadvertently pulled her toward him and away from the tracks. By this time a crowd had gathered and Tyrone was chased out of the subway, grabbed on the street, and held until the police arrived. At his arraignment, the Division for Youth recommended that he be returned to the foster home, but the request was denied. He was sent back upstate to the same unlocked facility, the most stringent option allowed in New York for a boy his age, no matter what the offense.

Rodney R. had already served eighteen months for robbery involving sexual abuse when he was put in a lineup with some other boys around his age, which was fourteen at the time. One of the other boys in the lineup had identified Rodney as his accomplice, but the victim could not do so. She had described the attack, in which her purse had been taken and she had been left torn and bleeding, and she could identify the other boy, whose face she had seen when he raped her, but she was unable to positively identify Rodney as the one who had sodomized her. She was crying as she shook her head to indicate that she could not pick the second boy out of the group. When it was clear that she could not identify him, Rodney's lawyer, appointed to represent him by Legal Aid, leaned over and hugged and kissed him. "Great!" she said, beaming at him. "We won!" Rodney was later identified as the perpetrator of another rape and sent away for eighteen months to an unlocked facility upstate, this time with the proviso that the Division for Youth could place him in a secure (locked) facility if he did not behave in the less restrictive one.

The cases of Billy L., Tony S., and the others are among those I became familiar with in the course of three years as an observer in the various parts of New York City's Family Court. In those three years I had a unique opportunity to glimpse a world and a process that, with rare and infrequent exceptions, are closed to press and public. This book is an attempt to explore some of the social, psychological, and political issues raised by these cases and to challenge some of the assumptions behind the laws and institutions that constitute the juvenile justice system today.

In the course of observing the proceedings in Family Court, cases of delinquency, neglect and abuse, custody, PINS (youngsters alleged by their parents to be Persons in Need of Supervision),* and more delinquency, I have found they form a continuum from the abused infant to the abusing adolescent. I have also found that what happens in the courtroom is never very much of the whole story, and in attempting to learn more of the background of the cases and of the people involved, I have talked with many of them—judges, lawyers on both sides, probation officers, social agency workers, court psychologists, the parents and grandparents of complainants

---

*While delinquents are underage criminals, there is a group of youngsters who run afoul of the law as status offenders, youngsters guilty of no crime, of nothing that would constitute a crime if done by an adult, but of acts that are only unlawful for juveniles. These are the truants, the runaways, the troublemakers in school, the ones who can't get along with their parents. In New York they are known as PINS—Persons in Need of Supervision. In other states they are known as MINS (Minors in Need . . .), FINS (Families . . .), JINS (Juveniles . . .) or CHINS (Children . . .). Various states define them as anywhere from under sixteen to under twenty-one, with under eighteen as most common.

and respondents (victims and victimizers) as well as the youngsters themselves—and recorded hours of taped comments, some casual, some more formal. These interviews put the issues in the words of those on the front line, words often more vivid than those of the battle correspondent who sums them up.

I have also talked with police officers, with teachers in "trouble" schools, and with staff members of upstate locked facilities, as well as with teenagers sent to these places for the most serious crimes—the ones I've found most interesting and most willing, even eager, to talk with me. Some of their ideas about their earliest encounters with the legal system are eye-opening. As far as I know, with the exception of a reporter for *The New York Times* and a TV documentary crew a few years ago, occasional visits from lawyers being trained to practice in Family Court, and a few members of the Juvenile Justice Committee of the Association of the Bar of the City of New York and the Vera Institute of Justice preparing reports and publications for their organizations, I am the only outsider to have visited these facilities recently and talked with the residents.

While my own observations have been made in New York City's Family Court system, official statistics, published results of research studies, news reports, and comments by juvenile justice officials elsewhere indicate that New York's problems—and the system's failure to solve them—are paradigmatic for other large cities throughout the country as well. From Los Angeles to Washington, D.C., from Detroit to Miami, similar patterns of increasing violence by the young accompany the disintegration of the traditional family and the breakdown of other social structures and institutions, from the neighborhood to the church.

By the beginning of 1987 it was clear that juvenile crimes of violence were on the increase. Shootings by teenagers drove homicide rates up, and crime rates in 1986 were on the way back up to the all-time record highs of the mid-1970s. In New York, Detroit, Los Angeles, and Chicago, drug-related crimes proliferated with the spread of cocaine and its derivative crack. New York, Washington, Atlanta, Miami, Boston, Philadelphia, St. Louis, Baltimore, and Dallas all reported steeply rising crime rates, with teenagers responsible for a growing number of killings, many of them over drugs and many others over things like a pair of sneakers, a fancy shirt, or a bit of loose change.

In the face of a growing nationwide incidence of brutal crimes of random violence by younger and younger criminals—often "mere children"—our present judicial response is inadequate and often inappropriate. It seems to give insufficient weight to the sufferings of the victims—most of whom come from the same minority underclass as most of the violent young criminals—and the effects on the rest of the community.

The obsolescent philosophy behind the present system of laws dealing with violent young criminals gives far more emphasis to their youth than to their crimes. It is a system grounded on the belief in rehabilitation and it was designed to deal with delinquents who stole hubcaps, not those who mug old ladies. It makes the courts a kind of sanctuary for the most vicious among the criminal young while paradoxically it fails at the same time to reach and effectively deal with those who might be deterred from a life of crime.

It is the failure of the present juvenile justice system either to restrain or retrain the violent young that is its most striking feature and the subject of this book.

1

The Violent Few

Chronic offenders started their violent harm early in life, and will apparently continue if allowed to do so.

> —Paul E. Tracy, Marvin E. Wolfgang, and Robert M. Figlio, *Delinquency in Two Birth Cohorts* (Washington, D.C.: Office of Juvenile Justice and Delinquency Prevention, 1985)

Persons under the age of adulthood are subject to a special set of laws. In New York the age is sixteen; in many states it is eighteen; elsewhere it varies from fourteen to twenty-one. The law defines a juvenile delinquent as someone over seven and under the age of legal majority who does something that would be a crime if done by an adult but who is not criminally responsible for what he has done because of his age ("by reason of infancy").

With minor variations, the process that follows the arrest of a juvenile is similar in all states. The individual is ordered to appear in the juvenile court, called Family Court in New York, where, in a procedure called intake, he is seen by an officer of the court. In New York, this is a probation officer.

At intake, cases are screened and may be adjusted (dismissed). This is sometimes referred to as diversion from the

8

(legal) system and is usually the option applied in first offenses and/or less serious cases. The other option is to send the juvenile on through the court process. In these cases, the next step, comparable to arraignment in adult criminal court, is usually taken on the same day, following intake.

A petition (a statement of the charges) is drawn up by the city's legal department, which will present (prosecute) the case against the juvenile. If he is detained (jailed, in adult terms), either because of the seriousness of the charge against him or because there is considered to be a risk that he will not return to court, he must be brought back to court within three days for a judicial hearing, the purpose of which is to determine whether there is probable cause to believe he has committed the act with which he is being charged. Less serious cases not requiring a probable cause hearing may go directly to trial.

At the probable cause hearing he will have a lawyer to represent him and argue the case on his behalf. If the judge finds that there is probable cause, the juvenile will be returned to court within the next ten days for a fact-finding hearing, a procedure corresponding to a trial in the adult system.

If the juvenile is not detained, he is paroled to his parents (or whoever is legally responsible for him) until the fact-finding hearing, which will be scheduled within six weeks of his first appearance at intake. If he is judged guilty at the fact-finding, a dispositional hearing will be scheduled about eight weeks later, when he will be returned to court again for what corresponds to sentencing in the adult system.

In the case of a juvenile in detention, the dispositional hearing must be held within twenty days of the fact-finding hearing.

On the basis of the facts as presented in court and the background information presented by an investigating probation officer and any experts, the judge must determine whether the youth needs supervision, treatment, or confinement. If none of these is required, the case may be dismissed and the record will be sealed. In other cases, the judge may choose one of several options: The juvenile may be placed on probation and referred to a social service agency; he may be given a conditional discharge, sometimes under the supervision of an official of the court system; or he may be placed in a special institution for juveniles. Such institutions range from small, informally run group homes in the city to large, high-security institutions in isolated areas of the state. Group homes may be run by private social agencies contracting with the city and/or state; limited-secure and high-secure institutions, referred to legally in New York as Title II and Title III, are run by the state's Division for Youth. Limited-secure facilities rely on close supervision by staff and on geographical isolation; secure facilities have locked rooms and razor-wire fences and are comparable to adult prisons. A juvenile may be placed in an institution for an initial period of up to eighteen months.

In any case that results in a disposition favorable to the respondent (the accused), the records will be sealed. This means not only cases in which the juvenile has been found not to have committed a delinquent act, but cases in which for some technical reason—such as the failure of victim or witnesses to appear or some procedural irregularity resulting in the inadmissibility of physical evidence or of the respondent's statement (confession)—the case has not resulted in a finding against the juvenile. This can result in a juvenile respondent having several sealed cases prior to the one being heard. The judge will know of their existence but will know nothing of their nature.

In New York, the most serious crimes of violence (including murder, rape, assault with a deadly weapon, kidnapping, arson) involving juveniles fourteen and older (and thirteen-year-olds in the case of murder) are not afforded the protection of the juvenile court and may be tried in the adult system.* The district attorney may, however, decide not to try the case in State Supreme Court,† but to refer it back to Family Court. Juries are often reluctant to reach verdicts that might result in the imposition of harsh sentences on the young. And even in the case of a conviction by a jury, the juvenile offender is not subject to the same penalties as the adult criminal.

In the courtroom, one sees a mere boy looking chastened, even frightened, his age very young, the charge against him just a word. Even if the word is murder, or rape, there is no victim present to bring the word to life. The blood has dried, it all happened some time ago, and the boy can easily seem pathetic—a troubled youth. Like Billy L., who led the attack on the bag lady. Here is the story of that August night, pieced together from what the three youths told the police later:

Jimmy P., who was thirteen at the time, and Frankie W., at sixteen, the oldest of the three, were on their way downtown when they met twelve-year-old Billy on the subway platform at 116th Street and Lenox Avenue. Billy had a reputation as a "mean dude." According to Jimmy, "We ran behind the gate. . . . Billy said why you all ducking me. . . . He said he ain't going to get us in trouble." The three of them

*In New York, these juvenile offender cases start in the adult system and may be referred down to Family Court. In a number of other states, they start in the juvenile court and may be waived up to the adult system.
†In New York, this is the highest trial court and the one in which felonies, crimes for which the penalty is a sentence of a year or more, are tried. Misdemeanors, crimes for which the penalty is less than a year, are tried in Criminal Court.

rode down to Times Square, where they went to a movie, and then walked uptown to Columbus Circle, where they entered Central Park. They saw a man in the park, and Billy came up behind him and "yoked him," put his arm around the man's neck from behind and held him, while Frankie and Jimmy checked his pockets. He had no money and they let him go. "We kept walking," Billy says, "and when we saw the old lady laying on the bench, Frankie said to her, 'What are you, dead?' and we started to laugh. Frankie pulled the bag off her and said, 'I want to fuck you.' Me and Jimmy laughed."

Jimmy says, "I held her legs and Billy said, 'One of ye all hold her hands' and Frankie held her hands. Billy was fucking her while she was on the bench and the old lady was saying, 'Oh, my God, help me.' She said it four times.

"Then Frankie said, 'Let me get the back,' and while Frankie had the back I was holding her hands. She was saying the same thing, 'Help me, God,' while Frankie was fucking her. Then Billy came on her legs. While I was holding her hands Billy said, 'Put her on the ground,' and Frankie came on her. I was holding her on the ground with Frankie while Billy went for a stick in the bushes. Frankie stood over her and jerked off on her stomach and her face. Billy came back with the stick and he hit her on the head about five times."

Billy adds, "She started hollering and Frankie slapped and punched her. Jimmy took his dew rag and put it in her mouth. Frankie kicked her in the face . . . and then he jumped on her head . . . I kicked her once to see if she was alive."

According to Jimmy, Billy kicked the woman in the head five times while she was on the ground and then jumped on her back. Then they started running.

As they left the park, they saw a police patrol car

coming. They went up to it and told the officers inside that someone had left a bleeding woman in the park, evidently thinking this would divert suspicion from them. For a moment, it did.

It was not until a vagrant who had seen the boys earlier gave a description of them—Billy was a particularly striking figure in his white hat—that the police put three and one together and radioed to another car to pick them up, which they did, locating them a few blocks away on Fifth Avenue.

During questioning, Jimmy had something else to tell the detective who was interviewing him: Frankie had told him that Billy had raped and beaten up another old lady in the park. What Frankie had not told him, or what Jimmy was not telling the detective at any rate, was that Frankie had been with Billy on that occasion, too, and that Billy, after raping her, had killed the woman. He had beaten her to death.

In cities throughout this country today, small groups of boys like Jimmy, Billy, and Frankie, acting "in concert," as the law puts it, are responsible for a large proportion of robberies and other acts of violence involving guns and other weapons. While young males are responsible for most crime, only a small number of them, perhaps as few as 6 per cent of all delinquent juveniles, are responsible for most of the violent crime committed by juveniles. What's more, those who commit serious crimes do so frequently—more frequently than statistical tables indicate. Many delinquent boys report having committed about ten serious crimes for every one for which they were arrested.

Youngsters who commit delinquent acts don't specialize in a particular type of crime, violent or nonviolent. They show a versatility of involvement in illegal behavior; but although they can't be divided into those who commit acts of violence and those who do not, there is a group that commits more frequent crimes, including more serious acts of violence—classified by the F.B.I. as "index crimes"—than others. It is not committing any one kind of crime but the frequency and seriousness of involvement in various kinds of criminal behavior that are the best predictors of future serious criminal activity. Moreover, those who commit the more serious crimes begin their careers with these crimes; they don't work up to them gradually, which leads one to believe they are a particular type of individual.

And in fact numerous statistical studies have consistently suggested a profile of violent juvenile offenders. They are most typically black or Hispanic males from unstable, often one-parent families in which there is a high degree of conflict; they are usually on bad terms with their parents, who provide little or no supervision, and were very young when they began to commit violent acts, usually in groups. They tend to be school failures with conduct problems as well as academic ones, and for all practical purposes are unemployable because they exhibit the same conduct problems on a job as in school.

Frankie, the sixteen-year-old involved in the August rape of the bag lady in Central Park, had four previous arrests, three of them for assault, including one incident in which he had thrown a woman teacher down a flight of stairs. Interviewed at the precinct house after being apprised of his rights in the presence of his father, Frankie offered some further information. He and Billy and another boy, Wayne M., fourteen, had raped another homeless woman in the park a month earlier, "and did the same thing as they did to the lady last night." Not quite the same, actually, since the first woman had been killed after she had been raped. Billy had beaten her to death after he and Frankie and the other undeniably troubled youth, Wayne, had raped and sodomized her and attempted to set her on fire.

The Kerbs Boathouse at the pond near Fifth Avenue and Seventy-second Street in Central Park stands between the statue of Alice in Wonderland and a children's sandbox. In the afternoons and on weekends, schoolchildren swarm over the statue and toddlers make sand pies under the watchful eyes of well-dressed East Side parents and uniformed nannies. Model-boat fanciers sail their craft in the pond, where boathouse members frequently hold races, returning them afterward to their stands in the boathouse. Strollers are reminded of the Luxembourg Gardens on the Tuileries in Paris. It's one of New York's pleasantest scenes.

On a night just a month before the August rape, the battered body of a woman had been found leaning against the wall of the boathouse. In the photographs taken at the scene she looks like a rag doll a careless child had thrown down and abandoned on the ground in order to go off and climb the statue or play in the sandbox. Her striped cotton dress is up above her bare thighs, her legs are apart, her feet splayed out in yellow socks and sneakers, and her head hangs to one side, her long gray hair partially covering her bruised face. She is covered with blood. According to the police report, a plastic bag with the word "ice" on it had been stuffed in her mouth. It too was covered with blood from inside her mouth. On the ground nearby was a green backpack containing, according to the same police report, "misc. items of food" and "misc. items of clothing." Also nearby was a golf club. The report identified it as a putter. It had been used, along with fists and feet, to kill Mary Evans (not her real name), fifty-one years old, who had lived in the park since the hotel on East Seventieth Street where she had lived alone had closed.

The mail carrier remembered Mary Evans. The only mail she received, as he remembered it, was from the Social Security Administration and a city agency concerned with Medicaid. "At no time did she ever mention family or friends," the report stated, "nor was she ever seen with anyone." Since she had begun to live on the street she had kept a post-office box and it was the post-office employee in charge of the boxes who went to the morgue to identify her body.

In an attempt to locate possible witnesses, a detective interviewed several people who were in the vicinity of the killing. Their addresses are given as "usually sleeps at Madison Ave. and 71st Street"; "sleeps on park benches"; "sleeps in park or downtown in the 60s along Madison Avenue." The interview report concludes: "The above-named persons were interviewed; no information concerning the homicide was obtained." None would be obtained until two of the three boys involved in the killing of Mary Evans were caught trying it again.

This is how Frankie described that July incident:

"We walked down a hill towards a house and then we saw this lady sleeping on the bench. Billy said, 'Let's drag her behind the house.' I smacked her on the side of her face and she said, 'Hey!' Billy put his hand over her mouth to keep her from screaming and then we all dragged her behind the house. We started taking her clothes off. Billy took off her panties. Wayne pulled up her shirt. I took off her shoes. We were feeling on her body. She was fighting us back so I smacked her and Billy smacked her twice and Wayne smacked her once. Then she stopped fighting. She was lying on the ground. Billy climbed on top of her and [the police officer who took down Frankie's statement, perhaps reluctant to offend or embarrass the members of the grand jury to whom it would be read, here did a bit of bowdlerizing and wrote down Frankie's next words as "inserted his penis in her vagina"] while Wayne and I held her down. I held her hands back over her head while Wayne held her feet apart. When Billy finished, Wayne got on her and Billy held her hands while I held her feet."

Leaving Wayne to manage on his own, Frankie and Billy walked over to the boathouse a few feet away and "we climbed up to the window and bent the metal bars back. I boosted Billy so he could get in the window. Then I went back to the woman. Wayne had finished and was fixing his clothes. I put my knees on her shoulder to hold her down. . . ."

While Frankie took his turn, Wayne went over to the house, where, according to Frankie, "Billy passes out to him a golf club and a stick. . . . Wayne helps him climb out of the window. Then Billy and I help Wayne into the window. The woman was laying on the ground . . . She started to get up and Billy ran over and pushed her back down to the ground . . . Billy is beating the woman on the ground with the golf club all over her body. I go and help Wayne climb out of the window and then he goes over and starts hitting the woman with the stick . . . Before we left we brought some twigs and put them around her body so we could set her on fire . . ."

Frankie continues: "We headed home while we talked about what we did. We all agreed not to tell anybody on the block about what we did." Wayne—who was arrested the morning after the August incident, having been named by Frankie as a participant in the earlier rape and killing—claimed, "All I did was hold the lady" for the others, who did all the raping, sodomizing, and beating of Mary Evans while he simply continued to look on. ("I did not get on top of the lady, I just held her" [while] "she was beat with the golf club and hands.") He ends the story in what could almost be a parody of a scene from *The Adventures of Tom Sawyer:* "We left the park and went to Fifth Avenue. We made an oath not to tell anybody about it . . . We all put our hands one on top of the other while we made the oath. We said that whoever tells and breaks the oath, they would be beat up by the others."

Juvenile crime has changed in the last two or three decades. The most important studies of juvenile crime have shown interesting and highly significant shifts in the nature of criminal acts since the 1960s. Of some 10,000 males born in Philadelphia in 1945, fewer than 7 percent were found to be responsible for more than half of all juvenile crimes and over two-thirds of the violent crimes committed by juveniles. When the study was repeated with 14,000 males born in 1958, a comparably small percentage of chronic offenders was again found to be responsible for the majority of crimes by the young—with this difference: In the second group, raised during the turbulent 1960s and 1970s, the rate of rapes and aggravated assaults had doubled, the rate of murders had tripled, and the rate of robberies had increased fivefold.

Not only do we know that a small group of young males is responsible for most violent crime by juveniles; we also know that these offenders start early and finish late. Studies have demonstrated that a substantial proportion of the violent few continued to commit crimes as adults and, of those who did, most had been arrested for the first time at the age of twelve or even younger.

On the New York City Police Department's Juvenile Arrest Report filed on the August morning after the boys had been

taken to the precinct house, Billy L. was charged with second-degree murder and assault in that he "w/2 others did
assault one Evans, Mary, causing to her death . . . weapon
poss/used: blunt instrument."

He was not charged with first-degree murder because it is
a capital offense and New York State has no death penalty.
However, even the second-degree murder charge did not stick.
Billy never admitted to the July killing, about which there
was only the evidence of his two companions against him.
The statements of co-perpetrators are not sufficient to convict
without independent corroborating testimony. Although both
Frankie and Wayne had told the same story with the same
details in separate interviews without having had a chance to
talk about their versions of the events beforehand, it was Billy
who had the last word. He maintained coolly, "I don't know
nothing about no killing," and added, "You ain't got nothing
on me." In the matter of the August rape, in which he had
beaten the victim bloody, and her blood was found on his
shoes, he pleaded guilty to attempted rape in the first degree.
The victim, who had lived on the streets and in the park since
being released from a mental institution, was unable to testify
against him, since it was her belief that the attack was part
of a government plot against her. Billy was sent to Camp
Tryon, an open facility in upstate New York, for a period of
up to eighteen months.*

A little over a year after the rape of the bag lady, Billy
was moved from the upstate camp to a facility called a youth
development center, the first step in DFY's community re-

*There was no authorization granted for placing him in a locked facility. The
law does make provision for the Division for Youth to extend the placement for
another twelve months at a time, after a hearing, and this can continue until
he reaches the age of eighteen. DFY can also release him if they feel there is no
need to provide him with further services because he has been rehabilitated or
if they feel they are unable to provide him with further services because he is
incorrigible.

entry program. The center was further upstate, but there were more frequent home visits. On one of these, Billy disappeared. A member of the Corporation Counsel staff, who remembers Billy, thought she saw him in Central Park one morning while she was jogging, the day after a derelict was found beaten to death and sexually mutilated. "It was his m.o.," she says.

2

As Children Apart

A main objective of [the] special system of law . . . for treating young juvenile offenders is to hold them as children apart from usual methods and ineradicable consequences of the criminal law.

—from Notes of Decisions, *Family Court Act* (1983), Article 3, Part 1, Separation of Juvenile Offenders

It was the weekend of the Shavod Jones case. All the newspapers had just finished covering the historic Fourth of July ceremonies celebrating the centennial of the Statue of Liberty, events for which the city had been blanketed in blue with uniformed police in evidence on almost every corner from the Battery to the north end of Central Park, and which ended with no violence to report beyond a couple of small boats sinking during the harbor festivities.

The next day, with police coverage returned to normal, a released mental patient went berserk on the Staten Island ferry and attacked several people with a saber, killing and wounding at random. And the following weekend, a young officer on anti-crime patrol in Central Park approached three suspicious-looking boys near the lake at the north end of the park. He'd observed them fanning out as they approached a bicyclist and recognized the usual preparations for stealing a bike.

As twenty-nine-year-old Steven McDonald approached, clearly identifying himself as a police officer, one of the three boys, fifteen-year-old Shavod Jones, turned around, removed a .22-caliber Saturday night special from his pants waistband, turned back, and shot Officer McDonald three times. One of the bullets hit McDonald in the neck, fragmenting in his spinal column and leaving him paralyzed from the neck down.

The papers reported the facts about McDonald, a third-generation New York cop, and his young wife, pregnant with their first child, but most of the coverage was on Jones.

Shavod Jones, who was referred to consistently in *The New York Times* as a "troubled youth," had a history of violence. Several arrests had resulted in dismissals and the sealing of the Family Court records that would have revealed the pattern of dangerous behavior; for example, a charge of robbery and assault at knifepoint had been dismissed because no witness could be found who would testify in court.

Jones had been arrested again and indicted by a grand jury in May; the case was being tried in State Supreme Court because of the seriousness of the armed robbery charge. Jones pleaded guilty and, his previous arrest record as a juvenile having been sealed, the judge deferred sentencing and released him without bail until July 3 and then again until July 18 after being assured by Jones's Legal Aid lawyer that there were plans for him to enter a residential treatment facility for emotionally disturbed boys, the Cedar Knolls School at Hawthorne, New York.

Why this should have made much difference is hard to understand. Jones had been at Hawthorne before and had run away. In fact, the school refused to take him back, calling him "unengageable," and he was left to his own devices, at large pending his reappearance in court. Six days before that scheduled appearance, he shot Officer McDonald.

Under the juvenile offender law, Jones would be tried as an adult in State Supreme Court for the shooting of Officer McDonald, but under the sharply restricted sentencing provisions for minors, he could get as little as three and a third years and no more than ten years in prison.

To the *Times* reporter covering the case, Shavod Jones was "a classic example of a severely troubled youngster who had slipped through the system." A court official described him as "a kid . . . in trouble" who "fell through the cracks," seeming to imply that the right treatment existed somewhere if only it had been provided. In fact, he hadn't fallen through the cracks at all. He had been admitted to various facilities, including a psychiatric hospital, at one time or another and had either absconded or been removed by his family. The various social service agencies involved in trying to find a way to help or at least contain Jones had, as an official of one of them put it, "no knowledge of these other criminal matters."

The identities of Jones's two companions on the night of the shooting, a fourteen-year-old and a thirteen-year-old who had been his accomplice in a previous armed robbery, were withheld since they were being charged as juveniles in Family Court. They were both found to have committed designated felonies—assault in the first degree and conspiracy to commit a robbery—and, over the objections of the District Attorney's office, which had asked for a restrictive placement, they were placed in a Title III limited-secure facility for up to eighteen months. They remain anonymous because of their tender age.

Shavod Jones was found guilty of attempted murder in the second degree, aggravated assault on a police officer, and criminal possession of a .22-caliber revolver and, in January, six months after he shot Officer McDonald, he was given the maximum sentence allowed by the law. It was three and one-third to ten years. The evening television news broadcasts that reported the sentencing also carried, in a touch worthy of a novelist, the news of the birth of a son to McDonald's wife in a hospital not far from Bellevue, where McDonald remained paralyzed for life.

MOM: IT'S SYSTEM'S FAULT and MOTHER PUTS BLAME ON SYSTEM read the *Newsday* headlines, and the mother of Shavod Jones said, "I feel like my son's being railroaded; he's the victim." He was "a very troubled kid," she said, "who needed help."

A spokesman for the city's Department of Juvenile Justice remarked that "there's no all-seeing agency that can hold them within its gaze at every step of their lives." There used to be such an agency. It was called the family.

While the Jones affair filled the papers, inspiring indignant columns and editorials in the tabloid *New York Post* and *Daily News* and thoughtful, understanding background pieces in the *Times*, more routine criminal activities were going on as usual.

Twelve-year-old Joey N. decided to spend the evening of Sunday, July 13, killing his sister's boyfriend. Joey took a .22 and some bullets and rounded up his friend Benjamin T., eighteen, to help him with the shooting.

Joey's thirteen-year-old sister was living with an older man (some said thirty-five, some said forty) who ran a shooting gallery, that is, an apartment where addicts came to take drugs. What Joey had against him is not clear, but the older man seems to have turned the girl on to hard drugs and may have been abusing her, although whenever the police removed her at her family's request, she went back to him.

Joey and Benjamin went up to a rooftop where they waited for Joey's "brother-in-law" to appear. When he did,

Benjamin fired the loaded gun in his direction but missed. He later claimed to have shot wide of the mark on purpose. They then went to Joey's family's apartment to get some more bullets, but Joey's mother's live-in boyfriend couldn't find any.

Back out on the street, Joey and Benjamin bumped into fifteen-year-old Anthony B. They showed him the gun and he joined them. With the gun and the remaining two bullets the three boys strolled down to 100th Street and Central Park West, where they kept themselves busy trying to rape, rob, and murder before they were caught and arrested.

First they tried to break into a parked taxi, but hadn't managed to break the window before they noticed a woman entering the park and decided to rape her instead. That plan was dropped because, luckily for the woman, Joey was afraid of dogs and she was walking two German shepherds. They then set upon a couple they found sitting on a park bench, intending to rob them and rape the woman. Anthony asked Joey for his gun so he could kill the man (in order, as he later explained, to leave no evidence), but Joey later claimed that while pretending to load the gun he threw the remaining bullets away and so when Anthony aimed the gun at the man's head and pulled the trigger point-blank, nothing happened. Joey had found a piece of pipe, but before he could put it to use, the couple managed to get away. They ran out of the park and collided with a Transit Authority policeman who went back into the park with them, where the three boys were found and arrested.

Benjamin and Anthony, because of their ages and the seriousness of the charges, were held for appearance before a grand jury prior to trial in Criminal Court. Joey spent Monday in Spofford, the city's juvenile detention center in the Bronx, and was brought to Family Court on Tuesday, July 15.

At his arraignment, Joey looked small and harmless, even

pleasant. His hair was close-cropped, and he was neatly dressed and quiet.

Joey's court-appointed lawyer asked that he be paroled to the custody of the New York State Division for Youth. As a matter of fact, Joey was already in DFY custody Sunday night, at the time of what is referred to as "the incident," having run away from a DFY facility, a small group home in Brooklyn to which he had been transferred from the Eddie Parker Residential Center, an upstate camp to which he had been sent after an earlier delinquency finding.

DFY's court liaison officer said that since Joey was already in their custody (in the sense in which an AWOL soldier can be said to be still in the army), they would accept responsibility for him. This time, the assumption was that he would be returned to a more restrictive facility than the one from which he had absconded.

The assistant Corporation Counsel objected to this proposal. "Your honor," she said, "I think it would be a waste of the taxpayer's money sending the respondent upstate and bringing him down again for the various hearings. He can stay in Spofford."

The judge said, "These are vicious charges and even if they are half true, he is a danger to the community," and she remanded him to Spofford until the probable-cause hearing the next day. Joey could stay in Spofford until fourteen days after his arraignment if it were determined that there was sufficient evidence to believe he had committed a crime for which he should go to trial, or, in the parlance of Family Court, probable cause to believe he had committed "an act that would constitute a crime if committed by an adult" and for which a fact-finding hearing should be held.

The two weeks are provided to allow both sides to prepare for the trial, or fact-finding hearing. In this time, the Corporation Counsel would have to have the gun and any bullets that could be recovered analyzed by the police laboratory, gather testimony from witnesses, police records, and the grand jury minutes on the two accomplices who, if indicted, would be tried in State Supreme Court.

On the next day, July 16, the judge ruled that there was probable cause and sent Joey back to Spofford until the fact-finding hearing.

Joey had a family history of neglect. He was nine years old when he first appeared before the court on a delinquency charge. At that time he was no longer living at home.

Court documents relating to that 1983 case state Joey's father's "whereabouts unknown" and give his "parent substitute" as "mother's paramour." Joey's mother, the ninth of her mother's twenty children, was abandoned by her own mother in the hospital when she was eight days old and then given away to an aunt "because her paternal aunt had a drinking problem and it was thought that having the responsibility of caring for a child would help her stop drinking."

Joey's mother had been a drug addict since the age of seventeen. She acknowledged that Joey had been staying out late, "associating with undesirable companions and being involved in robberies and pickpocketing," but "stated she felt that Joseph would interpret being placed on probation as punishment and it is possible that Joseph would react to being placed on probation by reverting to his previous acting-out behavior." This opinion was also that expressed by the "parent substitute," who had been legally married at one time but no longer knew the whereabouts of his wife or son and had never contributed to the support of his son.

"Mother's paramour," as he is referred to in the Probation Department report, is described as "a man who has a drinking problem that led to the children being placed by SSC [Special Services for Children, New York's child-care agency] when it was alleged that while under the influence of alcohol, he allegedly beat the mother's infant son." Joey had been returned to the family home from placement in Children's Village, an open facility for troubled children in Rockland County, north of the city, at the time the report was written. While he was in Children's Village, Joey and two other boys had stolen a car. They were very young, no one was hurt, and it may have been a prank, although a dangerous one. They were arrested for "unauthorized use of a vehicle" and Joey, the youngest, was given a conditional discharge. If he didn't get into any more trouble for a year, there would be no further consequences.

The probation officer's report says "the family has a history of problems that include difficulty in supervising the children." Of Joey's mother's five other children, three were living with other relatives at the time and the oldest, sixteen, was pregnant and had dropped out of school. Nevertheless, despite Joey's behavior and family history, his mother's drug addiction, his father's neglect, and the "parent substitute's" abuse, the probation officer concluded that "it seems that residential placement is not currently needed" and recommended that Joey be placed on probation, trusting that "this would provide an additional authority figure to monitor his behavior and provide additional support to enable Joseph to avoid further difficulty with the authorities and remain in the community."

It was almost three years to the day after the report was written that Joey was arrested in Central Park. In the meantime, he had not remained unknown to the court.

He was arrested again in September of 1984 when he went into a McDonald's, became loud and abusive, was ejected, and came back and threatened the security guard with a bottle. This time he got the full treatment. There was a psychological evaluation as well as an investigation and report by the Department of Probation.

The Mental Health Services psychologist, who saw him three times, found Joey, despite his vulnerable childlike appearance, to be manipulative and evasive. Joey explained his five previous arrests as resulting from the actions of others. "My friend gets [me] in trouble." He showed no embarrassment or remorse. Eventually he said, "I'm hungry for money," and told about taking part in robberies with others. "A lot of times we had a .22." When asked why he repeatedly ran away from foster care and group homes, he replied that he wanted to remain home because, "You don't have to be told what to do, what you don't wanna do."

The psychologist thought Joey "may be a danger to others, is completely oblivious and unconcerned about his anti-social behavior, and is in need of a high level of structure." He recommended that Joey be placed in a setting where "limit-setting would be helpful to him" because of his history of absconding and his difficulties with others, and to prepare him for academic remediation (he was, at eleven, in a third-grade special education class, from which he had been suspended for having a knife in his possession) and perhaps eventually for psychotherapy, although he felt Joey would not be able to make use of psychotherapy at this point.

The psychologist's report of his interview with Joey's "stepfather" found the man affable, although he was "unkempt and smelled bad." This "possible resource" blamed all of Joey's difficulties on the other boys he'd been involved with in various delinquent acts. He referred to Joey—"almost affectionately," in the psychologist's words—as a "fucking punk" and did not think he should be punished but "should be given another chance at bat."

The various hearings relating to the September incident

at McDonald's went on from January of the following year to late March. The probation report to the court notes that "we were not able to request a written school report because the respondent's aunt [with whom he was living at the time] was not present to sign release forms." If a school report had been obtained, it would have revealed that Joey had been suspended from the special education class in which the Committee on the Handicapped had placed him. The educationally or emotionally handicapped were forgiven a lot, but they were not supposed to carry knives in the classroom.

The Evaluative Statement section of the probation report described Joey as "a youth with little or no insight into his delinquent behavior. He was very angry and hostile during the interview. His prognosis for further contact with community appears to be poor." ("When question [sic] respondent about future goals," reads the report, "he indicated that 'I'll probably rob old ladies.' ") All things considered, including his future career goals, placement was recommended for Joey.

Efforts to find a place that would take him went on into April. Seven agencies rejected him. Finally, "in view of the fact that respondent has a history of absconding from open settings, and there appears to be a need for a high-structure setting," Joey was placed with DFY Title III for up to a year and in May of 1985 he was sent to Eddie Parker. He was now eleven years old.

Eddie Parker is considered to be one of the better facilities of its kind. There is minimal hardware, with reliance instead on what a DFY worker describes as "a staff-to-kid ratio of almost two to one, which means there is almost constant eyeball supervision." The setting, some fifty miles north of the city, is rural. There is nowhere for a runaway to go. At Eddie Parker, according to the DFY worker, "they take smaller, less violent kids who might get stomped on elsewhere," and they have a reputation for doing well with many of them, although there are no follow-up statistics available. It costs approximately $54,000 a year to keep a boy at Eddie Parker.

After about a year there, Joey was found not to be adjusting well and DFY petitioned the court to extend his placement—and move him to a *less* structured facility. In the spring of 1986 he was sent to a group home in Brooklyn. He was AWOL and back on the street in less than a month. A warrant was issued but no attempt was made to enforce it, and in July, while technically still in the custody of DFY, Joey was roaming the streets with a gun in the company of two other youths not unknown to the courts.

The tape recording of their conversations with the detective who interviewed them at the precinct house to which they were taken immediately after their arrest tells the story of the evening in their own words. Detective Dunn later said the boys had made these statements as casually as if they were ordering a hamburger at McDonald's. (It's not clear whether he knew about Joey's earlier experience there or whether his choice of example was just a coincidence.) And indeed, the tone of voice of all three boys on the tape is flat. There is no audible sign of emotion. They sound at ease and as if they are comfortable with what they are saying.

The first to be interviewed was Benjamin. After giving his name, age, and address, he told Detective Dunn that he had been arrested twice before, once for stealing a bike "and one for fire."

D: What do you mean, fire?
B: In a school.
D: You set a fire in a school?
B: Yeah.
D: How long ago was that?
B: Long time ago.

After establishing that Benjamin knew where he was, Detective Dunn said, "Before we go any further I'll advise you of your rights. I'll read them from a card. See the card I got in my hand? What's on the back of the card? You read the date."

B: March 19, 1983.

D: March or May?

B: May.

D: Okay. You have the right to remain silent and refuse to answer questions. Do you understand that, Benjamin?

B: Yes.

D: Anything you do say may be used against you in a court of law. Do you understand that, Benjamin?

B: Yes.

D: You have the right to consult an attorney before speaking to the police and have any attorney present during any questioning now or in the future. Do you understand that, Benjamin?

B: Yes.

D: If you can't afford an attorney, one will be provided to you without cost. Do you understand that?

B: Yes.

D: Without an attorney available you have the right to remain silent until you've had the opportunity to consult with one. Do you understand that?

B: Yes.

D: Now that I've advised you of your rights, are you willing to answer questions without an attorney present?

B: Yes.

After establishing that Benjamin was aware that the conversation was being tape-recorded and that he understood the charges against him, Detective Dunn asked, "Do you want to tell me what happened today?" Benjamin began to do so, and the following are excerpts from their conversation.

D: Before you go any further, where did you—what time did you meet the other two fellows?

B: I met him on my block. He had the gun I had [when arrested].

D: Which kid is that?

B: The small one, the one who's twelve.

D: What's his name?

B: Forgot his name.

D: What do you call him?

B: I think his name was Joey . . . Joey something . . . So he told me let's go kill somebody, right? His brother-in-law, 'cause he sells drugs. So we went there and went to the roof. We shot a shot in the air. So we left. And after that we went to—

D: Why did he want to kill his brother-in-law?

B: . . . I don't know. He making her use crack. That's what he told me to do . . . Yeah. And I saw him. I wasn't going to shoot at him. I told you. I missed. 'Cause I didn't want to shoot no guy . . . Yeah, instead of shooting down I shoot the other way . . . He was walking there. So Joey told me, "Yo, Ben, shoot him up there." So I said all right. I hit the corner, I shoot the other way and I missed. So I said, "Yo, let's leave . . ." So after that we left and went to 110th. That's where I met my friend Anthony. And we went to Central Park. No, we went to his house to get some bullets for his gun . . . We went to Central Park. We saw a girl with two dogs. And my friend told me, "Yo, Ben, let's rape her." I said, "No, man, forget it, man, let's go home." He said, "Now you're scared . . ." I say I ain't scared to do that so we went along. A girl with two dogs, he was gonna rape her, I said, "No, don't do it."

D: Who wanted to rape her?

B: Anthony. 'Cause he's a criminal. He rape, he raped his nine-year-old cousin in the roof.

D: When was this?

B: That was a few days . . . that was last year, long time ago.

D: Did he get caught for it?

B: Nah. They didn't do nothin' to him. So I said to my friend—

D: His cousin never pressed charges?

B: I don't know. That's another story.

D: Who else did he rape?

B: He rape a lot of people.

D: Well, how do you know he raped a lot of people? Did he tell you or did you see him do it?

B: He told me. He told me. In Central Park, a lot of people. He steals bikes. He did a lot of bad things. That what my friend told me, he do heroin . . .

D: All right, back to this thing again . . .

B: . . . So we went all around to Central Park, we saw two guys, a guy and a lady. So he said, "Yo, she's got a good butt," so he said, "What?" and he say it again, I say I shoot you right now. So I came and put up the gun in the air . . .

D: And the two people, what were they doing?

B: They were kissing and everything, so Anthony say—

D: What's the guy look like? What color was he?

B: The guy was Puerto Rican, mustache, curly hair. His wife was short, long hair, dark skin like me. They were sitting down.

D: Whose idea was it to vic 'em?

B: Anthony.

D: What did Anthony say?

B: Yo, yo Ben, let's rape them, take their chains, take their money. So I said, "Yo, I don't wanna . . ." He said, "Nah, you're scared." So I took out a gun, shoot a bullet in the air . . .

D: Where'd you get the gun?

B: Joey gave it to me to hold . . . So I said, let me get it . . . throw the bullet in the air. So we left walking. He didn't pay no mind to it. And that's when my friend Anthony came and said, "Yo, give me the gun." I gave it to him . . . So I told Anthony, "Don't point to the lady. Let the lady go." He said, "Fuck it . . ." He went to the guy and said, "Yo, give me your chain and your money." So I told my friend, "Yo, Anthony, leave 'em alone, leave the girl and the guy alone. Let's leave." He said, "Fuck it, I'm gonna, you know, do something." So he went and the guy started running. So my friend, the little one, picked up a pipe. He was gonna hit the guy . . . That's when the dude took out a knife. And we walk. And the officer came and pulled out a gun and said, "Yo, you're under arrest." And so Joey threw the gun there . . . So I tell myself in the car, I'm gonna tell him the truth, and I told him the gun was right there. 'Cause that kid was lying, 'cause I knew I could get in trouble 'cause I'm eighteen and they can get away with anything. So I said, forget it, I gonna say the truth. So I told 'em the truth and that's how everything happened.

D: It was Anthony's idea then to go out and do vics today?

B: Yeah. He said, "Yo, Ben, let's vic some people today." So I said all right. So we went around over to these two people making out.

D: Who'd you see before that?

B: Before that? Before that we see, oh, white lady walking her two dogs.

D: Why didn't you take her?

B: Nah.

D: What changed your mind? I mean, you went out looking for vics. Something must have changed your mind. Big dogs or little dogs?

B: Like German shepherds. I say to 'em, I say, "Forget it,

man, let's take a taxi." I say, "Yo, I wanna go home 'cause
my mother's worried. Say, forget it." That's when we saw
the two guys. You know what I'm talkin' about?

D: Where does Anthony like to do his robberies?

B: He like robbin' an' killin'. He go up to you and kill you
right there. Lucky that gun have no bullet. He would have
kill the girl right there. That's why I took out the bullet and
threw it in the air 'cause I knew he was gonna shoot the lady
or the guy . . .

D: How do you know he's not a bullshit artist? You know,
just trying to run his mouth and be cool on the block.

B: I don't know about that. The only thing I know is he
beat up somebody bad with a bat, a kid.

D: Did you see that?

B: Yeah, I seen it. That was on the corner of 111th between Madison and Lex . . . He beat up the dude with a bat.

D: And when was this? How long ago?

B: That was a few days ago.

D: Two days ago?

B: Yeah.

D: Do you have anything else to say?

B: Nah.

D: You don't know anybody around with a silver gun
that's raping people, do you?

B: Nope. The only one I know is him . . . Joey. He's up
to kill his brother-in-law. That's what he's up to do . . . I just
met him. I never done nothin'. This is my first time in here.
'Cause I go to church. This is the first time in my life. I know
what could happen to me 'cause I'm old. And they get away
with anything.

D: That's all you have to say?

B: Yeah.

D: You made this statement of your own free will?

B: Uh-huh.

D: Nobody threatened you or beat you or anything like that?

B: Nah.

D: You were treated nice?

B: Yeah. With respect.

Joey was the second to be interviewed by Detective Dunn, who read him his rights as he had Benjamin, and then said, "Okay. I'm going to explain to you using [plain] English. 'Cause these are big words for your age."

D: You have the right to remain silent means I can't force you to talk. Understand what I'm saying? I can't beat a confession out of you or threaten you or promise you anything. You don't want to talk to me, you don't have to talk to me. That's under the Constitution of the United States. Okay?

J: Yes, sir.

D: Anything you tell me, though, I can take into court. Play it before the judge and your attorney in the Family Court. Do you understand that?

J: Yes, sir.

D: Okay. You got the right to have a lawyer present. That means you can have a guy here who's a lawyer giving you advice. Now if you don't have the bread to buy one, the city will pick up the tab. You know what I'm telling you?

J: Yes, sir.

D: It ain't coming out of your pocket. These people are spending it. New York City. Ed Koch's got a big barrel of money. They'll take some out and give it to your lawyer, okay? Now say you had your own private attorney. I mean, you know, you got a family friend and he's out in the Bahamas someplace and you can't get to him today. That means, you know, you can just sit back if you don't want to talk to me and wait for him. But you don't have your own private attorney anyway, right?

J: No, sir.

D: That's what your rights are. I have to tell you that. Basically what I'm trying to find out today, Joey, is the truth. And I spoke to Benjamin and it sounds like you got some problems.

J: Yes, sir, I got big problems.

D: Maybe I can help you with your problems.

J: Yes, sir.

D: Earlier today I was talking to Benjamin and Benjamin tells me he met you last night and you asked him to do you a favor and off your brother-in-law.

J: My so-called, my so-called brother-in-law.

D: What's he doing, shacking up with your sister?

J: Yes.

D: How old's your sister?

J: Thirteen . . .

D: Why did you ask Benjamin to shoot him?

J: No cause. Yo, he wanted to, see . . . like he wanted to use the gun too.

D: That was your gun, right?

J: Yes. My friend's gun. That he lend me.

D: What's your friend's name?

J: His name is Ray. They call him Ray.

D: Ray what?

J: I don't know his last name.

D: Where does Ray live?

J: In the Bronx.

D: Where in the Bronx?

J: I don't know the avenue.

D: Where did you meet Ray that he gave you the gun? You must know him pretty good if he gave you a gun to borrow?

J: Yeah. Yeah. And he got the license for it too.

D: How do you know he has a license for that gun?

J: He told me and he showed me the papers.

D: How old's Ray?

J: I don't know.

D: Roughly, how old? As old as I am?

J: Yes, about thirty or something.

D: Where do you know Ray from?

J: From the building. He's a security officer.

D: From your building? He's a guy—he's a thirty-year-old man, has a job as security and he lends you a gun? That don't sound right.

J: Yes, sir. I needed it so he lended it . . .

D: What'd you tell him you were gonna use the gun for?

J: Like I had business to take care of. Indio [his sister's boyfriend], right?

D: He knew you were gonna off Indio?

J: Yes.

D: And he loaned you a gun?

J: Yes, sir.

D: He must be a nice friend to just give you his gun . . . Did you go to your mother's house to get bullets?

J: Yes, but my father [sic] said he didn't know where he put 'em at so he didn't give me none . . .

D: When did you hook up with Anthony?

J: When we were walking down to 110th . . .

D: What did Anthony want to go do?

J: Oh, rob somebody.

D: Who did he want to rob?

J: A man or a lady . . .

D: You only met Anthony last night?

J: Yes, sir . . .

D: So now you went hunting for a cabbie and you didn't find one?

J: We found one but we tried to break the window and . . . after Anthony seen this lady walking down through Central Park, he stopped.

D: What did the lady look like?

J: She was white and had blond hair with two dogs.

D: And what happened then?

J: He wanted to, you know, grab her.

D: What did he want to grab her for?

J: I don't know. To do something to her.

D: Do what to her?

J: Like do sex to her.

D: He wanted to rape her?

J: Yes.

D: What did he say? What were his exact words?

J: He said, "Come on, we could get some off of her like." Like get some off of her. Like get in her pants.

D: That's what he said?

J: Yes.

D: Then what did you do?

J: I said, I don't know, because she got two dogs and I ain't messin' around with no rapin' no lady. That's serious trouble right there.

D: If she didn't have the dogs do you think Anthony and you guys would have done it?

J: I wouldn't have. That's—

D: There's a big difference between doing a car and going out raping. I mean that's some heavy shit.

J: That's why I didn't get involved with that.

D: And then what'd you do?

J: And then we were looking around. We seen this dude, right, with this girl, right, and he, and you know, he was kissing her, and he said, "You can't handle that."

D: Who said that?

J: Anthony. He said, "You can't handle it." He said, "What boy?" He said, "You gotta beef?" Anthony said, "You gotta beef?" He said, "What's up?" And the other dude said, "What's up?" And we were walking back where he was at. And he said, "I'll blow your head off."

D: Who said that?

J: Anthony. He said, "I'll put a bullet, a bullet in your head." You know. And I found the pipe. I wasn't gonna chase them or nothing and hit 'em . . .

D: Anthony had the gun now?

J: Yes.

D: Who fired the shot?

J: Yes. When he fired the shot up, pow, right? Ben fired the shot up and I went in my pocket and I found one more bullet. Right? I put it in the cartridge but I knew what I was doing, so I said, forget about it. And I clicked it back and the bullet fell out of the gun. And I knew it fell out and I just gave it to him 'cause I knew he was ready to shoot him. I gave it to Anthony. And he went like that . . . and then the dude, he said, "Oh, homeboy, you got it, you got it this time . . ."

D: And he started running or did he stay there?

J: And then he stayed and Anthony said, "Sit down and give me all your stuff, right?" He said, "Give me all your jewelry and stuff, right?" And he pulled out a big Rambo knife. And that's when we ran back and started walking.

D: Did you give the gun to Anthony?

J: No, he passed it back to me, right?

D: What did you do when he had the gun and the guy had the knife out?

J: We ran. 'Cause the gun went click and there was no bullets in it.

D: He pointed it at the guy and pulled the trigger?

J: Yeah.

D: And then when they knew the gun was empty the three of you ran?

J: Yes.

D: And he gave the gun to you?

J: Yes, and when the police was coming I threw it inside a garbage can . . .

D: Anthony, Ben and you were going out to do a rape and a robbery then.

J: Not me.

D: You were gonna watch?

J: Yes, I just was with 'em.

D: Who wanted to do the rape? Ben and Anthony or just Anthony?

J: Anthony.

D: What were you gonna do, just take the money and chains and let him get the pussy?

J: Probably, I don't know. I got some of my own chains, probably I get some money . . . I need money . . .

D: Do you use drugs?

J: No.

D: Now do you have anything else to say?

J: No.

The last of the boys to be interviewed was Anthony B., who was no stranger to the court. At his first appearance in Family Court, Anthony had been charged with burglary; the case was adjusted (dismissed) and the record sealed. The next time, a burglary charge was dropped when he admitted to the lesser charge of grand larceny; this time he was put on probation. At the time of the incident in Central Park in July 1986, there was a warrant outstanding against him for violation of probation. He had missed twenty-one days of school, and the judge who had put him on probation and then issued the warrant had finally agreed that he should be placed in non-secure detention. The warrant became obsolete when he was arrested in the park and charged as a juvenile offender with attempted murder and attempted robbery in the first degree.

Anthony's history was one of serious psychological problems for which he had been treated at a city hospital clinic for several years after he had tried to castrate himself with a pair of scissors. He had been accused of sexually molesting his six-year-old cousin, although charges were never brought, and he admitted to stealing bicycles, adding that he was sorry that he had gotten caught. It was obvious that Anthony was a boy in trouble, a boy with troubles, and a boy who would make trouble for others.

An attorney who had spoken with him in connection with one of his earlier cases said, "Anthony will kill somebody. He's one of the only two kids I've ever seen who really want to kill someone. The other one was Billy L. [who, at twelve, as described earlier, had raped and then beaten to death a derelict woman he came upon sleeping in the park one summer night in 1983]. When they're that cold-blooded it shows up at an early age."

As he had with Joey because of his age, Detective Dunn, because of the seriousness of the charges against fifteen-year-old Anthony, explained the Miranda rights after he had read them and asked if Anthony understood them. He told him, "I can't beat a confession out of you, I can't make you talk, I can't threaten you to talk. You talk to me 'cause you want to talk to me. You want to clean your conscience, you want to get all this off your chest, and it's gonna be the truth. All right?

"Everything you tell me, I can tell the judge, I can tell your attorney, I can tell Family Court, the Corporation Counsel, or Criminal Court, the District Attorney. I can say

this and say, well, you told me this, and I can use this 'cause
you're telling me this . . .

"If you can't afford a lawyer, the city picks up the tab.
They'll turn around and say, 'Anthony needs a lawyer, get
him a lawyer, we'll pay the bill.' All right, you got your own
lawyer, a friend of the family or something like that, and he's
not around. He's in Puerto Rico or maybe playing golf so you
can't call him on the phone, you can sit and be quiet until
we get ahold of him for you. You understand that? If you
want your lawyer here, your lawyer's here, makes sure your
rights are taken care of and advises you.

"So right now we're talking, me and you, all by ourselves
with no lawyer and you're doing this of your own free will.
I haven't threatened you or anything, nobody's beaten you,
no deals are being made or nothing like that—we're gonna
be straight with each other?"

To which Anthony answered, "Yes."

D: What happened last night?

A: Well, Benjamin and Joseph went to pick me up at my
block . . .

D: Did they show you something?

A: Yes, the gun. Benjamin show me that gun. I say it was
fake and then he say, "Take a walk with me, I'll show you,
but we gotta go up to my friend's house first to get the bullets." So I walked, I went with them . . . and me and Benjamin wait outside and he got the bullets and came down. I
told him, Let's go rob. And we went to rob.

D: What else were you gonna do besides rob?

A: Rape.

D: What does "rape" mean?

A: Beat somebody up.

D: What do you mean, "somebody up"?

A: Beat a lady up.

D: And what do you do after you beat her up?

A: Rape her.

D: And what does that mean when you rape her?

A: Put your penis in her.

D: In her what?

A: Twat.

D: In her twat. Okay. If you don't know the big words use the words you know. You know, if you call it a pussy, call it a pussy. If you call it a cunt, call it a cunt.

A: All right.

D: We're not here taking a test or anything. Whatever you're comfortable saying, you say . . . but you have to be clear on it because, you know, if they don't understand it they'll just leave it blank. "Do" means anything, so you gotta explain, so they know what's in your mind. That's what's gonna come on the tape recorder.

A: So we're gonna break into this taxicab and we got the gun and took it out and tried bang on the window and couldn't break so we left it alone. We saw this white lady with two dogs.

D: Where did you see her?

A: Hundredth Street and Central Park.

D: And what did you decide to do with her?

A: Rape her.

D: All of you or just you?

A: Me.

D: Just you?

A: Yeah.

D: And what were the other two guys gonna do, watch?

A: I don't know . . .

D: Well, were they gonna join in? Were they gonna take turns?

A: Yes.

D: Did they say that?

A: No, but I knew they was gonna do it . . .

D: Who had the gun?

A: Joseph.

D: Are they gonna rob her after you rape her?

A: Yeah.

D: They said that or you just know they're gonna do that?

A: They said that. We all made agreement. So we followed her . . .

D: How come you didn't try to grab her in the park?

A: 'Cause they was, Ben and Joey was scared of the dogs.

D: So you let her go and then you started looking for somebody else?

A: Yeah. We found that man and that lady kissing . . . So I walked around and said, "Fuck her, fuck her good . . ."

D: This is to the two people on the bench?

A: Yeah, and he said, "What?" And Ben had the gun . . . and he fired it up . . . He shot it up. He said [noise]—

D: He shot it up in the air?

A: Yeah. And Joseph pass me the gun and I was aiming for him. I thought it was—

D: Where were you aiming at him?

A: His head.

D: You thought the gun was loaded?

A: Yeah. So when I clicked it—

D: When you pointed the gun at his head, and aimed at his head, did you know that would kill him? If you hit him in the head?

A: Yeah.

D: Why did you want to kill him?

A: I didn't want to leave no evidence.

D: So you had no doubt in your mind you were gonna shoot him in the head.

A: Yeah.

D: And then what happened when you heard the gun click?

A: I got scared a little bit 'cause if he would have heard it he would have chased me with a Rambo knife.

D: He had a Rambo knife?

A: Yeah. And he would have stabbed me.

Having told how they ran out of the park, Joey carrying "a pole" or "a stick" and throwing the gun away when they were stopped by the police, Anthony provided some information about how he had been passing the time the previous fall after being paroled by a sympathetic Family Court judge.

D: Did you ever rape a woman before?

A: Yes.

D: And when did you do this?

A: Last September.

D: Are you sure in September?

A: Yes.

D: And who were you with?

A: My brother.

Anthony talked easily, almost casually, about accompanying his twenty-one-year-old brother on three occasions when his brother had raped women and about the time in September when he had raped one of those women himself. Anthony had been hiding in the bushes, "watching and looking out for the cops," when uniformed police arrived on the scene. Anthony's brother ran and the police went after him, leaving the woman, who was—according to Anthony—"knocked out cold."

D: So while they're chasing him, that's when you fucked the lady?

A: Yeah . . . both ways.

D: What's both ways?

A: Ass and pussy.

Anthony described the three women. One had been an older woman, walking her dog in the evening, another had been jogging late at night "where that river is at in Central Park."

D: Oh, around the reservoir?

A: Yeah. And he pushed her down . . . he didn't beat that old lady up, 'cause I didn't let him.

D: What did he do to her?

A: . . . Suck his dick . . . and he banged her . . . to her ass . . .

D: And he's in jail now?

A: Elmira.

D: How much time did he get?

A: Three years.

D: That's just on the one rape? They didn't catch him on the other two?

A: No . . .

D: Everything you told me is the truth?

A: Yeah . . .

D: You have anything else you want to tell me?

A: No.

Anthony and Benjamin were indicted for attempted murder and attempted robbery in the first degree and jailed to await trial in Criminal Court. Joey's case didn't go to trial. He pleaded guilty on July 28 to attempted robbery in the first degree, the highest of the nineteen counts with which he was charged (the lowest was menacing, a misdemeanor) and was ordered to DFY for eighteen months—the maximum time allowed.

It was the opinion of the court that Joey should be followed closely. It was the opinion of the borough chief of the Corporation Counsel in Manhattan Family Court that he would eventually wind up where his two accomplices were—across the street in Criminal Court. "He'll be back," she said wearily, and added, "I sent two boys to Title III today, Joey

and another one, and they have similar histories and may
wind up at the same facility, but they are different. The other
one will probably turn out all right. A lot of the boys we see
here are obnoxious teenagers who, in a different tax bracket,
would be sent off to prep school. They grow out of it, would
grow out of it whatever we did with them. Others, like Joey,
grow up to be hardened criminals, and probably would have
no matter what. Everything that matters happens long before
they're twelve."

The aging, soft-spoken black man in charge of the detention room in the Family Court agrees with her. He's seen
them all over the years. He thinks the other boy will probably
do all right. Joey is different though. "There's something
calculating about him," he said. "Cold-blooded," was how
Detective Dunn phrased it. "And that," said an assistant corporation counsel, "is nineteen years on the force talking."

A lot of boys like Joey are walking around our cities. Many
of them have never been arrested. Others have, and have
been paroled to their families and put on probation. Some
have run away from non-secure detention facilities—small
group homes in the city with no locks on the doors. Eleven
days after his guilty plea, Joey will go upstate to a DFY Title
III facility—*not* secure.*

Joey could not be held more than eighteen months even if
he had killed someone—even if he had killed several people—
because he was twelve years old at the time of the act in
question. DFY can file a petition for extension of his place-

*The court can give DFY authorization to move Joey from placement in a lim-
ited-secure facility to a locked one if he doesn't adjust well in limited-secure: if
he runs away, starts fights, or makes trouble in other serious ways. In Joey's
case no such authorization was granted. A DFY court liaison officer stated that
even if authorization had been granted, DFY would be reluctant to put a thirteen-year-old in secure placement.

ment beyond eighteen months, in which case there will be a hearing at which he has the right to contest the extension. Meanwhile, he will have home visits. And he can always run away again, as he had done at the time he was picked up for this crime.

Normally, DFY has complete control over who is released and when. DFY officials can, in the absence of a special court order, parole anyone at their discretion without notification to anyone. Even in Joey's case, notification is not a statutory requirement for release by DFY, an agency that is, in regard to juvenile delinquents, a law unto itself. Even the requirement for notification is just that—notice of the release. There is no way the court or the lawyers on either side can prevent DFY from releasing anyone they choose, even if they do so the day after he's been placed.

This is a good system insofar as it prevents a youngster who's done nothing seriously wrong from being sent to jail for an indefinite period and forgotten there. There was a time when it was possible for a boy who was merely obstreperous or who committed a petty theft to be thrown into a "reformatory" and to languish there. But the times seemed to have changed.

There is nothing unique about the case of Joey N. and his two companions. Unlike that of Shavod Jones and his companions, their case never even made the papers. It was just a routine, run-of-the-mill, everyday sort of case. Nobody was killed, no cop was involved, and so there was no press attention paid to Joey and Benjamin and Anthony. Not this time. Maybe next time.

3

From Wise Parent to Due Process

*Consider the child not as upon trial for commission of a crime,
but as a child in need of care and protection of the state.*

—Penal Law, New York, 1909, para. 2186

The present Family Court was established in 1962 to replace
the old Children's Court, Girls' Term, Domestic Relations,
and other special courts and bring together all proceedings
concerning children and family life—child support, child
abuse, juvenile delinquency—with the exception of separation and divorce.

The building that houses the Manhattan Family Court is
a stark angular structure. Its shiny black facade, broken by
small windows here and there and set off by an abstract sculp-
ture, could not be a more appropriate design to represent
what goes on inside its walls. Abstract. Based on a theory that
has lost connection with the realities of human need. And
reflecting very little sense of the community with which it
should be connected and whose needs it is supposed to serve.

This is the center of the juvenile justice system in New
York City. And in every major city across the country there

is a building like this dealing out justice—or injustice, as some critics of the system believe, suggesting that it has contributed not only to the increase in juvenile crime but to the increase in its brutality.

In the seating area outside the courtroom, a police officer from an anti-crime unit waiting to testify in a drug sale case, tired, bored, cynical, says, "Kids used to do things for kids' reasons. Now they do them for money."

Charles, who looks about nine, is sitting nearby. He's here with his mother, who is here to ask for an order of protection against her boyfriend, who menaced her with a knife, broke the glass in the door to get in, and wrecked her apartment. Charles gives his father's occupation as "drug dealer." He has been convicted of grand larceny. Charles says he doesn't understand why his mother "goes from one jerk to another."

A fourteen-year-old pleads guilty to mugging an old man. There's no possible defense and he has several priors, although neither fact is actually acknowledged in these proceedings. A recidivist with an alias and a record, he is, as they say, known to the court. Cynical smiles all around the courtroom as the boy is asked his name, his age. The mood is expressed by an assistant Corporation Counsel, who says under his breath, "Eddie, we're going to put you away but first we're going through with this very expensive procedure to be absolutely sure you got a fair shake." The judge even instructs the defendant's lawyer to make a motion she has overlooked in order to make sure he has the most complete defense. Corporation Counsel cites appellate rulings as precedent in answer to the motion, which has to do with the degree of force that distinguishes a robbery from a larceny. There being no reasonable doubt that it was Eddie who indeed robbed and beat the man, the boy will be off the streets now for eighteen months—after which, says the assistant Corporation Counsel,

"He's sixteen and he's not my problem anymore." No, I think, but he's still mine. The mugging occurred in the neighborhood where I live.

The parents of a four-year-old, who is sitting on the lap of a social worker, dressed in a frilly white pinafore and with ribbons in her hair, argue in a child support case. The father, an obese and sullen black man, insists he doesn't harass the mother. "The onliest times I bother her she be gone. I don' be botherin' her except for the child." The issue is whether the mother is ever there when he comes to see the child, whom he says he finds alone or in the care of a neighbor child. The mother looks at him wrathfully, turns to the judge, and demands, "I'm sayin' what about me!" She wants more time to herself, wants him to pick up the child and deliver her to the public day-care center, where the girl stays from eight-thirty in the morning to six at night. Neither of these parents seems to have any interest in the child.

At the time of its passage, New York's Family Court Act of 1962 was considered a milestone in the development of national policies on family law. The law provided counsel for accused juveniles in a court that was intended to be, in the words of the legislators who drafted it, a "special agency for the care and protection of the young and the preservation of the family."

In accordance with its non-punitive and rehabilitative purpose as "a special agency for the care and protection of the young," the court, while following many of the same procedures as criminal trials, avoids the language that would stigmatize the young accused. They are not defendants but "respondents"; they do not have trials but "hearings"; they receive not sentences but "dispositions."

Statutes and case law set down in a series of early decisions defined the objective of juvenile proceedings as seeing that the "delinquent youth is properly subjected to therapy which would rehabilitate, retrain, and change the attitude of mind of the child and give him a sense of social responsibility." Written in 1944, this statement about the purpose of Children's Court—explicitly distinguishing its purpose from punishment—was carried over to the Family Court Act. The purpose of the court was to reclaim the child, to retrain him, not punish him, and to restore him to the community. It sounds good—the sort of statement everyone would like to subscribe to, but is it realistic? Is it even possible?

Observing in the various parts of Family Court is like watching a demonstration of human nature in all its forms—the comic, the poignant, the revolting, the foolish, occasionally the admirable.

A gray-haired, sweet-faced woman with a cane sits outside the courtroom waiting for her case to be recalled as soon as a worker from Special Services for Children can find some papers she's gone off to get. The woman wants custody of her grandchild, now in the agency's care. She says she can make a good home for her. She shows me a vivid color photograph of a little girl with lots of braids and hairbows, clasping a doll and looking right into the camera. Then she shows me another snapshot, somewhat blurred, of a young woman she says is the child's mother. "My daughter." Then, sadly, "The pressures of life are a bit too much for her." I wonder why they aren't too much for this elderly woman who's here to ask for care and trouble and responsibility at a time of life when all that could be expected to be behind her. I take her hand and wish her luck. Later, one of the courtroom guards comments, "Like parent, like child—but a lot of the time it skips a generation."

The old and the very young are the innocents here, the

ones involved in custody cases or in other ways dragged in by other people's actions—a mother who's on drugs, a grandson who steals. Among the adolescents, some are more mischievous than menacing, brought in for behavior that is less than criminal by parents who can no longer handle them.

Phil Dobbs, the Probation Department's Family Court liaison officer, thinks PINS cases don't belong in court; they should go to a social service agency.* A thoughtful man, Dobbs has been in the system for over twenty years, and his experience in every aspect of probation work—intake, investigation, supervision—gives him a unique perspective on what goes on in the court.

"People want to avoid responsibility," he says. We're talking in the waiting area, trying to hear each other over the din of English, Spanish, Chinese from the crowd of kids, parents, social workers, lawyers, waiting for the court officers to call their cases. We've just come from the courtroom where we've been listening to an irate mother venting her anger through an interpreter. "When you have an institution that has power to compel," Dobbs says, "people will dump everything on it. They try to make the courts function as parents."

The mother had brought a PINS petition against one of her daughters, who then became pregnant while in placement and now plans to keep the baby with the help and approval of her boyfriend's mother, who is in the courtroom and whom I recognize from an earlier court appearance. Her son was the respondent in a juvenile delinquency hearing I attended some weeks previously. He'd been accused of stabbing another boy. The girl is a beautiful sixteen-year-old. The

---

*Since this was written, new legislation requires PINS cases to go through a mandatory referral process, which can take up to several months to complete, discouraging all but the most patient and resourceful parents from pressing court action, and, in effect, weakening whatever authority the threat of court action gave to beleaguered parents of acting-out or truanting adolescents.

judge cautions her about the responsibilities of parenthood. She smiles and nods. Yes, she wants to keep her baby. Her mother can't contain herself, interrupts, and, as she talks, the judge gets visibly angrier and angrier.

MOTHER: Why do you leave her there [in placement, an open group home]? Why don't you make her . . .

JUDGE: I have no power to compel a person her age . . . this court can only place her in—

MOTHER: Why don't you tell her—

JUDGE: Do you want her to come home to live with you? Do you?

MOTHER [pause]: No.

JUDGE [sternly]: Well then?

MOTHER [bitterly]: This is—democracy. This is how you do things here. Everybody can do whatever they want.

JUDGE: It took years and years for Carmen to get where she is today. If it makes you feel better to blame this court, I can't help that. [Her face is red. She is furious—I imagine both at the interruptions and at the attitude.]

The interpreter remains impassive, translating almost simultaneously, so that one is struck both by the calmness of the voice conveying the words we've just heard uttered in such angry tones and by the perceptual dissonance one feels in the momentary delay between the emotion-laden sounds and the expression of what they mean. One guesses that nothing surprises these bilingual virtuosi. They've not only heard everything, they've said everything. One of them is something of an actress, albeit more intuitive than studied. Translating for a mother who insisted to an investigating probation officer that she would not tell her husband about the trouble their son was in "because it would kill him," she pronounces the words with the same sense of urgency one hears in the mother's voice. It's hard to believe she's not speaking for herself when she explains that the man must earn the bread and not be bothered with these things; it is the woman's job, her job to look after the children.

One of these children attempted to commit a robbery with a loaded gun. He will probably be away for a year and a half. Does she think her husband won't notice? Or does she find herself unable to deal with more than the day's ration of pain at one time? The investigation reveals her to be a mildly depressed, deeply religious, somewhat superstitious woman who hardly leaves her house, tries to keep her children safe and out of trouble by keeping them in the house, too; in eighteen years in New York, she has seldom ventured beyond the corner bodega, never learned to speak English. Somehow hers seems less of a cautionary tale about social policy than a matter of individual pathology: a frightened person not up to coping with the world around her, who might have gotten by in a less complicated, less demanding rural setting. Her pathos and her predicament seem to have more to do with the timeless human condition than with specific social conditions in New York in the 1980s. Her story could have come out of Balzac.

It is impossible to sit in Family Court for a single day without being struck by the enormous expenditure of time and money and the wastefulness of it all.

The court is considering the case of an abandoned baby. Left with relatives shortly after birth, the baby has now been in an institution for several months. The mother and father have made no effort to find it and the mother did not keep appointments with social workers who had traced her through relatives. Hours and hours of agency time and court time have been logged on this matter, reams of papers fill bulging files, and meanwhile the baby spends its most formative months in an institution cared for at public expense. The court takes the attitude that it's the responsibility of the agency to pursue the

mother, that nothing can be decided about adoption meanwhile. As I often do here, I think of Dickens and the Victo-
rian picture of the impoverished mother and child. In these
romantic tales of tragic separation, the pathetic victims of the
system longed only to be given a chance to provide for their
own children.

What we see here are people who seem to feel no personal
responsibility for their own children. Everything seems to become a public, a societal responsibility.

The outstanding feature of New York's Family Court Act of
1962 was the provision for appointment of counsel for all juveniles appearing before the court. The law guardian was to
be the "wise parent," concerned with the general welfare of
the child, not just the advocate of his legal rights. When the
Act was written in 1962, it permitted the appointment of a
law guardian when requested. With the landmark *Gault* decision five years later, appointment of a law guardian was no
longer an option; it became a mandate in all juvenile delinquency cases.

In re Gault was the Supreme Court's review of a case in
which a fifteen-year-old boy was committed to a state indus-
trial school for six years—until he reached adulthood—for
making "lewd phone calls." The complainant, who never appeared at any of the hearings, reported the remarks in question as "Do you give any?," "Are your cherries ripe today?,"
and "Do you have big bombers?"

In response to her complaint the boy was picked up and
detained without notification to his parents. He was not informed of his right to a lawyer, was questioned without a
relative present, and was sentenced to remain in an institution until he reached the age of twenty-one. The maximum
penalty for an adult for this charge was two months and a
fifty-dollar fine. It is important to remember these facts and

conditions in order to understand the justification for the *Gault* decision. The decision hit at the juvenile court's reliance on informal fact-finding and afforded juveniles all the protections accorded to adults except for bail and trial by jury.

Most important of all, *In re Gault* made appointment of counsel a constitutional requirement in every delinquency case.

By the early 1970s, various procedural technicalities of criminal law increasingly came to be applied to juvenile matters. Family Court decisions required proof beyond a reasonable doubt, *Miranda* warnings at the time of arrest, and numerous stipulations relating to the admissibility of evidence.

With the due process revolution ushered in by the *Gault* decision, the juvenile courts moved away from the concept of benevolent protection to that of procedural rights, and the system began to resemble the adult criminal justice system.

Since 1967, some critics assert, *Gault* has spawned precedents by which a violent juvenile who is clearly guilty, sometimes even by his own admission, can be set free on a technicality that makes the evidence of that guilt, although it exists, inadmissible in court. Such suppressions are the result of the swing of the pendulum from one extreme to another.

In granting many due process rights to children that had previously been reserved for adults, *Gault* also ensured that juvenile cases would become adversary proceedings, a situation Justice Potter Stewart, in his dissenting opinion, called "a long step backwards" that was "sadly unwise." As the Justice predicted, *Gault* brought lawyers into the courtroom in force.

In the courtroom, B.J. and Daryl look around casually, unconcerned, while their lawyer insists the evidence against them should be suppressed even though they've signed their own handwritten statements of what they did and how and when. The issue is whether the officer who read them their rights—the Miranda warnings—may have forgotten to have them initial their affirmative responses when asked if they understood what had been read to them. "These kids know Miranda," says one cop, "the way we knew Mother Goose." B.J. and Daryl seem to know it's a game they can beat if they're smart and cool. They see their lawyer is making up a likely story on their behalf. Again, I think of the children in Dickens, misapprehended, awestricken, fearful, pathetic, and therefore highly appealing, with a resonating grip on our romantic imaginations. Was it as false then as it is now? What of the victim, the teenage boy whom B.J. and Daryl robbed and beat up? His testimony is easy to criticize, but its inconsistencies seem to indicate a difficulty in conceptualizing time frames, maintaining sequences in his mind, rather than any lack of veracity. His account of what happened is believable. And so is his misery. One wonders how he was persuaded to appear. He will have to go back to the neighborhood where they all live, and there is no assurance at this point that B.J. and Daryl aren't going back there, too.

Rafael is a nice-looking boy. He waives his right to a hearing and pleads guilty to attempted grand larceny. The judge explains his rights very clearly and very carefully, making sure he understands that he is giving up his right to face witnesses against him, to have a lawyer argue his case, to remain silent without prejudice, and that by his admission he gives her the right to decide what to do with him and that he may be sent away from home for a period up to a year and a half. He understands. She asks him to tell her what happened.

"Me and these two friends decided to go uptown to see these girls. We didn't have any money so we decided to get a

purse and we saw this lady on a bike . . ." He tells this story
in the same tone in which another boy might say, "We decided to go to a movie," or "I decided to look for a job after
school," the tone in which one recounts normal, expectable
behavior.

Rafael is a nice-looking boy and both of his parents are
present in court. That in itself counts for a lot. The judge
paroles him to his parents' custody pending an I and R (investigation and report by the probation department) and an
MHS (a mental health study by the court psychologist).

Later, an assistant corporation counsel confers with her chief
on the case of a little girl accused of having set a fire. I see
the child with her mother in the waiting area, neatly dressed,
well-behaved, a pretty little girl with braided hair and a
frightened expression. Corporation Counsel doesn't want to
try this case; it wants to drop the charges if the mother will
agree to psychiatric treatment for the child. Nobody thinks
she should be treated like a juvenile delinquent. She is nine.
Her Legal Aid lawyer agrees. I had almost expected her to
insist on a hearing on principle. But she's one who combines
compassion with common sense, who once said to me, "We
see them as neglects at two, PINS at eleven, delinquents at
fourteen."

The inefficiency of the system is staggering. What must it cost
to keep all these people here all day when so much of their
time is wasted? Over and over again a case on the calendar
cannot go forward because "the probation officer isn't in today, the DFY person can't be found, one of the lawyers is
arguing a case in another part." There must be a better way
to coordinate these proceedings.

The seemingly endless waste of time is part of every day
in every part of the court. Witnesses don't show up, docu-

ments aren't ready, calls to locate them are delayed by busy phone lines or the information that the computers are down again, counsels are elsewhere, and meanwhile the judge sits in an empty courtroom waiting, while the clerks and guards and the court steno stare into space, chat, write letters, do a crossword puzzle.

A court clerk, an elderly man who's been working here for twenty years: "A book? You writing a book about this place? I been waiting to tell somebody. You should write this: We can't make them whole here. It's like Humpty-Dumpty. The average kid—forget it. He gets lost in the shuffle. This system is geared for the ones with a high IQ and the handicapped. The kid like Robert, the one who just got put on probation for taking something off another kid, he falls through the cracks, he'll never see the sun here. He can't read, he can't understand, he doesn't go to school. What can the court do for him?"

By 1976 there was a public perception that urban street crime had increased, and that most of it was being committed by young teenagers. There were more and more news reports of elderly people in New York and other cities being victimized—robbed and often beaten as they fumbled for keys outside their apartments, or set upon in little mom-and-pop stores in poor neighborhoods. In response to the public outcry, the New York legislature passed the Juvenile Justice Reform Act of 1976. It defined certain "designated felonies"—including murder, kidnapping, rape, arson, armed robbery—and established new "dispositional alternatives" (i.e., sentences) in such cases. There were still certain limitations on age (no one under thirteen could be tried for a designated felony without a serious previous history—for instance, two prior felony findings). The intention of the Act was to add the protection of the community to the considerations of Family Court, where up to then the interests and wishes of the child had been the primary—and often the only—consideration.

But even the 1976 law didn't go far enough for an increasingly anxious public made aware by the press of a number of designated felony cases. Even after the Act's passage, a number of cases of juvenile crime made the headlines, notably those of Willy Boskett, a subway murderer whose sentence as a designated felon was three years, and Felipe O., also placed for three years for a murder in which he was reported to have laughed while pulling the trigger.

In 1978, the legislature established the category of juvenile offender. A juvenile offender is a thirteen-year-old who kills intentionally, or a fourteen-, fifteen-, or sixteen-year-old who kills, rapes, robs with physical injury or deadly force, sets fires—any of the worst crimes of violence against another person. The juvenile offender may be indicted and tried by a jury in Supreme Court like an adult—although the sentencing will still be different—or tried in Family Court, where his offense usually becomes a designated felony. He can have been convicted of two previous felonies and still be tried in Family Court. What all this boils down to is that—by definition— only juvenile delinquents are tried in Family Court. No one twelve years old or younger—*no matter what he does*—can be tried as anything but a juvenile delinquent or thus anywhere but in Family Court. Therefore, *nothing* done by anyone under thirteen can earn him more than eighteen months' initial placement, the most stringent "disposition" allowed under Family Court law, unless he is already a designated felon—a juvenile with prior findings of the most serious nature. This is a fact not unknown to kids in the area the police know as Manhattan North, where the guns they play with are not infrequently real ones, or to the area's thriving drug dealers, who offer them good pay to be "yos." A "yo" just has to stand around outside a building or on a corner or beside a car and look out for the cops. If he sees them he calls out "Yo" and tries to disappear fast. If he doesn't make it, no matter. There's not much that can happen to him, and just to make sure that nothing does, there's always a lawyer.

By 1982, when the J.O. Law, as it is referred to in the system, had been in effect for five years, 5,000 juveniles were arrested in New York State for crimes subject to adult prosecution. Of the 830 of these convicted as juvenile offenders, 679 had been sentenced by 1982. Of these, 280 (41 percent) were put on probation and 92 (14 percent) were given sentences of under four years. All in all, the incarceration rate for *convicted* juvenile offenders—guilty of murder, rape, attack with a gun or a knife—for the period 1978–82 was 59 percent. In other words, four out of every ten convicted murderers, rapists, and armed assailants never spent a day off the streets.

When the Family Court Act was written in 1962, delinquents were for the most part petty thieves, troublemakers, disobedient truants whom their parents complained they couldn't control. Well into the 1970s, the most common act for which juveniles were adjudicated delinquent was "jostling"—picking pockets with no physical confrontation involved.

Today's young criminals seem to be a different breed. Changes in society—the breakdown of the family, the weakening of religious and other forms of authority, the prevalence of drugs and the high cost of addiction, and the cynical knowledge about how little they have to fear from the law— all seem to encourage youthful predators of a kind the laws and institutions of a previous generation could not have anticipated.

4

By Reason of Infancy

'Juvenile Delinquent' means a person over seven and less than sixteen years of age, who, having committed an act that would constitute a crime if committed by an adult . . . is not criminally responsible for such conduct by reason of infancy . . .

—Family Court Act (1983), Article 3, Part 1

In colonial America and into the nineteenth century, children "convicted of any stubborne or rebellious carriage against their parents or governors" were committed to the House of Correction alongside adult criminals.

In 1824, the Society for the Reformation of Juvenile Delinquents in the City of New York was established by New York State with the avowed purpose of rehabilitating children under sixteen by placing them in a special supervised facility—the New York House of Refuge—instead of adult jails or penitentiaries. A similar institution, the Western House of Refuge, served upstate communities. The regimen at the House of Refuge was strict, a long day of classes and labor, but probably no harsher than life for most working people at the time.

By the end of the decade, Boston and Philadelphia had established similar institutions, to which juveniles convicted of crimes were sent along with orphans and neglected chil-

65

dren. Until well into this century the typical juvenile criminal was a boy caught stealing coal from the railroad yards to take home or a group of boys stealing copper fixtures from an empty building to resell. After serving some time, these youngsters were apprenticed to adult masters in the community to work out the remainder of their sentences as servants or laborers. By the end of the century most states had established separate correctional facilities for juvenile criminals. By then they were known as reformatories or training schools.

The movement to separate children from adult criminals led to the establishment in Illinois in 1899 of the first juvenile court. In 1905, the Pennsylvania case of *Commonwealth* v. *Fisher* denied the child's right to trial by jury on the grounds that children were not brought before the court to be tried but to be saved, "if a worthy subject for salvation." It was a clear declaration of the judicial philosophy of the state's discretion over the welfare of its children. It was a philosophy that was to rule the juvenile justice system until the 1960s.

By 1909 the law directed the courts to "consider the child not as upon trial for commission of a crime, but as a child in need of care and protection of the state" and to deal with him accordingly. Thus from the earliest years of this century the law was designed to meet the needs of the child and protect his best interests.

The "child savers" of the late nineteenth-century reform movement saw the task of social work as overcoming the effects of the environment of urban poverty. They focused on child labor legislation and on living conditions in the overcrowded slums and city streets. They also spearheaded the establishment of juvenile courts, training schools, and reformatories intended to deal with delinquents, as a juvenile court judge of the time put it, "as a wise parent would deal with a wayward child." Instead of being tried as a criminal, the youthful miscreant would receive, in the wording of the

Standard Juvenile Court Act of 1909, "the care, guidance and control that will conduce to his welfare and the best interests of the State," which would act as his parent.

By 1910 there were juvenile courts in most states. They were an expression of the progressive philosophy of urban social work and the child development movement in response to the need to integrate large numbers of immigrant workers and to educate their children to citizenship.

In the philosophy that guided the new institutions of children's courts, juveniles could not be considered criminals. Treatment, guidance, supervision replaced accusation, guilt, punishment as the thinking and language of social work replaced that of criminal law. The very idea of a juvenile court grew out of civil rather than criminal justice, in particular the medieval English doctrine of *parens patriae*, whereby the Crown could step in and take the place of the natural parents in cases where a child's welfare was deemed to be at risk. By 1920, every state in the union had established a juvenile court based on the doctrine of *parens patriae*. The aim was the rehabilitation of the child; the means, whatever was in his best interests.

A 1932 decision made it clear that since "the state was not seeking to punish a malefactor" but "seeking to salvage a boy who was in danger of becoming one . . . the proceeding was not a criminal one," and therefore constitutional procedural safeguards were neither necessary nor desirable. The informal *parens patriae* system was thus in place. Delinquency proceedings were considered civil rather than quasi-criminal matters, and their purpose was to rescue and change a child gone wrong.

Thus, for good or ill, for over a hundred years we struggled to separate the misdeeds of children from those of adults and to be guided by the doctrine of *parens patriae*—the benevolent state as wise father devoted to the rehabilitation of his errant children. In the 1960s, all of this was swept away. In the landmark 1966 *Kent* decision, Supreme Court Justice Abe Fortas characterized the system as a failure. Fortas wrote that as the system actually operated, "the child receives the worst of both worlds . . . he gets neither the protections accorded to adults nor the solicitous care and regenerative treatment postulated for children."

Morris A. Kent, Jr., was fourteen when he was arrested in Washington, D.C., in 1959 for housebreaking and purse-snatching and placed on probation. He was interviewed from time to time and a social service file accumulated on him. In 1961, an intruder entered a woman's apartment, took her wallet, and raped her. In her apartment the police found fingerprints that matched those in Kent's juvenile court file. Kent was arrested and taken to police headquarters. There, under questioning, he admitted to the rape and robbery and volunteered information about several other robberies and rapes he had committed. His interrogation lasted from midafternoon until late in the evening, when he was taken to the Receiving Home for Children. The next morning he was returned to police headquarters, where he remained until 5:00 P.M.

Kent remained in detention for almost a week, during which time there was no arraignment, no formal charge. The day after his arrest, his mother had retained a lawyer. The lawyer's requests for the juvenile court records were denied, as was his motion for a hearing on the basis of psychiatric testimony reporting that Morris Kent was "a victim of severe psychopathology" and recommending hospitalization. Instead, with no hearing on any of these issues, the juvenile court judge waived jurisdiction and sent Kent to criminal court to be tried as an adult.

No reason was given for the waiver. Kent was indicted by

a grand jury and tried in criminal court. The defense held that he was not criminally responsible because "his unlawful act was the product of mental disease or mental defect." The jury found him guilty of six counts of housebreaking and robbery, for which he was given a thirty- to ninety-year sentence, but found him "not guilty by reason of insanity" on the rape charge, and he was committed to St. Elizabeth's Hospital, a mental institution, to serve out his sentence.

In a series of appeals, the case made its way to the Supreme Court, the first case in which the Court considered juvenile court procedures. A number of grounds were given for reversal, all of which addressed the issue of violation of due process: the failure to notify his parents of Kent's arrest; his interrogation in the absence of counsel or parent, without warning of his right to remain silent and to have a lawyer present; his detention without a probable-cause hearing; and the use of the fingerprints from his juvenile court files in violation of the confidentiality implied in the rehabilitative intent of the juvenile court system. However, while agreeing that these were all matters "of substantial concern," the Court limited itself to consideration of the judge's decision to waive Kent's case to the criminal court, which it declared to be invalid. Kent's indictment was dismissed on the grounds of procedural irregularity.

In a decision that would have far-reaching implications, Justice Fortas wrote, "The theory of the . . . Juvenile Court Act . . . is rooted in social welfare philosophy . . . its proceedings are designated as civil rather than criminal. The juvenile court is theoretically engaged in determining the needs of the child and of society rather than adjudicating criminal conduct. The objectives are to provide measures of guidance and rehabilitation for the child and protection for society, not to fix criminal responsibility, guilt and punishment. The state is *parens patriae* rather than prosecuting attorney and judge. But the admonition to function in a 'parental' relationship is not an invitation to procedural arbitrariness."

Kent called into question whether the courts could be relied on to function in the interests of children "as a wise parent" in the absence of due process requirements accorded adults. As a sixteen-year-old, it held, Kent was "entitled to certain procedures and benefits as a consequence of his statutory right to the 'exclusive' jurisdiction of the juvenile court." Instead, he had been tried and sentenced without counsel, without a hearing, without a finding, without reasons—"without ceremony."

Since *Kent,* ceremony has been introduced to the juvenile court system with, one is tempted to say, a vengeance. *Kent* was a decisive step in the direction already taken in California as well as in New York to replace the *parens patriae* model—which was perceived as having betrayed its original promise of looking to the welfare of the minor—with the criminal justice model.

With the Court's ruling in *Gault* the following year and subsequent lower-court decisions, *parens patriae* was replaced by due process and most of the rules regulating criminal proceedings were brought into Family Court, with the result that the focus on the needs of children is now often replaced by an emphasis on the rights of children—and they are not always the same.

The waiting areas in Brooklyn Family Court always seem to be more crowded than Manhattan's. On a steaming summer day in 1984 they are flooded by a sea of young and old, children and grandparents. It is like a Hogarth drawing except that everyone appears well-fed, and no one is dressed in rags or looks sick. A man and woman in their twenties are arguing. A little boy rests his elbows on the woman's knee, looks up into her face raptly. It is a mask of anger as she rasps at the man, "I've got more balls 'n you'll ever have!" A few yards away, standing outside the courtroom door, a large elderly woman wearing a button that reads "You must be born again" says to Albert, a teenage boy, "Don't forget. You got your rights." It's like a hospital waiting room. There should be a loudspeaker calling for various specialists—a philosopher, an economist. How do we separate rights and needs? For that matter, how do we balance human needs and fiscal ones?

Brent is the complainant, stabbed by another boy in the school corridor. He explains how it happened. "Me and him was riding the train, see? And he messing with me. You know, staring like. So I stare back at him. So we gets to school and we're putting our books in the lockers and he starts messing again and he calls me 'pussy,' so I put up my hands and then he took a knife out of his bookbag." The defendant slashed him—he has superficial cuts on his shoulder and his jacket is ripped—and ran away but was caught by the school security guard. Brent is over six feet tall, wearing the largest and whitest sneakers I have ever seen, laced widely and untied in the current fashion. He does not seem upset, says he wouldn't be there if the guard hadn't caught the other boy and the school officials and police hadn't intervened. His mother sits by, sullenly chewing gum, a large impassive woman in a striking red wig. "Does your husband live at home?" asks the investigating attorney. "Sometimes." "Does he work?" "Off and on." There is a normalcy about everyone's tone that seems inappropriate to what is being said, what has been done, until you've been in Brooklyn Family Court for a few hours. By then it begins to seem normal enough.

Albert, his grandmother wearing her born-again button, has come before the court now. His Legal Aid lawyer wants him released until the next court date. "You can't put this kid in the slammer for six months!" Albert has been charged with deviant sexual behavior with a retarded boy who lives in the same housing project. There are no sanctions to protect the complainant from Albert, because Albert is a juvenile.

As we sit in a coffee shop near Brooklyn Family Court during a lunch break, one of the young attorneys working for the Corporation Counsel tells me about Hector and his two friends. Hector, described as an angelic-looking little Hispanic kid of fifteen, was indicted with another fifteen-year-old and a sixteen-year-old for rape. The girl was sodomized and when they'd all raped her, they stuck a gun up her vagina and tore her up. Hector bragged to the police about his prowess and seemed surprised at their attitude. "Hey, man, you shouldn't be mad at me," he told one cop, "I was the nice guy," and he told them he had put her handbag under her head so she would be more comfortable during the attack.

Four boys have been accused of trying to steal money and a calculator from another boy outside the junior high school they all attend. The complainant has failed to appear and so the charges will be dropped. The mothers are angry, shouting at the Corporation Counsel attorney who has been handling the case. Now their sons will have a record. (One of them, a tall boy wearing a ski hat—it's the middle of summer—and brand-new Nikes, has an open robbery 1 case involving a gun, which seems to limit his credibility.) The attorney explains these arrest records will be sealed "unless they get arrested again." One of the mothers snaps back scornfully, "How I going to see to that? I work twelve hours a day!" Another of the mothers asks the attorney if she'll be responsible if her son gets into trouble after he turns sixteen. The attorney explains that the boy would then be tried in criminal court as an adult.

Later, he remarks wearily, "We don't even hold the *kids* responsible for what they do. How can we hold the parents responsible?"

Somewhere along the way, the protection of the minor client's interests (the concept of "helping them express their wishes to the court") and his due process rights as an accused in danger of being deprived of his liberty have taken precedence over the idea of his need to be retrained, rehabilitated, salvaged, returned whole to the community.

And the aim of the lawyers who defend him has become wholly adversarial: to keep him from being found to have committed an act which if committed by an adult would constitute a crime, and—ironically—thus to keep him from being given any of that help, rehabilitation, training, which was supposed to be in his own best interests and those of the community. "For better or for worse," reads the commentary accompanying the written text of the Family Court Act of 1983, "the adversarial nature of Article 3 [delinquency] and Article 7 [PINS] proceedings has increased and been accentuated beyond anything the original drafters of the Family Court Act probably contemplated." In fact, according to the *Manual for New Attorneys* of the New York Legal Aid Society's Family Court Branch, the handling of a delinquency case should be indistinguishable from the defense of an adult criminal prosecution. Whether the child in question has been accused of killing, rape, sodomy, or violent assault, the law guardian should disregard not only his personal feelings about either the child or the nature of the crime, but also "the possible need for incarceration. His duty is to defend the child with zeal."

A boy has attempted to rape a little girl at knifepoint in the elevator of their housing project. His Legal Aid lawyer tries to get him put in an open facility between this fact-finding and the dispositional hearing a month from now instead of in secure detention at Spofford. She loses, but seems to be in her element, defending some principle that has left common sense and humanity behind somewhere.

And yet . . . sitting here day after day it's hard not to get caught up in the game of definitions, rules, exceptions. A bit like a crossword puzzle. Or a board game. Can she make it around? Can the procedure be made to work here? Can the evidence be discredited, the statement be thrown out, the witness caught out in a contradiction? Lost sight of in the game aspect of it all is the human reality. And many—although not all—of the Legal Aid lawyers, particularly the women, seem not just to be providing the mandated legal defense necessary for a fair hearing on the charge but to be emotionally overidentified with the respondents. I wonder to myself, for instance, whether ordinary people, members of the public that are never present here, would be offended to hear the Legal Aid lawyer call the boy she's representing "Sweetie"?

The courtroom empties, refills. A court-appointed lawyer is here to protect the rights of the mother in a custody case. Two caseworkers are here on behalf of the agency that has placed two of the children with foster parents who want to adopt them. The foster parents are here, too, with their lawyer. The natural mother is very young, small, wan, uncaring. Various facts emerge. The children, all fathered by different men, are being supported publicly. For those still at home, Welfare provides Aid to Families with Dependent Children. In addition to rent and food, there is day care for the children and psychiatric care for the mother. ("She's fragile," says the mother's lawyer.) She looks absent, glazed, the only one in the room who doesn't seem to care what happens. She has difficulty answering a question about when she last visited the children in foster care. Trying to organize her thoughts, she looks pained. "When was it? I dunno. It was cold out . . ." It's as close as she can come to dealing with time. Thousands of dollars an hour are being spent here, thousands more worth of psychiatric tests are ordered to show what we all can see—that she's out of it, can't possibly be competent to care for her children . . .

Observing the proceedings in Family Court inevitably leads one to question two of the system's basic assumptions. The first is that it is always dealing with children whom it is possible to rehabilitate and that bringing about this change should be its primary goal; the second is that the proceedings should be conducted in secret and records of them should be unavailable to the press.

Often the court seems more concerned to avoid "the possibly stigmatizing effect of a delinquency finding" than to protect the child from himself, let alone protect the community from him. The business of the court is "to avoid for one who has the defense of infancy the stigma attached to defense or conviction of 'criminal charges,' " reads the law in a 1981 decision. How appropriate is the concern for the privacy of these hearings? Why, I wonder as I sit in the courtroom, doesn't the public have a right to know what goes on here, and why should no stigma be attached to repeated offenders, whatever their age?

In another courtroom a Legal Aid lawyer refuses to let me be present in the courtroom because, he says, his client objects. With a straight face he says, "My client feels it's an imposition, an embarrassment . . ." His client is nodding in a chair, eyes closed. It's unlikely he cares or would even notice the presence of another person in the courtroom. It's the lawyer's own decision. *He* feels it's an imposition and might become an embarrassment. It cannot always be easy to insist on the rights of some of his more brutal clients. You have to keep your mind on abstract principles and not look too closely at the kid or even at the facts.

In 1976, the purpose of the system was enlarged to include a new element, specifying for the first time in the Juvenile Justice Reform Act passed that year that the court should consider not only the needs and best interests of the alleged delinquent but also "the need for protection of the community." Inevitably, the two stated goals would clash.

While the best interests of a wayward juvenile and the protection of the community might appear to be the same in a case involving no serious harm or loss to another person and where benign intervention might turn still impressionable youths around in attitude and behavior, there are not too many of them. Not very many of today's young criminals seem that malleable, and the resources available to deal with them have not been applied that successfully. Nor is there any reason to expect them to be. Violent crimes are usually committed by someone who got an early start and has gone on considerably from there before being apprehended for the first time. The data seem compellingly clear on this point. Habitual street criminals are typically youngsters who have failed to form attachments to others early in life, who have no structured families or community institutions like schools or churches to which they feel responsible, and who are careless of life, both their own and those of others. They see no reason to change, and the system doesn't really give them any. It offers neither sufficient rewards nor punishments to make a real difference, until it is too late. And with a violence-prone, uncontrollable teenager who feels that his best interests are served by being sent back to the streets, his law guardian is expected to try to help him do so in every possible way. The lawyer has at his disposal a whole arsenal of procedural rules, the infringement of any small part of one of which will get his "client" off.

The legal question, of course, is not what he did—or may even admit to having done—but what can be proved. In a typical case, a boy ran away from a policeman who then caught up with him, put his hand in the boy's pocket, and found drugs. The evidence was suppressed. The drugs were inadmissible as evidence. Illegal search. A loaded gun found on another boy was inadmissible because the search that revealed the weapon was not based on probable cause. The loaded gun was there, but only in actuality, not in probability.

In criminal law these safeguards make sense because of the potential penalties involved in a felony conviction, but the sanctions are markedly different in the juvenile court system. It is the schizoid nature of the juvenile system—unable to make up its mind whether it is a civil process designed to help the wrongdoer or a criminal action in which rules must protect the accused because he is at risk for serious sanctions—that is the problem.

If the evidence is so overwhelming that there is a finding (conviction), the law requires that the court should order "the least restrictive available alternative." The boy may be sent to a residential treatment center, a limited-security facility outside the city but without locks, or he may be sent to a non-secure group home in the city from which he can go and come—if one will take him. If he's too intimidating, he may be refused and, rather than send a "child" to a lockup, a judge may order probation. Back on the streets—most often, to repeat the process and eventually wind up in the adult prison system.

Mario is back in court because of his violent behavior in the group home to which he was remanded for non-secure detention pending the disposition of his case. He's been throwing furniture around, fighting with the other kids. His MHS suggests instability, recommends placement where he will have more help controlling his impulses instead of the freedom to act on them. The judge has another approach to boys like this. A former Legal Aid staffer, with more experience in the juvenile justice system than most of her judicial colleagues put together, Judge Kathryn McDonald remains incorrigibly optimistic. The child, to her, always deserves the benefit of the doubt.

She tells Mario, "I understand how you feel. Psychiatrists are a pain in the neck, aren't they, always snooping in your own business. Now you liked the social worker at Beach Avenue, didn't you? We have to find a place for you·to live where you'll like the people you have to deal with so you can learn to be the kind of guy you want to be and that other people want you to be . . ." She is unfailingly kind, her tone of voice always friendly.

"It's time to smarten up, son. You say these dumb things you don't mean but people don't know whether you do or not. What would you do if you were the psychiatrist asking the questions and the answer was, 'I'd beat his head in'?" Mario is looking down. It's impossible to tell what effect this is having on him. To another boy this morning, Judge McDonald said, "I understand you have family problems but that's the kind of thing that makes you sad, makes you cry, but it doesn't make you sell cocaine."

Later, in the empty courtroom between cases, she says of Mario, "I'm not worried about him, he's got a lot of defenses." Phil Dobbs, the court liaison officer who has just walked in, says, "Yeah, like knives, guns . . ." She laughs, then adds, "He's not intimidated by all those professional types hovering over him. I don't know that that's so bad, do you?" Thinking about some of them, I'm able to say, "No . . ." But I don't sound convinced, even to me.

The fifteen-year-old was involved in a brutal gang rape shortly after being released from a Title II facility (no locks) where he'd spent a year. The Corporation Counsel attorneys didn't want to tell me what the boys had done. They said it would have been better for the girl if they'd killed her. She would never get over it. It was the only time I remember them being reluctant to provide the details of a crime. The I and R from the Probation Department said he had "little bond for any particular person." It's this lack of attachment to other human beings that seems to make possible these acts of random violence. Are these the kind of people who could run concentration camps or preside over political torture?, I ask myself.

The psychological report describes him as "not aggressive," which the psychologist explains doesn't mean that he's not capable of being criminally violent but that he isn't capable of handling life situations in an assertive, competitive way. The failure to establish normal affection for others early in life is connected with the ability to confront others later with a healthy degree of aggressivity.

The history is depressingly predictable. Mother, sixteen at time of his birth. Father unknown. Shunted around among various relatives. Mother in a series of relationships with sometimes brutal men, treated for heroin addiction. Placed in special classes for the emotionally handicapped; a record of failure, truancy, and finally dropping out. A life lived mostly on the streets, occasionally turning up at some relative's for a night or two, sometimes returning to the apartment mother shares with current man, sometimes being kicked out. Becoming well known, as they put it, to the court. The only open question about his future is whether he will make it to the adult prison system before he kills or gets killed himself.

"There are too many cases like this," the Corporation

Counsel attorney says, "kids who've committed serious crimes, released after a year and a half, and they go out and do it again."

Too many cases, and too few people in the courtroom with any sense of how to deal with them.

If there is a model Family Court judge it is probably Judith Sheindlin, who was sitting in Bronx Family Court when I visited there (she has since been transferred to Manhattan). She is thoughtful, fair, and above all firm. "They're *supposed* to be afraid of me," she says of the boys who appear before her. "I'm not supposed to be their pal, call them son." She is clearly in charge of her courtroom and everything that happens in it and commands the respect if not awe of both Legal Aid and Corporation Counsel, whose Manhattan Family Court division she headed before being appointed to the bench.

A small woman with dark curly hair, Judge Sheindlin wears high heels and a lace collar on her black robe; nevertheless she exudes a no-nonsense attitude. Fathers waiting to have their support cases heard ask with some trepidation, "Is *she* in there?" After hearing her conduct one such case, I could see why.

To the bitterly quarreling parents, she said, "Don't tell me you don't want *her* to have him, or *you* don't want *him* to have him. He's not *your* child, he has *two* parents. Custody is not something you give or withhold from the other parent. The child has a right to maximum exposure to both parents."

The battle was between a mother who had not remarried and lived in the city and a father with a suburban home who would be away on naval duty for months at a time, leaving the child to be cared for by his second wife.

Once the facts were established and the situation clear, Judge Sheindlin called the lawyers for both sides into her chambers and pointed out to them that it was in the child's interest for them to reach an agreement without prolonged litigation. To facilitate that, she would tell them what she was likely to do. She would not, she told them, award custody to a parent who would be absent on the high seas while the child was taken care of by a step-parent when there was a natural parent available who was not an unreasonable choice. So why prolong all the acrimony and bitterness? Why not try for an agreement?

The father's lawyer looked impressed, seemed to get the idea. He would get to work on it. Meanwhile, Judge Sheindlin ordered visitation arrangements. She obviously knows these situations, knows what she wants. It's a relief for everybody involved, a benefit for the child.

Her next case was a boy who'd been caught stealing bus transfers and selling them. His mother was there, anxious to tell her story, obviously soured on the boy. He's difficult, she says, gives her trouble all the time, truants, then when she tries to talk to him, "he bangs on the wall, hits it with his fist." So far there's been no violence against other people.

Judge Sheindlin paroles him to ATD (an Alternative to Detention school program in the community), and tells him, "Michael, you've got smarts but you're not using them. You could be something when you grow up, but only if you use your smarts to learn something now, and you're not going to learn it on the streets, unless your friends are a pretty intellectual bunch, which I doubt." Michael will get remedial schoolwork and counseling. The hope is that he'll stay out of trouble in a better setting than his present school or his home.

A good judge can make the system work. The trouble is not only that there are so few judges who use it wisely but that there is just so much that the system—any system—can do to redirect the energies of a fifteen-year-old who's missed out on everything that should have been an influence in his development up to then. Perhaps Judge Sheindlin knows that, which makes her efforts all the more impressive.

The next case is a more serious matter, a boy up for "rob 1." Robbery in the first degree involves a deadly weapon. We've gone beyond kid stuff now. Both parents are in court, an unusual thing here. The father, a big man, keeps glaring at his son every time the probation officer or the psychologist says something about the boy's motivation or character. The mother is withdrawn, weepy, resigned. They are separated. The father, a sanitation worker, says he has no trouble with the other children. He's ready to move back in to the family home if it will make a difference on disposition.

The boy is sullen, lethargic, seems to feel no connection to the proceedings, nods off. Judge Sheindlin asks him if he's been given any medication at Spofford. He says yes, for "gongorea."

The probation officer is none too bright, none too organized, none too articulate. She was impressed with the family and the home and suggested paroling the boy to his parents. The psychologist is bright, organized, and articulate. He thinks the boy is impulsive, prone to violence, needs a highly structured environment to modify his behavior. He explains: Under close supervision, there will be increasing responsibility, rewarded if he does well by more freedom and more responsibility. If he regresses, then less freedom. Remedial schoolwork is another necessity for this boy. The probation officer is weak when questioned by the assistant D.A.—he's on the case because it's a designated felony—but the psychologist comes across as credible and persuasive. The case is adjourned until the following week to hear testimony by a psychiatrist. Meanwhile, the boy will stay in Spofford.

The New York Youth House for Boys, now the Spofford Juvenile Center, was opened in the Bronx in 1957 as a detention center for delinquents. From the beginning it was over-crowded and for some time it housed status offenders—non-criminal juveniles like runaways—along with delinquents. In those pre-*Gault* decision days, children could be locked up on a complaint without a formal court procedure or an official order. But all that has changed.

The visitor to Spofford today is greeted by a no-nonsense administrator, director Rose Washington, a black woman with experience in working with youth groups and a realistic attitude toward her charges that is neither punitive nor sentimental.

Boys are sent to Spofford in some cases because the seriousness of the "incident" for which they were arrested—usually a robbery—caused them to be remanded rather than sent home, in other cases because no adult family members could be found to assume responsibility for them until their scheduled court appearance. Some are there only a few hours; others may remain as long as several weeks.

The first thing the visitor to Spofford is shown are the impressive medical facilities, in many ways—including the individual attention—superior to public health and dental clinics in the outside community. Classrooms are attractively equipped, and the school day, lasting five and a half hours, takes place in a part of the building named for a black historian. The cafeteria and swimming pool compare favorably with those of most public schools, and inmates who follow the reasonable-enough rules earn extra privileges—including cigarettes and recreational time for playing basketball or watching television.

The boys in Spofford do not look happy, but it's hard to blame that on the place itself.

The most restrictive alternative for an under-sixteen who has been found to have committed an act which if committed by an adult would constitute a crime is one of the New York State Division for Youth's locked upstate facilities.

In one of those Title III secure facilities, Goshen, I talked with a tall, gangly boy who was sweeping the hallway between the residents' rooms. Small rooms, they contain a bed, a chair, a locker for clothes and personal effects, and pretty much whatever the boys want to put on their walls. Posters of basketball players and rock stars mostly. A lot of Michael Jackson. This boy showed me his room. Over his bed, pictures of a little boy I guessed was about four. Three, he told me proudly. Big for his age. Like his daddy. In one of the pictures he's holding a basketball. In another he's with a girl who could be his big sister. His mother. The boy leans on his broom, looks right into my eyes, tells me he never wants to do nothing bad again, just wants to get out of here, he has six months to go, then he'll get a job and take care of his old lady and his kid. He seems harmless, sincere, nice. He's harmless enough here, of course, surrounded by high walls and security guards, and he sincerely wants to impress a visitor who might be somebody important for all he knows. I wonder how nice he seemed when he was doing whatever it was that got him here. It would have to have been pretty bad, and he'd have had to have done it more than once. Later I found out. A robbery with two other boys. They killed the elderly store owner.

5
Beyond Advocacy

The use of the term 'guardian' as part of the title assigned to legal counsel in the Family Court would seem to connote an intention on the part of the Legislature to expand counsel's role beyond advocacy alone. . . . The role of the 'wise parent' has, in effect, been transferred from the court itself to the law guardian.

—from Practice Commentary, *Family Court Act*, Article 2, Part 4

The Legal Aid Society is a private agency established in the 1870s to provide legal services for those who could not afford to pay lawyers' fees themselves. When New York's Family Court was established in 1962, the Juvenile Rights Division of the Legal Aid Society was created to provide youngsters who could not otherwise retain a lawyer with the law guardians now mandated for all juveniles in all proceedings before the court. Today, Legal Aid represents virtually all of the children, including almost all of the delinquents, who are brought to Family Court. Funded under contracts with the city, state, and federal governments, the Juvenile Rights Division is almost entirely supported by public funds. It operates, in effect, as a government agency, yet it has no public accountability.

When I came to the court in the summer of 1984, I was welcomed by the staff of the Corporation Counsel, the city

85

law department's "presentment" (prosecuting) agency in Family Court. Most of the attorneys I met there were eager to talk about the court and what goes on there and enthusiastic about drawing public attention to the workings of the system and its manifold problems. The Legal Aid staff were less welcoming. In fact, they did everything short of posting an off-limits sign outside the courtrooms—and they probably would have done that if they could.

I was there at the discretion of the judges, but whenever possible a Legal Aid lawyer would raise some objection to the presence of "a member of the press," would argue for the right of his or her "client" to privacy, and would try to have me excluded. Sometimes a judge would be persuaded, and I would have to leave. Most of the time I was allowed to stay.

Some members of the Legal Aid staff agreed to be interviewed, but any questioning of their basic assumptions about the use of procedural rights in juvenile court, about the criminal as victim of society, met with coolness. A few of the older staff members seemed dedicated and scholarly. Most of the younger ones were not especially effective at articulating a point of view about what they did or why it needed to be done. They were, like the committed of any political orthodoxy, hard to engage in real discussion. The Legal Aid staff soon perceived that I was more searching than right-minded, and eventually, by mutual tacit agreement, our contacts became less frequent. I belonged to the "other side."

I had gradually come to feel, as the days became weeks, and months went by in the courtrooms, that the original intent of legal representation for the young lawbreakers I saw there had been corrupted, that their real interests were often sacrificed to their legalistic entitlements. And the Legal Aid argument that protecting their rights protects us all began to ring hollow when I saw how the system was used—perverted, it sometimes seemed—to deny the rights of their victims, past and future, and, by sending them right back where they came from to do it again, to deny their own right to any measures that might stop them, change them—yes, save them. Somewhere on the way from protecting the innocent we had wound up protecting too many of the guilty.

Legal Aid is interested in winning cases, not helping children. Or so it seems to the observer watching Family Court proceedings. The child's real interests often seem at odds with his expressed wishes, which are what Legal Aid is committed to represent. As one Legal Aid lawyer put it, "Whether he did it or not is not the point." Legal Aid wants the child to get away with it, not learn to change his ways. What can he learn from this experience, I wonder silently, but contempt for the law and the other institutions of society?

The Legal Aid lawyer, an attractive young woman with a long full mane of wavy hair and a pretty face and pleasant manner, claims, "I never met a kid I didn't like." Since she has met a number of killers and rapists, as well as sodomists of smaller children, this seems an extraordinary statement. Has she really looked at any of these "kids" at all, as people, or does she see them only as representatives of a theory? Juvenile crime, she explains patiently, is caused by socioeconomic factors. It comes about because the government—"society"—is not doing its job. She doesn't ask if individuals—mothers, fathers—are doing theirs, doesn't see it as a matter of individual responsibility. She concedes that the growing number of violent youth is in part the result of the increase in the number of children born to teenage mothers, but she sees the problem as "a lack of support institutions for them." The problem is always that there is something wrong with societal institutions—the schools, the police. The answer is always more spending, more money for more programs. She specializes in appeals on termination of parental rights.

"For the child to remain in the family," she explains, "is presumed to be in the best interests of the child."

Always? Any family? What about the child who has been burned with cigarettes or had his ribs broken? Is an abusive family still a family? She doesn't ask. She is committed to certain principles. Her philosophy blames crime and other social ills on the failure of government agencies to care properly for children. But how can an agency be a parent, I wonder?

The Legal Aid diagnosis and prescription for our social ills is expressed to me by Lenore Gittis, the attorney-in-charge of the society's Juvenile Rights Division: "No child of fifteen or sixteen is hopeless. Basically, [those who commit crimes] are classically depressed because they have no hope. . . . What is needed is a federal commitment, like the Marshall Plan." Money, according to this way of thinking, will solve the problems. Charles Schinitsky, perhaps the man most responsible for the sweeping changes in Family Court in the 1960s, agrees. "Probably nothing *can* be done in our society," he told another investigator of Family Court. "Not enough money is voted."

It was Schinitsky who, at the request of the Legal Aid Society in 1960, undertook a study of what was then known as Children's Court. It led to the publication in early 1962 of an article entitled "The Role of the Lawyer in the Children's Court," which was published by the Association of the Bar of the City of New York. The article provided the impetus for the requirement, when the Family Court was established later that year, that children in the new court had to be assigned lawyers to represent them. The Legal Aid Society was asked to provide that representation. In effect, this was the end of the attempt to adjudicate on the basis of the child's welfare or even that of the community. The name of the game now was rights. In Schinitsky's words, "If you have fifteen different people in a courtroom, you have fifteen opposing expert points of view. I thought, with a room full of experts there ought to be one person who would stand up and say, 'I don't have any idea what the best interest of this child is. I'm here to tell you what *he* wants. I'm here to look out for his rights.' " To Schinitsky, the "procedural safeguards" in question are designed to protect "innocent kids."

Twelve-year-old Rabhu B. was out on parole on a charge connected with the rape of an eleven-year-old girl (he had held her down for the fourteen-year-old who raped her) when he was arrested for criminal possession of a loaded weapon. The weapon was a .38, a big gun, capable of even worse harm than the usual Saturday night special. He was one of three boys who, when caught, seemed to be attempting what Corporation Counsel attorney Peter Reinharz calls the great train robbery: three boys get on a subway train and one stands at either end of the car while the third goes down the length of the car demanding the passengers' valuables at gunpoint. As soon as the train stops at the next station, they get off and make a run for it.

This time they didn't make it. Rabhu, the one with the gun, was remanded to Spofford, the city's secure juvenile detention center in the Bronx, to await his hearing. A dangerous kid, the judge thought, and said so. Locked up on the gun charge, Rabhu was still technically on parole on the earlier charge. After three days, his lawyer was not ready for the fact-finding hearing and the judge ordered another three days' secure remand. At the hearing, Rabhu was found guilty. He was remanded for ten days to Spofford. At the end of that time, when his lawyer was still not ready for the dispositional hearing, Rabhu was remanded for another ten days of secure detention. On the twentieth day his remand on the gun case

ended and Rabhu pleaded guilty to unlawful imprisonment—
a felony—in the rape case. The judge then gave him an open
remand on the gun case and he was placed in non-secure
detention.

Peter Reinharz, who was trying the case, was indignant.
"Before the finding he's in secure. After his guilt is determined
he's put in non-secure, where 'detention' means he'll get a
weekend pass to go home on the subway." When he chal-
lenged the ruling, Reinharz was told "his I and R isn't that
bad." Reinharz's response was, "Not that bad? He's out on
parole on a rape case. He doesn't go to school, he's on the
subway with a loaded gun . . ." Then he was told "his MHS
isn't that bad." Reinharz read the report and found it stated
that Rabhu needed "to be taught the ways of socialization
and concern for others." This was too much for Reinharz.
"This kid doesn't know how to live in society. And they're
going to teach him in NSD? They're talking about *re*habili-
tation? This kid is at ground zero. He tells them he didn't
intend to rob anybody and they take his word for it."

Reinharz brought the matter to the attention of his boss,
James Payne, then the head of the Corporation Counsel's
Family Court Division, and Payne went to Frederick A. O.
Schwarz, Jr., then the Corporation Counsel of the City of
New York, who took the matter up with the commissioner of
juvenile justice, Ellen Schall, and succeeded in having Rabhu
sent back to Spofford. It all seems like a great deal of time
and energy spent bringing the agency around to doing what
common sense would have suggested in the first place. Peter
Reinharz, shaking his head, says, "What we had to go
through. And even in the weeks just following the Shavod
Jones case. Rabhu was like Jones—another walking time
bomb." The Title III facility to which Rabhu was finally sent
was what they call limited-secure. No twelve-year-old is ever
sent to a locked facility.

Whether a twelve-year-old is charged with grand larceny or murder, with stealing your wallet or killing your son, the maximum possible penalty is the same: up to eighteen months' placement in a limited secure—that is, unlocked—facility.

As noted earlier, no one can be placed in a secure—that is, locked—facility unless he is thirteen or older, even if he has committed a designated felony like rape or murder, without special authorization from the court, which is rarely granted.

Fourteen-year-old Samuel S. was arrested and charged in connection with the savage beating of a boy who resisted a robbery attempt by a group of boys on a subway platform. When the others started to walk away, leaving the boy lying there, Samuel turned back, picked the boy up, carried him to the edge of the platform, and was about to throw him on the tracks in front of an oncoming train when a woman's screams startled him and he dropped the boy at the edge of the platform just as the train rushed by.

Because this was his first offense and there was nothing to indicate that Samuel would not appear in court at the time of his scheduled hearing, the judge paroled him. As he read the law, this was in accordance with a recent decision against preventive detention for juveniles.

While he was out on parole, Samuel and two of the other boys who had been involved in the robbery attempt accosted the victim and threatened to kill him if he testified against them in court. The victim reported this to the assistant Corporation Counsel, who asked the judge to remand Samuel for tampering with a witness. The judge refused.

Still roaming the city on parole, Samuel was arrested again shortly afterward for his part in a gang rape. This time he was arraigned in Criminal Court as a juvenile offender and tried in Supreme Court.

One young woman attorney on the Legal Aid staff had her wallet stolen in the Family Court building. She told a member of the Corporation Counsel staff she would press charges if the theft was committed by an adult, not if it was done by "a child." She felt, she said, that children must be treated differently, no matter what they do.

"What," asked the other lawyer after she had gone, "if she were beaten up or raped, or her child was?"

The infancy defense sounds good on paper and it appeals to those who take their compassion neat, without diluting theory with the reality of repeated violence and its victims. It's an attitude expressed at its most extreme by the judge in a New York Supreme Court case in 1981 and reported by the mother of the victim, her only son, a talented young student killed by teenage thugs in a subway robbery attempt. Impatient with the prosecutor's attempts to call attention to the defense lawyer's delaying tactics, the judge said on the record, "This is only a murder . . . only a murder, and we are talking about an eighteen-year-old."

While many of the Legal Aid attorneys do believe in the rightness of what they are doing, it becomes apparent to an observer of the daily scene in Family Court that some of them negotiate cynically. "What you gonna give me on this one?" a law guardian asks an assistant Corporation Counsel. Another says, "I'm a garbage man. All I do is collect garbage around here and put the shit back on the streets."

The inconsistencies of the Legal Aid philosophy that continues to prevail in Family Court have often been remarked. "Family Court," says a lawyer who practices there, "was set up for little boys who stole candy from the newsstand or broke somebody's window. Not for teenagers on drugs who carry guns—and use them." A probation officer adds, "Rape is an adult crime whoever commits it."

To Peter Reinharz, the positions Legal Aid takes in Family

Court are glaringly inconsistent. "If all these kids are here because they're victims of their backgrounds, because the homes they come from are neglectful or abusive—then why does Legal Aid fight to put them back in those homes by paroling them to their families?"

Another issue on which Reinharz and his opposite numbers in Legal Aid disagree is whether Family Court should be opened, like criminal court, to press and public. "It's coming," Reinharz says. "There's bound to be a challenge to the constitutionality of the closed courtroom. It may come about through case law, which is the sloppy way. The better way is if the court is opened by legislation, which can define the parameters—for instance on what is brought out about the family, and about the victim—clearly. Once the court is opened you will be able to know who the respondent is."

Sometimes, despite the inertia of the system, a well-meaning judge or lawyer makes a difference where it counts. A twelve-year-old in Bronx Family Court was arrested on a robbery charge and admitted to having been involved in several robberies before that. He and other boys and girls in his building were being used as runners by a crack dealer who was paying them with the substance. The boy had lost weight, looked ashen, was trembling and crying. So was his mother, who seemed desperate. The assistant Corporation Counsel on the case was willing to let him take a plea. He would go along with the boy pleading guilty to the lowest of the charges against him in the expectation that he would be placed in non-secure detention.

The boy's Legal Aid lawyer objected. "No way," he said. "His mother's here, it's a first offense, we want him paroled. Or at most on probation." At that point an 18B lawyer (a private lawyer appointed by the court from a panel) who was representing one of the boy's accomplices in one of the robberies sat down with the boy and his mother and talked to the boy. "If you take a plea and get sent to NSD and behave yourself there, don't give them trouble, you've got a chance. Otherwise, you're dead. It's just a matter of time."

The boy went to a group home on Beach Avenue in the Bronx and after a couple of weeks was admitted to Lincoln Hall, a private, non-secure residential treatment facility, where he settled into the school program and began to talk about choices open to him in life—what he wanted to do later on. Too soon to call it anything but a beginning. A possible beginning. . . . Whatever the odds, they are bound to be at least somewhat better at Lincoln Hall—even with everything that can and sometimes does go wrong there and at other places like it—than back on the block he lives on. With luck, this boy, when he does go back to the neighborhood, will be stronger in ways that will help him stand up to the old pressures and climb out of the life there.

Whether or not he makes it, I find myself thinking as I watch the proceedings, the system ought to be designed to give him a chance. Not a chance to go back where the strongest influence is the crack dealer but where he's presented with some alternatives. Whether or not he makes use of them is up to him. Giving him the opportunity to do so is what used to be called the best interests of the child. What has replaced it is the legalistic aim of securing his "freedom"—which means sending him back where he came from, to everything that has brought him where he is.

6

In Support of the Petition

The corporation counsel . . . shall present the case in support of the [people's] petition. . . .

> —*Family Court Act*, Article 2,
> Part 5, Section 254

The Court shall consider the needs and best interests of the respondent as well as the need for protection of the community.

> —*Family Court Act*, Article 3, Part 1, Section 1 (italicized section added in 1982)

In Family Court, the office of the Corporation Counsel is the equivalent of the District Attorney's office; it presents the people's petition against the respondent. These gentler terms are substituted for "prosecution" and "defendant" in one of the many ways in which the Family Court Act gives special definitions to the actions of those under sixteen years of age. Peter Reinharz, then the deputy chief of the Family Court Division of the Corporation Counsel, is a trim bespectacled young attorney with a quick smile, a rapid delivery, and a scholarly mind, who loves the prosecutorial stance. "In theory," he says, "what we've tried to do in Family Court is wonderful. In practice, it's abominable. The court was set up in 1963 to bring all matters pertaining to family law under one jurisdiction, but I don't think the designers realized what they were doing. It's become a miniature version of the criminal system."

When the Family Court Act was written in 1962 to replace the former Domestic Relations Court, Children's Court, Girls' Term Court, etc., it defined the primary purpose of the court with regard to the juvenile delinquent as rehabilitation. Its aim was to handle all matters pertaining to children and families in an ameliorative and non-punitive way. Determination of guilt and affixing punishment were not to be the goals of its proceedings. Every child had the right to be represented by counsel (known as law guardians) and "the defense of infancy" required that "the least restrictive alternative" be found for any person under sixteen found to have committed an act "which if done by an adult, would be a crime"—including murder, arson, rape, assault, etc. Although there were relatively few such serious crimes being committed by teenagers at that time, their numbers have increased markedly since then.

When the 1967 *Gault* decision granted all due process rights to juveniles, legalism replaced the last vestiges of the best-interests-of-the-child concept, and every hearing on a delinquency matter became an adversarial proceeding. Procedural exclusion of certain evidence because of how it was obtained became common.

Reinharz says, "The biggest change in the system has not been in the police, the judges, or the prosecutors—it's been the defense lawyers. Of course, the case against a child should be proved, like any case, beyond a reasonable doubt. But the problem is, when you start talking about criminal rights, you've got a little mini-criminal system here for *all* offenses."

In what seems like legal logic gone mad, a child's special status at law was no longer to mean that experienced and well-meaning adults would decide whether it might be better for him to return to his home or be sent somewhere that could offer him greater chances of growing up self-sufficient. In-stead, he was to be assigned a law guardian to represent his interests *as he saw them*, even though his wishes might be self-destructive in the long run and destructive to the com-munity in the short run.

"Ten years ago," says Reinharz, leaning forward over a pile of legal folders and notebooks on the desk in his small, crowded office, "a lot of the kids that come in here would never have been arrested and brought to court. We get kids brought in on criminal trespass cases who may have hopped a fence or entered an abandoned building and been in the wrong place at the wrong time, or on a robbery charge be-cause they lifted another kid's sneakers. Is it really vicious behavior or a kid's prank? Time was when the cop on the beat would have gotten hold of the kid and taken him home and talked to his mother. He couldn't do that today even if he knew the neighborhood, the family. He couldn't do it be-cause of the procedural requirements.

"Everything in these kids' lives has become part of an ad-versarial system. No decision gets made without some sort of a trial. Even the schools. A principal can't suspend a pupil for anything without an administrative hearing. When I was a kid, the teacher's word was law, and parents just assumed the teacher was right. Today the parent comes into school and says, 'You have to prove it against my child.' These kids have no respect for any authority. They just tell the teacher off and walk out. And we find the greatest common denom-inator among delinquent kids is that they don't go to school.

"As prosecutors, we have to look to the good of the whole community. And we have to ask, 'Is this a kid doing some-thing or a criminal doing something?' and separate the two kinds of cases. But the emphasis on due process has made that tough and it's resulted in a lot of kids coming through here who shouldn't, and a lot who should be sent away being put back on the streets. We have competing rights here. And the courts aren't recognizing the right of the rest of the community to be secure."

James A. Payne was the chief of the Corporation Counsel in Family Court for all five boroughs in the summer of 1984, when I first talked with him. A tall muscular black man with a high forehead and a thin mustache, he paces and chain-smokes while he talks, gesturing with his cigarette to make a point. Says Payne, "I don't think the judiciary is looking to the best interests of the citizenry in the way they deal with juvenile law. It's an ivory-tower perspective—no appreciation for the trauma and the terror of the public. You see some kids here who are going to be bent on destruction as long as they're on the street and I don't see why we should go on giving them opportunity after opportunity."

Payne thinks much of the problem has to do with the way Legal Aid lawyers function in their capacity as law guardians.

"At arraignment, we're required to serve the kid with a copy of the petition. Most of them can't even read 'See Dick run.' What makes the legislature think a twelve-year-old who hasn't been in school for half the year and reads on a third-grade level can sit down and make judgments about something he can't even read? But that's how Legal Aid functions. They take a position 'because their client wants them to.' They ask the kid."

As Payne sees it, some of the Legal Aid lawyers make the child who's committed a serious offense feel that he is the aggrieved party, that society is picking on him—like the lawyer who congratulated and hugged a boy in court when he beat a rape charge because the victim couldn't make a positive ID.

"We already had two pending cases on him and he's a

walking violation of the law. But she makes him feel he's just an innocent victim and the court is out to get him for no good reason at all," says Payne. "Unless the kid realizes that his act is so anti-social that society is not going to condone it—and not only not condone it now, but the stakes get higher and you get to a point when you get older where we're not talking eighteen months' placement in a group home, we're talking five years in Attica—unless you want him to end up there you have to change that attitude."

As a black man, Payne can say things no white would be comfortable saying in public today. "There are too many people around here bleeding over these kids, encouraging them to believe they got a raw deal. And as long as you believe society is to blame for your problems . . . And we reinforce it. Academics, sociologists, psychologists want to blame anything but the individual himself. You make a choice, either you're going to obey the rules or not. Most of us decide to, but some of these kids at some point decide, 'I don't give a damn about anyone else, I'm out here for me.' "

Payne crushes out a cigarette and takes another one he forgets to light while he goes on heatedly. "These kids identify with a certain type of life, the ability to do nothing and get fast money. They figure that rather than work, say, off the books at the corner store for two bucks an hour and at the end of the week have fifty or sixty bucks in their pocket, they can get the same fifty bucks if they can catch you at ten o'clock at night coming home with your handbag, and it only takes about two minutes. They've got the same amount of money, and with no sweat. And they know if they get caught, by the time we read them their rights and everybody's played his role here, they'll be right back on the streets . . .

"You can't say it's poverty that causes crime. There are about one and a half million people in this city living below the poverty line and only a fraction of them ever commit a crime. But it's the *same* fraction, over and over again. And jobs don't stop crime. These kids' only responsibility is to go to school and they don't even do that. What makes you think they're going to get up at seven, put in a full day's work? They're not out there committing crimes for economic reasons, to pay the rent, or feed themselves, or take care of a sick mother. They're not buying milk for the baby. They're either putting it in their arm or up their nose.

"When I was twelve years old somebody said to me, 'If you want that twenty-dollar pair of sneakers you've got to go out and get a job. You've got to earn all or part of that money.' So I hit the brakes and went to every store in the neighborhood and said, 'Could you use me for an hour after school, could you use me weekends?' I listen to the politicians and I want to tell them the last thing I need from them is another generation of black people sitting around on their ass waiting to be taken care of.

"My father was a product of the old system that said if you get into trouble, join the army or go to jail. If you join up we won't prosecute. That's illegal now. But I was in the army and I know the military gave me some discipline. And I cared about not embarrassing my mother. I have some appreciation for what went before me, of which these kids have no idea. My grandfather worked on the Pennsylvania Railroad back in the Thirties. In forty-two years he got called more 'niggers' than these kids'll ever hear but he took it because he had three kids to raise and he needed that job. These punks think times are bad now? They don't know what it was like in the Thirties and Forties and the sacrifices the people before them had to make. They have no sense of history, and I don't mean the kind of history you get in school . . ."

Payne stops to take a phone call from one of his assistants in Brooklyn Family Court and answer a question from one of the young attorneys who's recently joined the Manhattan staff.

She's apprehensive about a fact-finding hearing scheduled for the next day—her first. He assures her she'll do just fine and reviews some of the salient points with her before going on.

"The white liberal establishment and the black political leadership have decided we owe the poor a whole series of things that only seem to have made things worse for them." Payne pauses, then says: "I have no easy answers, but I do know what we've tried hasn't worked. We're just raising a lot of kids with a predatory mentality.

"We're not seeing the escalation of offenses we used to, starting out with minor offenses and working up to more serious ones. We're seeing more kids starting at the top. Robbery, rape the first time out. That's the new wrinkle—kids starting right out with violent crimes."

Reinharz, who's been listening, nods his head vigorously and says, "The Founding Fathers came up with a wonderful bunch of rights for a civilized society, but we're applying these rights to people who have no respect for anything or anyone in the world. Juveniles come in here who don't care about life, theirs or anyone else's." A probation officer who has spent years in Family Court calls them "the new barbarians." And Reinharz adds, "We're very quick to hand out rights to these kids, but what about responsibilities? And what about the rights of their victims? The Fourth Amendment applies to everyone, not just the criminals. People aren't secure in their persons and houses when you protect the criminal's rights at the expense of the rights of the rest of us. When you throw a violent person back on the street by virtue of the exclusionary [evidence] rule, you violate the rights of everyone else in the community. The civil libertarian game doesn't protect my rights, it just redefines who the victim is—it's the criminal who becomes the victim of society. I believe everyone is entitled to effective counsel, but when we have cases of kids with long previous records of violent crime released because the cop didn't read the Miranda rights in the designated juvenile room of the precinct house . . . whose rights are we protecting and whose are we denying?"

Both Reinharz and Payne think punishment is the best approach to rehabilitation and prevention—at least until longer-term social solutions can be found. "If these kids had anything to be afraid of it might help them stay in line," Reinharz says. "But they know we can't do anything to them. They get sent to group homes or camps upstate and they may not like it but they don't get really upset until you mention Spofford. It's got a swimming pool, a basketball court, video games, and it's very social-work oriented, but it's locked, and once it's locked, it's a prison, and they don't like that."

Payne adds thoughtfully, "There is a liberal bias, a reluctance to talk about punishment. Yet there's a need to consider the various uses of punishment—as a means of rehabilitation to influence future behavior and bring about change and a better life; as a deterrent, influencing through fear of the consequences even where no change in character has occurred; as a way of protecting the public; and as vengeance, society's way of affirming its values, setting limits on what it will tolerate in the way of destructive and anti-social behavior and sending a message about how seriously it means to deal with it."

Payne believes that the Legal Aid people are patronizing, that they have a double standard for conduct and expectations from blacks. "Legal Aid are a bunch of ideologues," he says, "upper-middle-class whites bleeding for the poor nigger, teaching the kid society is at fault, not him. They practice objection law. They don't teach them how to try cases, they teach them how to make objections. They shoot up on sociology in school and get high on the idea of defending and helping the oppressed. The oppressed can help themselves. The Jews did it, the Irish, the Italians, now the Asians. The oppressed can help themselves if you give them a chance. We've been at it since the Sixties and we're not any better off. We're still unemployed, still in jail, still having too many babies. You don't rely on government help forever. What's needed is a positive attitude toward life—you can do it for yourself instead of sitting around waiting for the government to do it for you."

In 1985 Payne undertook the first systematic attempt to find out something about the results of the decisions that are made in Family Court. "What we found for the first three-month period we looked at was that forty-four percent of kids found to have committed a serious felony in that three months—homicide, robbery, rape, sodomy, sexual abuse— were placed in institutions. Of the non-serious cases—lar-ceny, robbery without violence—fifty-eight percent were placed. So the less violent kids get placed, and the more violent ones go right back on the streets. Many voluntary agencies will refuse to take a violent kid, and the judge may not want to lock a kid up, so he'll be put on probation.

"We're taking the worst offenders and sending them back into the community. Maybe they figure nothing's going to stop this kid but we have a shot at changing the non-violent kid. But even if we can't change the violent kid, we can stop him.

"How many times do we see another victim out there who wouldn't have been robbed and hurt if a particular kid had been put away for his last offense? That victim is on the judge's head for not having done what should have been done in the first place. It's high time we did a statistical study to find out if serious crime among juveniles is in fact on the rise, so we can see how many kids we've placed before are back with us again, what the pattern of recidivism is, which place-ments are worst in terms of prevention. If I can show that a high percentage of kids coming out of a particular facility commit another serious crime within ninety days of release, then I can say, 'Let's put the public's money to better use.' " It costs over $77,000 a year to maintain a juvenile in limited-secure detention upstate,* "about the same," Reinharz likes to say, "as four years at an Ivy League college, and it's about as hard to get a kid in."

"It would be interesting," Payne says, "to find out with what degree of accuracy one can predict which kids warrant preventive detention, whether you can tell anything about their future conduct from the past behavior of people who aren't even grown up yet. We can link up the juvenile records with the adult records and see where they went from here. Nobody asks these questions because if you're part of a system that's predicated on the possibility of rehabilitation, the one thing you don't want to find out is that rehabilitation doesn't work. How do you justify the money that's paid out of this building if rehabilitation doesn't work? If you have a twenty-five percent success rate? It's a terrible waste.

"The best rehabilitation is punishment. If you bring a kid in here for his first offense and you give him five days up at Spofford, the likelihood of him doing it again is decreased substantially, because he's on notice that you're not going to tolerate it. The problem is that they come in here and everybody mealymouths and takes the attitude that the kid isn't responsible for his behavior, it's society that's at fault."

Payne talks tough and believes in firmness, but he's also empathic and tolerant and is careful to distinguish between the teenager who's a transient troublemaker and will probably grow out of it and the dangerous one committed to a persistent pattern of violence, the potential career criminal.

---

*In 1985 DFY estimated the per-diem cost of limited-secure facilities (no locks, out of the city) as $213, and of secure ("hardware," locks, out of the city, strict "eyeball supervision," where the most dangerous cases—designated felons and juvenile offenders—go) as $224, over $81,000 a year per boy.

"All we're doing with those," he believes, "is reinforcing them.

"In spite of my reluctance to accept the theory of rehabilitation," he says, "it does work in some cases. Maybe there's a consistent thread in those instances. Maybe you could come up with a pattern if you looked at a number of kids and what happened to them and could see which institutions get better results and have the rest adopt their programs and methods. But nobody even tries to find that out. There are two agencies right in this building that could do it without spending a dime—Probation and the Division for Youth. All they'd have to do is pull out the records of a number of kids they've placed and have their records checked across the street in the adult court. But Probation doesn't even keep statistics on how successful they are. They have the same computer I have and more money, but do you think they've run even one sample of how successful they are on adjustments? Heaven forbid. Someone might be out of a job."

7

Saving the Children

They are born to it, brought up for it. They must be saved.

—Enoch Wines, *The State of Prisons and
of Child-Saving Institutions in the Civilized World,* 1880

Through a series of political obligations, favors owed and fears
of offending, a matter of luck and timing, suddenly, after
weeks of futile telephoning and being passed from one official
to another, I am given permission by someone high up, at
someone else's request, to sit in on probation interviews. This
is even more singular an exposure than sitting in the courtroom. Almost no one has ever been present at probation interviews, or even been given permission to interview
probation officers themselves, who will not talk to a writer
without such departmental permission for fear of losing their
jobs. A few years ago, members of a task force of the Citizens'
Committee for Children undertook a study of the Probation
Department, but when their interim report—a fairly mild
document, it seemed to me when I was shown it later—was
issued, the commissioner withdrew his cooperation, in-
structed departmental employees not to respond to requests

for information or allow themselves to be interviewed either about the nature of their work or their thoughts about it, and closed the door on any further intrusions by press or public.

Disbelief bordering on awe was the initial response of probation officers when I first introduced myself and presented the letter that documented my permission to talk with them and observe them at work. Gradually, they got used to me and accepted my presence. The branch chief confided to an attorney who later repeated her remark to me, "We'll live to regret this. She's going to burn us." At the time I thought she was wrong. Now I know she was right. And why.

The idea of probation was conceived by a nineteenth-century Boston social reformer named John Augustus, who undertook on his own to bail out drunkards and reform them. He counseled them and found them employment and brought them back to court sober and industrious citizens. Eventually he added juveniles to his caseload, seeing to it that they attended school regularly, and reporting to the court on their progress. He had bailed on probation nearly two thousand men, women, and children by the time of his death in 1859. It was not until almost twenty years later, however, that the state of Massachusetts officially made Augustus's invention part of the legal system, passing the first probation law in 1878 as a sentencing alternative for "such persons as may reasonably be expected to be reformed without punishment." When the first juvenile court was founded in Chicago in 1899, probation officers were appointed as members of the court to "present the interests of the child . . . furnish . . . such information . . . as the judge may require . . . and to take charge of any child before and after trial as may be directed by the court." Other states soon followed Illinois' lead in establishing juvenile courts, including probation services. Today, New York's probation service is no longer a court-administered program, but an independent agency of the city government. Subject to many of the ills that plague other city agencies, it has troubles of its own.

My first day in Probation. I find that I'll be observing three different Probation Department functions: intake interviews, in which the probation officer makes the decision whether to adjust, that is dismiss, the case or send the matter on to court; investigation interviews, which provide information on the family background and life circumstances of the respondent for a report to guide the judge on disposition of a case; and supervision, in which probation officers meet with the youths who report to them at intervals, ranging from once a week to once a month, on their progress in life, their school and other activities, during the period they're on probation. In the course of explaining these procedures, the branch chief, a pleasant middle-aged woman with a motherly manner, talks about the probation officer's job.

"You have to help the children deal with their anger," she says, and explains that many of them are frustrated because they can't read, that often when they are asked to sign their names they "act out" in order to hide the fact that they can't write. She suggests that the school system has failed them and that it is this failure to which the behavior that has brought them to the court is a response.

An intake interview. The boy, a slight fourteen-year-old, has been arrested for defacing public property. These graffiti charges are common, and one can't help wondering whether they really should be dealt with by means of the full procedural panoply of the court, requiring all the resources of a quasi-criminal trial, all the man-hours of hearings, investigations, examinations, reports, court appearances. Couldn't this kind of offense be dealt with on an administrative level, in the community, at the time of the arrest, leaving the full weight of the court's apparatus to be brought to bear on matters that involve attacks on persons, theft, violence, or serious destruction of some kind?

The probation officer is a slight, pale man with a gentle manner and a sense of humor that remains hidden most of the time. His suit is rumpled, his desk piled high with papers. These ubiquitous piles of forms and folders with papers spilling out of them seem like barricades in most of the department offices, erected to protect the people who work there from any possibility of being charged with not being overworked to the limits of their capacities. Look at all these cases, all these files, they seem to say. Most of the offices are dingy, too, the dust and the drooping plants seeming to testify to their occupants' preoccupation with other and more important matters than housekeeping chores.

The probation officer, Hy Gross,* asks, "Why the graffiti?" The boy talks about "my friend . . . I went along . . ." Why wasn't he in school? "It's a hangout school . . ." Why does he smoke marijuana? "The neighborhood . . ." His father, interviewed separately, had also blamed the neighborhood, the school. The probation officer accepts these replies non-committally. His stance is non-judgmental. He explains to the boy that he will have to make restitution for the damage he's done. His father will have to pay the costs of having it cleaned up. The boy asks, "How come? My friend didn't have to pay," and Gross explains that his friend was over sixteen and was brought to Criminal Court. (In one of the many ironies that abound in this system, that probably means that his friend got off more lightly than he; nobody wants to be bothered with these trivial offenses across the

---

*With the exception of Pat Brennan and Phil Dobbs, the names of the probation officers in this chapter and the following one are not their real ones.

street, not with so many cases, so few cells, no way of providing for simple restitution or working off a sentence or being forced to clean up one's own mess. Where the penalties are perceived as disproportionate to the crime, dismissal is the likeliest outcome.)

Gross asks the boy to read a paragraph in an article about boxing in one of a pile of sports magazines he keeps around for this purpose. The boy reads well, recognizes and pronounces words like "chronicled" correctly after only a slight hesitation. Gross urges him to study, to think about college.

I try to imagine the household the father has described. Several younger children at home, an older brother in jail. Mother in and out of a Bronx psychiatric facility. Father, unemployed, spends his time "waiting . . . watching TV." Then I try to imagine coming home to study in that apartment. Maybe placement would help this boy. One of the group homes, counselors to help with homework, encourage his efforts . . . But those facilities are reserved for more serious offenders, for whom they are often too little and too late, everything the law offers being applied beyond where it might do the most good. The principle is the least restrictive placement. The graffitist who might benefit from a non-secure placement will be put on probation, sent back to the family, to streets and neighborhood that don't seem able to contain him, and those group homes will be filled with boys who have already committed thefts, assaults, and who would probably benefit from a more restrictive and closely supervised environment.

The boy responds politely to the suggestions about attending school, doing his homework, not getting in with the wrong crowd.

While Gross takes the boy down the hall to talk with a representative of the Transit Authority, who will deal with the issue of restitution, I chat in the corridor with a supervisor who's been in the department for almost twenty years, seems to work hard and still try, but has a cynical, I've-seen-it-all manner not uncommon among the oldest staff members here.

"When I was in the field," she tells me, "the worst thing the kids did was threaten somebody with a zip gun. The judge threw them in detention upstairs for a couple of hours and they'd never come back. Now it's, 'I've got my lawyer, you can't do nothing to me.' "

"Wonderful." The word is enthusiastic but the tone is flat, expressionless. "How are things at school?" Mrs. Shine doesn't look at the girl she's asking the question of. She's looking down at the paper she's filling out, holding a pencil with some difficulty in hands knotted by arthritis. Her curly gray head is bent over the forms on her desk as she asks. "Fine," says the girl, tonelessly.

"Great." Mrs. Shine looks up and smiles mechanically. "Any problems?" A moment's silence. Then, "No, I guess not." Something in the girl's tone, her hesitancy, alerts me, makes me curious. I would ask again, making eye contact, trying to show I really wondered, wanted to know if there were problems. Mrs. Shine says, "Good," and beams again. This is proving a trouble-free interview. She looks relieved. The girl looks depressed. "Well, everything's all right then," says Mrs. Shine, and she writes a few more lines. Looking up, she smiles again. "And you came. That's terrific." There's a pause. No one says anything. The girl doesn't move. "Terrific," repeats Mrs. Shine, with more emphasis this time, as though to establish the fact of terrificness, as though someone might take issue with it.

"Well," she says brightly, "see you next week." Still the girl doesn't move. Then after a moment she drags herself up, as though she were much heavier than her slight frame appears.

"Good-bye," says Mrs. Shine, showing the first real warmth since the girl took her seat across the desk from her ten minutes ago. The girl's good-bye is so low I can hardly hear it from my seat about five feet behind her in this small airless room where all the plants seem to be on the verge of dying, the walls need painting, the posters ("Children Learn What They Live," reads one) have curling edges. They must have been put up a long time ago, when Mrs. Shine still had some enthusiasm for her task. Now she is waiting out the days until retirement and says so openly. She sees no reason not to. She will tell you things have changed, aren't what they used to be, but it's hard to get her to say what has changed, how things used to be. The statements have the same ritual quality as the interview she has just conducted and she is now going to spend a peaceful half hour—twice as long as the time she spent on the interview itself—writing up, describing, putting it into official jargon. ("Making progress . . .") I ask her what the girl's offense was, the act that has led to her being placed on probation and reporting to this official every week for a year. Mrs. Shine looks surprised, wrinkles her brow, shrugs. "I don't remember," she says. Now it's my turn to look surprised. She says quickly, "I don't think I should have in mind what they did before. I try not to think about that when I see them."

I can't think of a response. After a minute she consults the folder in front of her, rifling through the pages until she comes to the court records she is looking for. She reads a few lines, then says, as though she remembers now, "Oh, yes. She stabbed another girl in a fight." She reads on. "The girl needed twenty-one stitches." Whatever had led this quiet, pretty girl, carefully poised here, to an act of such violence, Mrs. Shine will never know, doesn't want to know. I have an impulse to follow the girl down the hall, stop her at the elevator, ask her to sit down and tell me what was on her mind, how someone might help with whatever it was one sensed lay behind her hesitation, her barely disguised readiness to be approached. The impulse to intervene is inappropriate, has to be resisted. One is here as an observer, a reporter, an audience rather than an actor.

One thing is clear. No matter what her life is like, no matter how things really are at school or at home or inside her head, this girl gains nothing from this meeting, finds nothing, learns nothing. She may manage to control herself, knowing she must stay out of trouble during the period of her probation, but nothing about the experience will have made any real difference, except perhaps to add to her despair.

Some kids on probation are luckier.

Pat Brennan is so full of life that being in the same room with her energizes one. A tall robust woman in her mid-thirties, her blond hair tucked behind her ears, dressed casually in a shirt and tailored pants, she exudes a sense of purpose and good humor. Humor may be her first line of defense. It is also her great charm. Her laugh is loud and infectious and punctuates her conversation in interviews with visitors as well as with the adolescents she supervises in their weekly visits to her office in the Department of Probation.

She is two things that make her unique there—involved and lively. She makes phone calls when her kids don't show up, threatens and cajoles, jokes and warns, pushes on her kids and listens to them—whatever she feels will get their attention, touch them, start them. She has no illusions about them and seldom gives up on them.

This afternoon she has asked two of them to come dressed as if they were going to a job interview. They'll practice applying for work—a situation as crucial for these kids as taking the College Boards is for others, and one for which they are far less well prepared. She'll joke with them and her big laugh will make them smile and put them at ease, but they feel her unbendable purposefulness underneath. They want to please her. They want to be like her. All of a sudden, an epiphany: I understand, after hearing it for years, what is meant by the phrase "role model."

Nicholas was arrested on an assault charge. When she visited his home in the investigation phase of the court process (this was a year ago now; home visits are no longer made: They are uneconomical and don't leave enough time for filling out papers) she noticed that his room was full of odd constructions, figures sculpted from objects found on the street or around the house. She didn't know anything about art, she says, but she was struck by the impulse that led him to make all these things and decorate his room with them. She suggested a special high school with an art and design program, kept after him until he filled out the application and turned it in, not a routine matter for a youngster in a disorganized home where such things are not routinely done, where in fact there is no routine to speak of. Now he sits across from her, smiling shyly, and giving her his news. He's made his application, has been encouraged to follow through on it, has to submit a portfolio of his work in September as the final step in the process of being accepted.

Pat Brennan doesn't say "wonderful." She just says "O-kay!" but her tone and her grin make it seem like a triumph. Clearly this is a triumph, for both of them. Now, she says, getting serious again, what about the portfolio? Tactfully, somehow managing to suggest he's been thinking about these things himself all along and she just wants to be filled in, she asks him what sorts of things he'll be submitting. Will there be a variety? She knows those cartoonlike figures he does are very good, he has a style of his own that's very effective, but it might be a good idea to let them see what he can do in other styles.

"Can you do realistic portraits?"

"If I work hard enough at it," he says, and I know there's hope for this kid.

What about other media? Does he have materials? What kind of paper is he thinking of using? Well, wouldn't pencil on ordinary notebook paper be likely to smudge and tear, look kind of woebegone by fall? Does he have any heavy drawing paper, any charcoal or pastels?

"I tell you what—how about we go shopping and see what's available? We've gotta outfit you with the right stuff! You may be my only art success." There's an art supply store right down on Canal Street, a few blocks away. She could meet him there on her lunch hour. When is Easter vacation, so they can go when he doesn't have school? He doesn't know. Never mind, she'll call the Board of Ed and find out. Having made the call and established that it's next week, she asks him about the time. Ten-thirty? He looks uncertain. Eleven? "Yeah," he says, "I don't wake up until ten." She takes this in good part, rummages in her bag, finds a subway token. A loan. Just to make sure he doesn't have a problem about carfare to get there. In return, she tells him, "Someday when you're rich and famous, you'll invite me to one of your openings."

It occurs to me that the assault charge that brought Nicholas into Family Court may have been the best thing that ever happened to him. It landed him on probation and brought him to Pat Brennan. What he had done was fashion a crude bow and arrow, something like a cross between a harpoon and a slingshot, out of some things he found on the street. He shot it in the playground and, aiming, he says, at a tree, hit a boy nearby in the shoulder. The wound was not serious but it had been inflicted with a weapon . . . and the unpredictable result of this imaginative if reckless act was to bring into Nicholas's life someone who actually suggested that if he

worked hard he might become accomplished at something—
even "rich and famous." She was doing things his parents had
never done—getting him transferred out of special education
classes ("We're in eighth grade now," she told me in his presence with her big grin, and later, when he was gone, that the
special ed class was "a snake pit"), even, at his mother's request, having a talk with him about sex.

After he's left I make sure I'm right about my hunch. She'll
be doing this—meeting Nicholas, helping him buy supplies—
on her own time, at her own expense. The other thing I've
noticed I don't have to confirm. How gratified she is at making a difference. How much she cares. And how singular she
is. Her colleagues, her supervisors, department officials all
acknowledge it. They can't reward it, though. After thirteen
years with the department she is earning $22,500 and she is
too tired at the end of the day to go out, and spends most of
her spare time following up on loose ends the department
makes no provision for.

A Taiwanese girl may be deported if she is not adopted by
the uncle who has brought her over. Pat suspects the girl is
being sexually exploited by the uncle but is ashamed to talk
about it, afraid of being sent home in humiliation. Pat is
trying to reach the girl through an interpreter, encourage her
to confide. She is in touch with the immigration people (two
lunch hours so far), trying to find out what provisions acceptable to the court would also be acceptable to them so the
girl can stay even if the adoption does not go through. None
of the other probation officers I've met here would do these
things. I have sat through numerous probation investigations
and supervisions with uncaring, incompetent, and unfeeling
adults facing hostile, passive, resentful, and unreachable boys
and girls. I've conscientiously made notes, storing up my
impressions while jotting down the words I hear, taking it in

but dying to get out, away from there, from the futility and the pain of it. In this room, with this woman, I am utterly absorbed. I don't notice the passage of time, don't want to leave, am terribly disappointed when her last appointment doesn't show up. A missed opportunity. For him. For me. As for Pat Brennan, she is beginning to talk about leaving, looking for another job. I understand why perfectly. The conditions of the work, the constantly imposed limitations on possibility, on imagination and effort, all militate against everything that makes her so good at it, makes her who she is. She's the only one who combines the character and the ability that are right for the job. And I have to admit she'd be crazy to stay much longer.

"This place is enough to make you crazy," Pat Brennan says. I've asked to come back to sit in on another of her supervision afternoons. She has just hung up after a call from a worker at a group home. A boy in placement broke another boy's jaw, wouldn't take any of the jobs on the campus because they were too menial. "A real sweetheart." Now he has been chosen to be sent on an educational trip to Nigeria. Before that, a conversation with a supervisor who tells Pat she can't visit the home of a relative willing to take in a teenage girl who has run away from a group home where she says she was sexually harassed by the older and bigger girls. The relative lives half an hour away in New Jersey and it's against the rules for a probation officer to go out of state. "It's like 'Twilight Zone,' " Pat says with her big laugh. "You get the feeling the rules have been changed and you're the only one who remembers the old rules."

Dennis is fifteen, what Pat Brennan calls "one of Hell's Kitchen's leftovers." He's one of the few white boys I've seen in the months I've spent in Manhattan, Brooklyn, and Bronx Family Courts, a member of one of the few remaining families in a West Side midtown area that's becoming gentrified, the old tenements being renovated and turned into apartments for rising young professionals, new high-rises going up all around them.

Like the tenement he lives in, Dennis is an anachronism. His father is a racetrack handicapper and an alcoholic, his mother a theater usher, his older brother is on drugs. Dennis was arrested for trying to steal a car along with another member of the neighborhood gang ("The Dirt Bags," Pat tells me the gang members call themselves). He has dropped out of school. "I ain't gonna stay in that school," he says. "It's all niggers." ("He has to look down on somebody," Pat explains dryly.)

Dennis works occasionally, shaping up on the piers, where he has an uncle in the union. He sits here in Calvin Klein jeans, chewing gum and occasionally snapping a bubble, slouched in his chair, combing his hair with a red comb he takes out of his back pocket every few minutes, tapping his feet, reaching out absently and moving things around on Pat's desk. Tall, well-built, handsome, he has no ambitions, no expectations, no real help from his family, and no interest in any of Pat's efforts to help him. He's been truanting again and now he's been picked up on another botched car theft. He's violated probation—three strikes now—one of Pat Brennan's few failures. The "niggers" he complains of are the only thing between him and the bottom of the heap, and he knows it.

Neal is so black his skin seems to have a blue shine to it. His school troubles are with the other kids. "If they see you trying to work they pick a conversation with you just to bover [bother] you," he says. He tells Pat fatalistically that his books were stolen from the bench in the schoolyard where he put them down for a few minutes while he shot a couple of baskets. His friend's hat that he'd borrowed was in the bookbag, and his friend has told him to come up with the hat or with three dollars to pay for it later that day or he'll beat him up. "I haven't got no three dollars and"—smiling a little—"he's bigger than me."

After some discussion Pat tells him she'll advance him the three dollars. "Advance?" He doesn't know the word. She explains. During the Depression, when her father made thirty dollars a week, he couldn't always make ends meet for his big family so his boss would sometimes "advance" him ten dollars out of his next week's salary. Neal likes that. He takes a little notebook out of his coat pocket and writes in it. "Ad-vance," he says slowly, writing the word down.

His year's probation is almost over and Neal will just be having another appointment or two. Pat asks him what he's learned from the experience. "What I learned," he says, "is stick to the bases and you'll get a chance to be something besides a criminal." On his way out, he turns to me and says, "Nice to meet you." By now I'm ready to offer him early admission to Harvard.

After he's gone Pat tells me she thinks Neal was testing her, wanted her to offer him the money. Does she think he'll pay it back? Yes (smiling), she'll make sure he does.

Manuel has a job. A slight boy with a faint mustache, he speaks barely above a whisper. He's having trouble at school, they're all suspicious of him because he's on probation, but he'll stick it out, wants to finish high school. He promised his father. He's obviously gratified by Pat's delight at hearing about his job, delivering for a dry cleaner after school. He gets paid off the books, but Pat seems understandably more interested in his having a job than in worrying about respect for the legal niceties here, one of the inconsistencies that inevitably arise as kids like this try to get around the system rather than beating it over the head.

She asks what he did with the money he's earned in the month since he's been working. He gave his father forty dollars, he says proudly. His father didn't want to take it at first, but Manuel insisted. And he bought some clothes for himself—sneakers, a fur hat for next winter. He grins, pleased with himself. She asks about his girl, who got pregnant last year when both of them were thirteen, and had an abortion. He tells her they've broken up. It was the girl's doing. She didn't want to go with him anymore after she heard he'd been arrested. He feels really bad about it.

Pat calls his home, his school, in order to set up a meeting with his parents and a teacher to work out some of his school problems. And she tells him, "Manuel, you haven't found a crime you do good yet, so you better stop." Tough, sweet, and funny, she strikes a note with these kids that seems to wake them up; the big laugh that bursts out of her is like an alarm clock in contrast to the soporific effect of some of the other probation officers. It's as though those other sessions are in black-and-white, hers in Technicolor. I remember the troubled girl who never uttered more than a monosyllable. (Everything all right? Terrific. You've been going to school? Wonderful. You came today? Here's a gold medal. Take it and go home.)

In contrast, Pat Brennan really probes. She gets them to talk, spends three times as much time with them as some of the others, opens a can of worms for herself with each one (Nicholas and the art supplies, the Taiwanese girl and the immigration office, Neal and the three-dollar advance, Manuel and the school appointment), but with her there's some point to the probation process. With most of the others it's a useless, meaningless formality, some of them too untrained or too unaware to do better, others just putting in time until they can retire.

A New York City cop sits filling out arrest reports in the office the Police Department maintains on one of the Probation Department floors in the Family Court building. Four kids have been arrested in Penn Station for stealing some cigars from a news vendor. One of them turned out to be an adult—that is, over sixteen. The other three are here in Family Court. Two of them have run away from upstate facilities. "We're talking a really nice place," the cop says. "They've got woodland and trees, nice rooms, good meals, education, people who care, and they run back to the South Bronx. The thing is, you can't do whatever you want up there. You can't be a shithead.

"These kids have been stealing from shops like Hoffritz. They hang around, harassing the shopkeepers, creating distractions. They rush in when it's busy, grab stuff, and pass it to another kid outside the shop so if they get caught they don't have it on them. Witnesses have seen them on the train with bags of the stuff they've taken.

"You can't replace the pressure of family criticism," the cop says. "But there's no name in the paper, no family disgrace . . . This isn't the suburbs. They live in a mob situation in a warren. They should be in the military, or something like the borstal system in England, the kind of place where you have to work, the kind of place you don't want to go to. Instead, here everybody's sitting around trying to talk them out of being a shithead. It doesn't work." Due process? "We're going to process ourselves right out of the city." Of some judges' reluctance to send kids to Spofford he says, "The judges don't ride the subways. They drive off to Princeton Junction or wherever they live and they never see these kids again.

They're dangerous." I'm not sure whether he means the judges or the kids—or both.

The mothers of two of the boys are sitting and talking in the waiting area. They don't look distraught, don't even seem particularly upset about the situation their sons are in. It's just part of life. What they do express annoyance about is having to wait. Instead of going to school their sons hang around the station and steal. Are they outraged? No, they seem to accept all that. There's no shame or humiliation attached to getting brought here. That's just how it is. An inconvenience.

The police officer tells me the boys gave false names, addresses, and dates of birth when they were arrested, making it difficult to check their prior records, and that he had trouble getting anyone to come down for them. He has spent twelve hours trying to get the information he needs to fill out the papers on this case. Boys and Girls High School in Brooklyn reports very poor attendance for all of them. Only one— the boy who actually took the cigars while the others crowded around him—gave the correct information about himself. When reached, his parents were angry and refused to come down and claim him. They said a night in Spofford would do him good. He turned out to have two priors, which had been adjusted at intake, meaning he'd been arrested twice before and brought to Family Court, where both times he'd been told in effect to go home and sin no more.

Hy Gross, commenting on the judicial attitude toward the young offender, gives me the example of a fourteen-year-old he'd interviewed recently at intake. The boy admitted to having held a mugging victim while the others punched him until he bled. When Gross asked if he felt any remorse, if he felt sorry for the victim, "he just put his head back and laughed.

But in the courtroom," says Gross, "he looks small and defenseless."

What if the consequence was defined by the act in every case—if you're proven to have done this, then that will happen to you—with fewer purely procedural exceptions and less attention to supposed motivations or extenuating circumstances? It's a question that begs to be asked but is hard to get anyone here to answer. After all, these are kids, and therefore we have to assume they're still malleable. This is the most common response, and it's always accompanied by a troubled look, a question in the voice, a trailing off into doubt. I feel the doubt myself.

Here in Hy Gross's office, a sparkling poster scene of snowy mountains contrasts with the miniature mountains of dusty papers, the grimy walls and windows, and the moribund plants. By now it's become like a stage setting for the familiar drama featuring the usual cast of characters—the weak mother, the absent father. This mother lives on public assistance, receives $323 every two weeks, has four sons, the oldest in jail, this one, Lisle, on probation. She is separated from their father, hasn't seen him in years. She was shocked, she answers, when Gross asks how she felt about Lisle being arrested again while on probation.

A few minutes later Lisle is occupying the seat across from Gross's desk. He is wearing a suede coat lined with alpaca and new-looking trendy suede shoes. He picks his nose as he answers Gross's questions. How many days has he played hooky this term? He grins. He doesn't know. Gross tells him. Twenty-five. He grins again, shrugs. What was he doing? "Jes' goin' places." He does have a favorite subject. "Language art." He complains about having to wait so long before Gross saw him, and the probation officer says, "If you commit a crime, you have to wait." Indeed, I reflect, it may be the only punishment he'll get.

Does he read? The *Enquirer*. Books? No. Does he have a
library card? No. "Why don't you study," Gross asks him
mildly, "instead of hanging around Penn Station?" The boy
grins again, spreads his arms over the back of his chair, and
leans back, legs outstretched, completely relaxed, somewhat
bored, slightly irritated at the inconvenience of having had
to wait and now having to sit here and answer these questions.

About "the incident": "He did it . . . we didn't know what
was happenin' . . ." He knows Gross knows he's lying. It's a
game. About himself: His father's age? "Don't have the slight-
est." He can't remember the last time he saw him. His last
report card? He failed three subjects. Gross's advice to him:
"Study and take notes every night." This is so hard to imagine
that I can't decide whether what keeps Gross going is a naive
sense of hope or a gallows sense of humor.

After ten minutes with Lisle, Gross will spend an hour and a
half on the paperwork. Now he sees the mother of one of the
other three boys, and then talks with the boy himself. Ken
can't think of anything he wants to do when he grows up.
What kind of books does he like to read? "Autobiography,"
he says, and while Gross is making a note he adds, "poetry.
And law." Gross looks up at him. Smiling faintly, he says,
"Take good notes."

I accompany Gross to his interview with the third boy, in
detention upstairs. Allie has been brought down from Spofford, where he's being held because no adult appeared to take
responsibility for him. The small interview rooms are all being
used and they talk across a table in what appears to be a
schoolroom-library. Where does he expect to end up? "I want
to go to college," Allie says matter-of-factly. "Computers."

"But you don't go to school," Gross says. Even his blanket
of imperturbability seems pierced this time. "You didn't at-

tend at all in December [this is late January and those are the most recent records available]. You failed every subject."

"That won't stop me," the boy says serenely. He spends most of his days practicing petty crime in Penn Station; his prior arrest there was dismissed, and nothing in his experience before or since seems to have impressed him with the reality of his situation, taught him anything at all about the relationship between cause and effect in life. What hope is there for him—or for Lance?

Lance was arrested for spraying paint on the walls of a subway station. His mother has three children by different fathers, none of whom married her; she has to stop to think which is whose father. The fathers have no contact with their children, no responsibility for them, economic or—a word that seems exotic in this context but surely relates to child-rearing—moral. They neither support nor socialize them, have no part in their education or growth. The family receives $265 every two weeks from welfare. The boys are in special education classes. A daughter, fourteen, has dropped out of school, is pregnant. The mother asks the probation officer about a PINS petition. She's angry because the daughter is promiscuous. "What does she expect?" the PO later asks wearily. This is after he has interviewed Lance.

Why did he do it? " 'Cause I wanted to." Has he done it before? "Lots of times." Why? "Nothin' else to do." Does he study? No response. Do his homework, the PO explains. Lance looks blank. Does he have a favorite subject? Still no sale. "Language arts?" the PO suggests. "What you mean," Lance asks, "talkin'?" What kind of work would he like to do someday? "Basketball player," he says. How was his last report card? "Okay." How many subjects did he fail? "Don' know." Then, "Two." What were they? Math, he thinks—and woodworking. (How can you fail woodworking, Gross and I are both thinking.) Why? "Don' like it. I didn' go."

He is not prepared to do anything requiring any effort. His answers are all the same: "I don't want to . . . I don' like it . . . I felt like it . . ." He remains forever an infant in a body that has already grown up. What hope is there for Lance?

Between appointments, waiting for a latecomer, I asked Hy Gross about his own family. He talked about his son, about the amount of homework he did every night, about the basketball game they'd gone to on the weekend and how they'd gone to a restaurant afterward. There, half an hour after the game, they recognized one of the players waiting on tables. "There's a black kid," Gross said, "who keeps up his grades, plays on the team, works after school. . . . Compare him with these kids here. They've got a sickness. The welfare syndrome."

There is a dreary sameness to the procession of adolescents and their families passing through the probation process—the inadequate parents, broken homes, contempt for school, lack of goals for the future—and yet every one is slightly different, a variation on the basic theme. Proof of Tolstoy's much-quoted adage, each unhappy in its own way. And sometimes even funny. You know you should not find this man funny, that his life is a hopeless predicament, his children doomed to failure, much of his fate and theirs a result of a personality so devoted to self-destruction that it would have found its way around any social policy constructed to contain it, but he is such an original, so outrageous, that it's hard not to laugh.

He is standing here in front of the probation officer's desk glaring down at her, in a soiled torn jacket, his hat still on his head, his arms akimbo, the very picture of righteous indignation. "I want my lawyer," he says. "My son shouldn't have been arrested and taken to the precinct, there should have been a summons issued." One thing is sure. He is in command of legal terminology, if nothing else.

The probation officer is a handsome black woman in her thirties, well dressed in a silk shirt and tweed jacket, and poised. She's not impressed. Not one to be bullied. She goes on writing. A portable radio on the windowsill is playing, mostly disco and commercials, all through the interview, all through the day, probably turned on with the light switch in the morning and off again at five. The constantly playing radio is a common feature of the offices along this corridor, along with the "Children Learn What They Live" poster and the dying plants.

Until a moment ago he was seated on the edge of the chair he's just gotten out of, answering her questions about his son and his son's offense. It was his third arrest. The first one was adjusted by probation at intake and sealed. The second was for stealing subway tokens from a turnstile with a pair of tweezers in order to resell them. He sounds like more of a menace to himself than society, a petty loser. This time it was—or was not—shoplifting from the supermarket at the entrance to the same subway. The father claims the police beat his son up. The PO looks through her files for the police report. It states, she says, looking up, that he was resisting arrest. The boy tries to interrupt. His father says, "Shut up. You got too much mouth." The police had no business arresting his son, the boy didn't do anything. Ask his brother— he was arrested with him. He gets in trouble because of the neighborhood ("it's the area, it's too near the subway"), and the police ("they're hostile"), and the school ("it's bilingual"). It's not clear what he means to say about the school, unless that it's largely Hispanic—this family is black—but it's hard to see what difference it makes since the kids hardly ever seem to go.

The PO stops writing, says to him, "Your son has to be responsible for his own actions." He ignores her. He is vehement, he will not stay for the court appearance scheduled to follow this interview. Yes, he's employed, he has told her— he works at the difficult job of raising four kids on public assistance. His occupation? "Househusband." His wife, who had a history of mental illness, left him in 1975. They have had no contact since. This is an inexcusable imposition on his time, he is saying now, because he should be spending the day getting ready to move to a new apartment from the welfare hotel in which the family has been living since they were burned out of their last one. She asks about counseling. "He was in it. But it was found to be false. They put him in Metropolitan Hospital for three days without my permission behind [after] me hitting him."

While he is talking, the PO is looking through the papers in the file in front of her, occasionally writing something on one of them. He stops for breath and she complains that all this paperwork takes up too much time. "There's no time to talk to the parents because I'm filling out papers instead." It's not clear whether this is for his benefit or mine. She seems disorganized, can't find a paper she's looking for among the piles of papers on her desk, doesn't remember the number of the boy's school or where she wrote it, but while she's looking for it she insists quietly over the father's increasingly noisy objections that the case must go to court. She doesn't feel she can count on him to keep the boys in line, see that they go for counseling, attend school, keep their probation appointments.

This stimulates a further outburst. Again, his son should never have been arrested, he was brutalized by the police, he's going to file a complaint, sue the city. He doesn't have time for this, he's going to leave. She explains that they're supposed to go to court this morning, asks him to wait out in the seating area until she has completed some forms. When he has left, still protesting, she says she's recommending that the court parole the boy to the custody of the father rather than sending him away. She hopes the court order will show them it's a serious matter and the father should make them shape up.

The interview has lasted for about fifteen minutes and the PO spends the next thirty minutes filling out papers relating to it. She never spoke directly to the boy or asked him anything about himself except his height and weight. Naw, he doesn't know how tall he is. "About five six," she guesses and writes. She asks him what he weighs, looks dubious at his answer, says, "You're no hundred thirty anything," ponders a minute and then writes another figure. She never asks him what he did, why he did it. She asks his class number at school. Class number at school? He can't remember. At one point during a lull in his father's tirade, he said to no one in particular, "I wasn't doing nothing, just standing there." She let the remark go by without comment. In fact, it was not clear to me sitting here and listening to all this just exactly what was alleged to have happened, whether the arrest took place outside the supermarket or at the subway entrance, and what if anything was found on the boy.

The father reappears at the doorway, demands, "Can't you fill out these papers another time?" Speaking of papers, he says, the arrest report is invalid. Pointing a finger accusingly, he says, "The date's not authenticated," then goes on, "I'm in a moving process, I shouldn't even be down here." She goes on writing. Still in the doorway, he is picking up steam. "You're making a big deal out of a minor offense. I been here over an hour. I did the same thing for the officer when he was falsifying his paperwork. He put eighty-four, not eighty-five." Triumphantly: "This whole thing's illegal!" Still writing, the PO insists he return to the waiting area.

Meanwhile, another figure has appeared in the doorway, asks to speak to the PO. It's a father who's brought a PINS petition against his daughter for truanting and absconding. He can't wait any longer, he says. She explains that he was late for his appointment and so she has taken someone else. She's now in the middle of a case and he will have to wait his turn. She'll see him next. He says he won't stay any longer and leaves. Truanting and absconding . . .

The first father reappears. He is still wearing his hat. It's been an hour and a half now. "I'm in a crisis," he says to no one in particular, "and all this is taking up my time. I shouldn't have to be down here. I got to get ready to move."

Wearily, she asks him to sit down. She offers him one of the papers from the pile in front of her, explaining that it's his authorization for her to request his son's school records. "I'm not signing no papers," he says. "I'm not putting my signature on nothing without a lawyer." When she tries to give him the slip of paper that tells him where to appear for the hearing on the courtroom floor above, he shakes his head angrily. "I should be working on my own business." (I think to myself, This isn't his business?) "I'm leaving." To the two boys who have been waiting outside the office he says peremptorily, "Let's go, y'all." Then, turning to the PO, "You want to find me, you know where I'll be. Issue a warrant." They're gone.

The radio is playing "New York, New York" ("If I can make it there . . .") and the PO goes on writing. Nothing has happened to the kids here, they have learned nothing, were told nothing about their actions. No attempt was made to tell them why they have to appear in court or to suggest they shouldn't do the things that have brought them there. For the next twenty minutes the PO is on the phone trying to get some information from the office of Special Services for Children, formerly the Bureau of Child Welfare. They can't find the records. While she is on hold she tells me about a now-defunct program in which she worked at a Harlem precinct house, adjusting those cases that could be resolved at the community level without being sent to court. At the precinct, she says, "we got a lot of good interaction between complainants and respondents."

The clerk at SSC is back on the line now. It appears that the father made a voluntary placement of one of his other children two years ago—one way, says the PO, to have the kid fed and taken care of. When she hangs up, her phone rings and she has a conversation about the union "rep" and the plans for a lunchtime meeting the next day. Two and a quarter hours have passed. She sits back on her chair. "I'm worn out now," she says. "This job is draining."

8

To Avoid the Stigma

Trial court's discretion . . . must be administered to avoid for one who has the defense of infancy the stigma attached to defense or conviction of 'criminal' charges. . . .

—*Matter of Robert M.*, 1981, 109 Misc.2d
427, 439 N.Y.S. 2d 986

Some of the goings-on in Probation are like the theater of the absurd. A young black college graduate with a social work degree tries to communicate with a Spanish-speaking mother who barely understands what she is doing here, cannot begin to comprehend his questions phrased in stilted social-workese, court jargon, and malapropisms. "I be aksing you," he scolds her, but even I cannot figure out yet exactly what it is he wants her to tell him about her son's educational history so he can fill out the form in front of him.

I had talked with Earl Roberts for the half hour or so we waited for her to appear. Hardly anyone is ever on time for these appointments. Talking about his work, Roberts told me that sometimes "my client don't come," and complained that "it's hard to keep up on the paperwork." I asked about his background.

"I had that Southern upbringing," he told me. "Disci-

132

pline. I was one of twelve kids and my father, he worked real hard. If you went to him, he'd say, 'You have to aks your mother.' She was very strict. If you got mad, you went outside and maybe kicked a can or a rock but you didn't talk back or even raise your eyes 'cause you knew what you'd get. You didn't get mad inside the house. We had delinquents— they did things like rob the school lunchroom—and if my mother saw me sitting in a car with them she'd pull me out by the ear and take me home with her. It was embarrassing but the whole community said they was no good, they was kind of set apart and everybody told you, 'Don't hang out with them' . . . Down the road there were these two old ladies who was always setting on the porch. They'd tell my mother if I didn't go to school—it seemed to us kids like it was their job—and then she'd whip me. Another kid's mother could whip you too if you did something wrong."

Later I told Peter Reinharz some of what Earl Roberts had told me about his upbringing. "And," said the lawyer bitterly, "the law took all that away in the name of rights. The right not to be disciplined. Great, isn't it."

After graduating from college, Roberts had come north and gotten a job with a juvenile delinquency prevention program. "The idea was to keep the kid in the community and with his family. We did family advocacy, we'd represent the family with the welfare or housing authorities, or in school, we'd represent the parent in a suspension hearing. The school is glad to have a social worker involved."

Francisco's mother has arrived, a younger son, Salvador, in tow, and Roberts begins the interview for the I and R ordered by the court.

A small, drab woman of indeterminate age, she answers his questions with a worried look, an ingratiating manner. She was born in Santo Domingo, left school at tenth grade, was raped when she was fourteen—her little boy, about six, is sitting next to her, chewing gum and listening, occasionally kicking the chair rung—and had Francisco when she was sixteen.

"Would you say your childhood was very troublesome, bein' raped and all?"

"No." She wrinkles her brow. Then, "My family, they did so many things for me, to not have the baby. They put things on my stomach, made me fall downstairs, but it didn't work, and there wasn't any abortion then." She never lived with the father of the child. "People told me he's in jail." After a pause, during which Roberts was writing, she asks, "They can't find out where he's at?"

He asks about the facts and figures that define the parameters of her life, noting down her answers. She gets a welfare check for $119 every two weeks in addition to $155 in food stamps each month and $270 for rent and utilities. She lived in a welfare hotel before moving into her present apartment. She was "scared to come out" there.

"As far back as you can recall," Roberts begins, "when did you originally go to the welfare hotel?" She looks puzzled. "What reason I go there?" she asks. They can hardly understand each other. His speech is indistinct, hers very rapid, and neither pronounces the words correctly or clearly. They don't really seem to have a common language.

When he asks what school her son attends, she can't remember. He has just started a new one. She has a purse full of papers, documents relating to welfare benefits, clinic appointments, school records, and now she looks for one of these. Why have there been so many changes of school? She keeps transferring her son, she says, to a school in a better neighborhood, or to one not so far away. I wonder how he can learn with no continuity.

"How do you feel," he asks her, "about the incident? Do you think he took that or that it was something brought on

him by someone else?" And then, "Do he have friends or do
he just be by himself?"

While he fills out the forms in front of him with the answers to his questions, she is trying to tell him her troubles.
Her neighbors terrorize her. They ask her to buy things for
them when she goes to the store and don't pay her back. They
break the doors. "The landlord don't wanna do nothing about
the holes, the leaks, the broken steps." She's going to Housing
Court on Wednesday . . . every day she goes to another court
or agency or clinic. It keeps her busy full-time, a kind of
career. She looks tired, worried. She's doing her best. What
else can she do, what is she fit to do? She has three kids—
Francisco, the one who's been arrested; one who's with her
mother and sister; and the youngest, the one who's with her.
She seems affectionate with this child, asks him to take his
jacket off, shakes her head and puts her finger to her lips
when the motor noises he's making as he pushes a little toy
car round his chair get too loud. He's a lively little boy.

"Do him and Francisco have the same father?" Roberts
asks her. "No," Salvador offers brightly. "All of us have different fathers."

"Has Francisco been evaluated by the COH?" She understands immediately what that means—the Committee on the
Handicapped that makes decisions on special placements in
the school. She tells him Francisco has been diagnosed as
learning disabled and has been in special education classes
since the second grade. He is now, at fifteen, in eighth grade.

Roberts refers her to a neighborhood youth project for
counseling, help in dealing with her landlord, the hospital,
the school. The government pays for the basic services and
then for these secondary ones to act as intermediaries between
the basic institutions and their clients, as they are referred to,
each service bureaucracy begetting another. Still, if anyone
needs a safety net, it's this helpless mother, and it would be

hardhearted indeed to begrudge the help she gets. She seems so beaten down, so lacking in the aggressiveness and posture of entitlement of some of the system's "clients." She thinks the group home in Brooklyn where Francisco has been temporarily placed in non-secure detention is "nice." She is grateful for small favors and probably couldn't function at all without this panoply of support systems. Roberts tells me these families are often in the hospital, a result of accidents, illness. "They're careless, and they don't know how to eat right, and a lot of the kids are sickly to begin with."

Roberts says, "Every mother worries about her kids," and adds that at puberty, Hispanic families begin to treat the boy like an adult. "There's a lot of peer pressure in that environment to prove you're a macho man." The mothers are protective of the boys, keep their secrets when they get into trouble, don't tell the fathers when they sleep all day and get up an hour before Father comes home and go out. He thinks this combination of pressure and indulgence leads a lot of adolescent boys into trouble.

"Probation Follies." It could be a musical revue. Familiar themes, rehearsed steps, the same routines, from the overtures at intake to the final curtain after the courtroom scene. Law meets boy, law loses boy, law gets boy—but by that time it's too late.

Angelo's mother had applied for voluntary placement because he was staying out late, wasn't going to school. Angelo wanted it too. He said it was hard for him to resist going along with his friends and getting into trouble. The placement was pending when Angelo was picked up again—three in concert—and now he'll be placed by the court.

Angelo's mother is smoking, the radio is playing, and she's trying to answer the probation officer's questions about her own background. She was one of eight children; she's not sure of her birth order among them—"somewhere in there." Since she told her parents about Angelo's arrest, "he doesn't dare look them in the face. He has more respect for them than for me." The PO, an attractive, well-dressed black woman in her forties, goes on writing. Not looking up, she says, "Yeah." Angelo's mother goes on. The Legal Aid lawyer told her Angelo should take a plea because he had the gun on him— passed to him by Eddie, he says—when they were arrested still hanging around on Columbus Avenue after a failed robbery attempt. Angelo's mother doesn't like Eddie. "I never allow them to bring friends in the house," she says. "One of them stole a bracelet once." She and the father of her youngest child have been together nine years "but we don't really live together. Sometimes he stays over." Angelo is the oldest. "He never sees his real father."

She gets a monthly check for $152 from Welfare in addition to $137 rent subsidy, and $32 for each child from Supplementary Security Income. Their father hasn't been able to work since an accident he had in 1976, she says, "but he never supported them before his accident."

She's a slim pretty woman in her mid-thirties, her hair cut fashionably short, wearing tight jeans that say "Sergio Valente" on the back pocket and high-heeled sandals. Angelo is afraid of being called a mama's boy, she tells the PO. He can't not fight if they pick on him; he wants to do what the other boys do—stay out late, hang out. The radio is louder than the interviewer's voice but neither of them seems to notice.

The PO's questions are mental-health clichés that suggest their own answers. "Has there been a behavior change in the last year? Has he seemed withdrawn?" The mother complies on cue. "Yes. Oh, yes." Angelo has been having psychological counseling at a neighborhood youth center, she tells her. "My son has emotional problems." She adds, as an afterthought, "My nerves are not too good neither." Angelo is a weak boy in a bad crowd, she tells the PO, "but he doesn't have a bad heart." He cares about other people. He helps his friends (like Eddie?), "he helps little kids—like when he was in Spofford and they were picking on one—and he'll help an old lady down the stairs. When the guy wouldn't give them his money, they let him walk away." Angelo didn't know Eddie had a gun, he has told her, until Eddie pulled it on the guy on Columbus Avenue. According to his mother, when Angelo said, " 'Please give us your money,' the guy looked at him like he was crazy and said, 'Get away from me,' and Angelo laughed and let him go."

This is the same story Angelo tells the probation officer in the detention room where he's being interviewed later that morning. They discuss the best place for him, what's available in terms of recreational facilities, psychological counseling, educational programs. It sounds like a student's session with his college adviser. Angelo would like to go upstate. He thinks he needs to get away from his friends. "We be doing human bebop." He grins. "They eat up my head." He tells the PO, "My education is important to me . . . I want to make clean money . . . I feel for my mom." He wants to go into the Army after high school, learn computers. Then how come instead of going to school, the PO asks mildly, he hangs out with his friends? He can't say no, he says with an ingratiating smile. The PO listens sympathetically, smiles back at this pleasant-mannered, good-looking young man almost flirtatiously, makes no effort to impress him with the consequences of his "hanging out," or what he'd better do if he wants to make good on his plans. She's more interested in hearing about what he and his friends do, besides robbery, while they're hanging out. He tells her about "snapping," which some kids call "ranking" or "dozens," a contest of escalating verbal insults intended to be witty. At her request, he gives some examples: "Your mother's so ugly she wears

army boots . . . They call your mother the Lincoln Tun-
nel . . ." Their parting smiles are amiable. It might have been
an ordinary social occasion. As a matter of fact, it occurs to
me, it was.

On a wintry afternoon on the west side of Manhattan near
the theater district, two young people on their way to work
at an off-Broadway theater were surrounded by a group of
marauding boys who started out demanding their purse and
wallet and, after a moment of what was probably more surprise than resistance on their part, grabbed them. They went
on to beat them both bloody, one of the attackers kicking
them in the head and on the body before they left them on
the ground and went on.

The case made the papers, students from the nearby high
school were questioned, rumors were followed up, someone
talked, someone else confessed reluctantly—under pressure
and given promises—to having been in the crowd and identified a couple of the more active assailants. Several witnesses
were found who identified the kicker. He was, as the expression has it, well known to the court, having been arrested
several times previously on charges involving violent confron-
tations with women or other youngsters on the streets or in
the subways. Duane was not shy.

Ellen Garcia, however, seemed to feel she had to draw
him out. A pretty young woman in her late twenties, wearing
a sweater and pearls under a tailored suit, she seemed dressed
for success in this atmosphere of failure. She might have been
a young executive at Citibank dealing with a priority service
customer as she sat with her pen poised over her notepad in
one hand, the other touching the beads at her neck, her
expression one of receptive amiability.

Like all adolescents, the boys in Family Court are searching for an identity. The boys in Duane's world distinguish

themselves by brand names, create a persona by means of Nike and Reebok sneakers laced just right, by Cazal sunglasses and various kinds of expensive leather boots, and by gold initials worn on chains around their necks. The one thing they will almost always get right on the witness stand is clothing. Their descriptions of what another boy was wearing are clear and specific, unlike almost anything else they are asked about. Most try to look like the rest. More daring dudes—the ones who scorn rules and feel in their hearts that they are exceptions—find further distinguishing marks. For Duane it is a gold front tooth.

Duane flashes a broad grin when the PO notes in her gentle voice, her manner open and friendly, that he was arrested twice in the same day and now has three open cases. His gold tooth gleams and I almost expect him to wink at her. Duane denies everything, smoothly and with no apparent discomfort about the charges or his situation. Somebody else did it. Each time. It just looked like him. "The man, it was like he done it," he explains affably. (There is sworn testimony from a police officer who saw Duane making a chain snatch, although, since he did it from behind the victim, she cannot swear it was Duane. Nor can the young stagehands who were kicked, since both victims had been trying to cover their faces and protect their heads during the attack.)

Duane exhibits no fear, no remorse. If they are there, his emotions are very well hidden. He keeps talking easily, explaining everything, rationalizing everything. He spreads his hands and grins as he talks away these mistakes of identification, misinterpretations of events, and the PO laughs and jokes with him. The reason they thought he had a gun on him, he explains (an abortive holdup, a short chase, and when he is caught there is no weapon on him), was because he had his hand inside his jacket to keep warm. "It was a bad day for you, wasn't it," she notes in a tone that if not sympathetic is certainly not unfriendly.

Duane knows the dates of all his scheduled court appearances. He has a busy agenda, like a lawyer or a CEO. "It's kinda funny, I know," he says, laughing and flashing his gold tooth again, referring to his statement that he didn't commit any of the several acts of which he's been accused. He tells a complicated story about the witness who has sworn she saw him beating up and kicking the theater pair. She was lying, trying to get back at him and his brother for some imagined insult.

"I got witnesses," he says with self-assurance, "on this one too."

"How did you *not* do this one?" the PO asks him with only the mildest irony. Is he going to claim, I wonder, that some other guy with a gold front tooth did it in every case?

Ellen Garcia asks Duane about his family, and he tells her his parents are not married. His mother has a drinking problem. He lives with his father and a half-sister, his father's child by another woman to whom he is not married either. She asks him about his mother's birth order and her siblings—nothing about the crimes—or, in PO terms, acts—with which he is charged. They compare notes about the streets in Jersey City where his mother lives, and about which are the best and worst parts of town. He is perfectly willing to oblige her by giving her whatever answers her questions seem to suggest.

"How did your mother take the news of your arrest? Was she upset?" "Yeah. Upset." "Upset or angry?" "Angry. Upset and angry."

His father is not here today because he is in court with Duane's sister. And his older brother? On Riker's Island. He informs her that his favorite classes are photography ("I like that too," she says) and Spanish (she is Hispanic). She makes a little pleasantry about his being a jock but doing a lot of reading now while he's in jail. Smiles all around. She joins him in mild disparagement of the school authorities and all that testing.

The room in which this is going on is barely large enough for a desk and two chairs. The door remains partially open and there is the sound of another set of voices, the actors on a daytime television serial. Everyone seems to accept the constant blaring of radio or TV, as though the violence on the dramas and in the music were the background for the violence in these lives. There is no reality for this "youth," as he is designated by the court, just a bunch of alibis relating to the various cases. As he juggles it around like an entertainer, the PO just listens and smiles, the perfect audience.

"Good luck this afternoon," she says as they part and he is taken back to the detention room to await his hearing. And on our way out she muses gently, "I don't understand . . . either he has really bad luck or he's a liar."

As I wait for her to sign out and for the key to be turned in the lock so we can leave the boys' detention area, I read the notice on the wall: "Legal Aid—Please do not furnish youth with cigarettes." Why not, I wonder. They are furnished with so much else—alibis, cynicism, contempt for the rules—that might be considered dangerous to their health.

It was in one of the intake interviews I sat in on that it all came together for me—a clear sense of who and what was most to blame for the mess, the perversity, the failure of the system to make a difference in these young lives, to help even in the limited way that intervention at age fourteen or fifteen might.

The young man across from Hy Gross was well dressed, neat, poised, and well spoken. He was appropriately polite, neither fawning nor sullen and withholding as many of the parents are in these interviews. As a matter of fact, he was not a parent properly speaking, but the older brother of the boy who was arrested, and had come in place of their mother. He gives the family history—the absent father, who deserted the family when both boys and their sister were small children, the mother's struggle to raise them, her inability to handle the younger boy, her disgust with his defiance, his school truancy, his late hours, her lack of control. Now he's been arrested for the second time and she won't come down to court. She washes her hands of him, wants to see him placed somewhere for his own good and so she can stop worrying about him for a while. She's asked his brother to appear for her and explain the family's position: they are not opposed to placement. Gross makes notes as he listens, from time to time saying, "Sure, sure."

My first thought is that this sounds irresponsible, shifting the burden of a kid's care to others, asking society to make up for a family's failure to socialize its children, presenting the public with a bill for private deficits. But something about this young man, so calm and articulate, so obviously better put together than most of the young or old family members one sees in Family Court, piques my curiosity. The telephone rings, the probation officer gets into a conversation about some misplaced records, a scheduled court appearance. It promises to be lengthy. For the first time, I break a rule and step out of my assumed invisibility. I start a casual conversation with the young man. Yes, he has some familiarity with the court; he's been here before. In fact, he's been through the system himself.

He's twenty-three now, employed in the construction business, with an apartment he shares with his girlfriend. They're planning to get married. When he was his brother's age, he got in a lot of trouble. He was wild and wouldn't listen to his mother either, wouldn't listen to anybody. Had to be a big man. Got in with a bad crowd. Got arrested. Drugs too? I ask. His brother is charged with criminal possession and criminal sale of a controlled substance. "No," he says matter-of-factly, "armed robbery." I can't believe it, looking at him. He nods. "They sent me away. Spofford, Goshen, then Camp Brace. It was the best thing that could have happened to me. Camp Brace was a good place. It taught me to discipline myself. They let you make decisions but you were strictly supervised. I missed things I'd taken for granted when I had my freedom and I decided if I couldn't make it one way I'd make it another way. I took my G.E.D. [high school equivalency test] and passed. They encouraged me to apply to college and I had three years at Oneonta."

So once in a while, with the right kid, rehabilitation does work. Maybe it would work for his brother. Maybe not. But it's understandable now, at least, why this family thinks placement is a good idea. The probation officer is off the phone now, the interview is concluded, and I hope my admiration and respect show when I say good-bye to the young man and wish him luck. Hy Gross gets his papers together, picks up his folders, and asks if I'd like to go with him to interview the younger brother in detention.

Upstairs, we ring a bell and a guard admits us through a locked metal door to an anteroom where we sign in and wait to be admitted to the locked room in which the boy is being held. The atmosphere is more like school or camp than prison. There are the ubiquitous posters on the wall ("If a child lives with criticism/ She learns to condemn. . . . If a child lives with acceptance and friendship/ He learns to find love in the world." They must have been ordered by the score when the building was put up.) There's a Michael Jackson poster, one of a basketball player I don't recognize, some kids' drawings in a style I'd call IRT graffiti, easier to appreciate on paper than on train walls; the clerks and guards are chatting easily;

an old black-and-white TV set is on, one of the daytime soap operas adding to the general level of noise although no one seems to be watching it. Only having to wait as a guard unlocks the door reminds me this is indeed a jail, even though it's a very temporary one. Kids brought down from Spofford for court appearances are held here for a few hours at most. Inside the room, which contains only a built-in bench and a toilet, the boy sits listless, eyes half-closed, barely taking notice of our entrance. He seems so out of it, so unconcerned, that I wonder if he's drugged. Next to him sits a tall, slender blond young man, impeccably three-piece-suited, whom I recognize as one of the Legal Aid lawyers. He says—it is not a question but a statement—he would like to be present during the probation officer's interview. "This young man is already my client."

Hy Gross objects. There's a short tug of wills, and Gross prevails. He is entitled to interview the boy alone at this point. The lawyer, I assume, represented the boy on his earlier case. Obviously annoyed, he turns at the door and says, "All right, I'm leaving, but I'm advising my client not to say anything." Pointedly: "Not to talk to you."

Gross shrugs and proceeds to ask the boy what happened. A short rehearsed-sounding reply: he didn't have the stuff, it was the other guy, he was only standing there, the cop is lying. It wasn't in his hand, it was "on the floor." (The arrest was made in a vacant lot on 122nd Street.) Gross shows no reaction, looks weary, asks the boy to read a paragraph from one of the boxing magazines he uses to test reading ability, asks the boy what his favorite subject in school is. "Social studies." No, he doesn't know how many days of school he missed so far this semester. He can't think of the number of his class. He doesn't know how many subjects he's failing.

Gross closes his pen, shuts his folder, stands up, and lets the guard know we're ready to leave. Nothing has been said on either side that adds to Gross's understanding of the boy, or to the boy's understanding of his situation. Only one thing is clear to me. This boy's last chance, his only hope, may be subverted by the system that has emerged from the Legal Aid philosophy. He will be accorded the rights due an adult criminal at trial. He has a lawyer, and that lawyer will tell him what to say, how to behave, so as to prevent him from being deprived of his liberty. It all has a noble ring until you begin to think about it. What it really means is that he will be sent back to the streets, unchanged, only perhaps a little more cynical and with less reason to fear the consequences of anything he does. He is almost sixteen. Next time he won't be back here, he'll be across the street in Criminal Court. And if they put him away, it won't be here among the juvenilia and the blasé but good-natured guards; it will be Rikers Island, the real thing. Chances of being rehabilitated there are not outstanding.

There is no way of knowing whether this particular boy would be reached by some counselor, touched by some opportunity, respond to some experience in the placement situation. His brother's was a more serious violent crime but something in his character did benefit from what he found at Camp Brace, the limited secure facility in upstate New York that provided his first taste of structure and supervision. Maybe this boy is too weak or too stupid or too mean-spirited. Maybe nothing can penetrate his druggy stupor or turn his imagination toward another kind of life, make gainful effort more satisfying than effortless gain. But we'll never know now. He has a smart lawyer who will try to "get him off" so he can go back to being an entrepreneur on 122nd Street. Whether he succeeds this time or not, he will be implementing the Legal Aid philosophy, which, in its determination to replace admittedly less-than-perfect attempts to provide for the best interests of the child and substitute perfect procedural safeguards at law, has ended up emphasizing the child's legal rights at the expense of his human needs.

Wade was arrested on August 20 and ordered to appear at Part A Intake at Family Court on August 29, at which time he was paroled until October 16. On that date his parole was continued to November 29, when it was again continued until January 8. After a fact-finding hearing on that date, Wade was paroled to February 19 while an I and R could be prepared by the Department of Probation for the court's use in the dispositional hearing. At disposition on February 19, Wade was put on probation. The assigned probation officer would have seen Wade and his mother that same day, but somehow nobody told them that and so they left the building when the hearing was over. The probation officer then sent a letter scheduling an appointment with Wade for March 8.

I sat with the PO waiting to sit in on the interview, but Wade failed to appear. It is hardly surprising. Why should he remember the appointment? He probably barely remembers the incident more than six months ago that led to his arrest, and at this point hardly knows why he was in court so many times. It made no difference in his life, didn't change it in any way. There was the inconvenience of waiting around to be called each time, but families like Wade's are used to waiting—at the welfare office, the unemployment office, the clinic.

The only consequence of Wade's failure to appear will be another letter setting a new reporting date and informing Wade's mother that failure to respond could result in court action. Not a very impressive result of Wade's first foray outside the law those months ago. It's no great wonder then that he will turn out to have tried his hand at it again before ever meeting with a probation officer. He is rearrested on March 10.

In an earlier time, before the establishment of the present Family Court system in the early 1960s, Wade would have been seen immediately, brought in on the day of arrest, at which time an intake worker would have decided whether to adjust the case or send it to court. Cases that went to court did so the same day, with a fact-finding hearing followed, after a short adjournment, by a dispositional hearing.

Alice Burns, a veteran supervisor in the Department of Probation, has seen it all. Her nearly twenty-year tenure in the department has spanned the time from the reorganization of the various lower courts dealing with women, children, and domestic relations into a single Family Court, through the increasing emphasis on the rights of the accused following the Supreme Court's 1967 *Gault* decision, to the tougher juvenile offender legislation of 1978, to "the present mess." She is convinced that once arrested, youngsters should go right to court the same day. "Otherwise they don't see the connection. Weeks go by and it's worn away by then."

We had lunch in the courthouse neighborhood at an old-fashioned bar and restaurant where everyone looks like a process server or like someone who forgot to go home several years ago. Portions are large and the food terrible. An anomalous place in the era of hi-tech atmosphere and nouvelle cuisine, it seemed a peculiarly appropriate setting for our conversation about old times and new problems.

"It started with Legal Aid," Alice told me over her sandwich. "They came in here as law guardians, to see the kids' rights weren't violated, but the emphasis on technicalities, on the rights of the accused got extended to saying to the kid, 'You didn't shoot her,' when the kid's already confessed. 'The cop did,' the lawyer will say, and the kid looks at him like he's crazy. So the interpretation of their rights has been extended to lying to get them off, even if placement would be good for them. To say nothing of the rest of the community they come from."

By the time we were having our coffee, Alice Burns had told me a lot about what she thought were the more egregious conditions of the system and what she would do if she had the chance.

"Some of the probation workers see themselves as advocates, taking the side of their client against the system. Drugs, illegitimacy are just part of a lifestyle. If there are six kids, I want to know if they have the same father or different ones. Even if he isn't in the house it can be a force for stability if it's the same father. The worker won't ask. She says it's not her business. It's their lifestyle.

"Is it deviant behavior we see here or normal? The parents say, 'All the kids do it.' If everybody in your family's been arrested, everybody in your building, everybody on your side of the street, everybody on the other side of the street, everybody on the block—is it abnormal behavior? It's not unheard of for there to be a family with four kids, every one of whom has been to Family Court.

"If there were one thing I could do it would be to give them words. If they have words, I can do something with them. I'd like to start day care in the schools at age two, use computers in kindergarten to teach them to read. Four-year-olds come to school now who don't even know the word for 'chair.' "

Almost a year after I'd sat in her office listening to her talk with the kids who were lucky enough to be assigned to Pat Brennan as a probation officer, I called on her again to find out what had become of them—and of her.

Pat had been transferred from Family Court to a task force set up to study the entire Probation Department—the adult system as well—and make recommendations for change. It was clearly a good thing for her, and just as clearly a bad thing for the Family Court system. There weren't enough probation officers like her to make her loss insignificant.

I asked her, now that she had the perspective that distance gives, how she would go about changing the Family Court probation system to improve things. She didn't have to hesitate a minute.

"We social-work the kids to death or else we treat them like dirt bags," was the first thing she said. "It's one extreme or the other.

"The training should be more practical. There's no on-site supervision. When you start as a probation officer you've never done it before, but you just have to wing it with whatever you bring to the job. It's all folklore. They do usually start you with investigations, not supervision, but there's no provision for observing how older, more experienced POs do it before you start doing it yourself.

"And there's no attempt to put people where they'd be most effective. Some are better at long-range supervision, others do better in intake, where it's just one, two, three.

"There should be a probation school for the kids, not just an after-school program and their regular school to go back to while they're on probation. These are high-risk kids; they need more control and structure if they're going to learn to take charge of their lives.

"There also ought to be some source of job referrals, some alternative for them to dealing in crack. At some point a lot of them say, 'Can you help me get a job?' What do you tell them? No? And if you *can* direct them to a job, you have to teach them how to deal with a job interview, how to act on a job—what's expected of them, how to handle themselves. Most of them have no idea."

I asked about the kids I'd seen in her office. What had become of them?

Nicholas is now an adult in the eyes of the law, having turned sixteen. He finished his two years of probation and he did get into the special school of art and design. Pat had met him not long ago in the subway station near the school. He was with a friend and he seemed busy and happy. He said he had a sketch, a portrait he wanted to give her. She told him he'd better make it in the next few days because she was leaving her old office soon, but he hadn't come.

As a result of Pat's persistence and in spite of the Bureau of Child Welfare, the Taiwanese girl was placed with a foster family on Staten Island and enrolled in a special school there with a large Asian immigrant population. The family was interested in adopting her. Five months later her father flew over and took her back home.

Dennis violated his parole, got involved in a series of car thefts with his brother, a drug addict. By the time of his latest case he was already an adult, eligible for Criminal Court and jail the next time he got arrested. At the parole violation hearing he pleaded guilty and agreed to go to a DFY Title III facility. Arrangements were made for him to go that same day, directly from Family Court. Pat saw him before he left. Looking around at the other boys in the group he was to leave with he said, "I don't think I'm gonna like it. There's a lot of nerds here."

"Listen," she said, "you think there are better-type guys in jail? That's where you'll wind up next time if you don't go here now. There are no success stories in your neighborhood. You've got to get away from there if you're going to stay alive."

Manuel's story was no more heartening than Dennis's. He'd gotten involved in crack and was stealing. His parents were covering for him and telling him not to tell his probation officer. He told her anyway, said he felt himself changing, asked her to send him away. He took Pat up to the family apartment and said, "See, they don't even clean the house or do the laundry anymore." Pat says, "Sure, you can say he's a big guy, could do his own laundry, clean up the place, but it's the whole attitude. I give him credit for having the guts to tell me when his parents told him not to." Manuel was accepted at Lincoln Hall and he seemed glad to go. He might turn out to be one of their success stories.

9
Guidance and Redemption

The Children's Court . . . intent had been defined, in case law, as providing for the guidance and redemption of neglected and delinquent children. . . . The 1962 Family Court Act continued the implied purpose.

—from Practice Commentary, *Family Court Act* (1983), Article 3, Part 1, Section 1

The earliest attempts at rehabilitation must often occur at school because many—although not all—delinquents begin life as abused or neglected children.

Increasingly, they are the children of teenage girls and boys with whom these young mothers have no lasting relationship. That means they grow up without fathers, the children of girl children who are in effect incapable of mature nurturing. By the time they come to the attention of the court, or even the schools, it may be too late for change, too late to influence their development in any meaningful way.

A case in point is Wayne M., who took part in the brutal rape and torture of a bag lady in Central Park—what the tabloids called the "thrill-kill rape and slaying"—when he was fourteen.

Shortly after I began observing in Family Court, and just a few days after the incident in the park, I received a call from a school psychologist I'll call Edith Gold. A mutual friend had mentioned my interest in the juvenile justice system, and she was eager to talk to someone about Wayne M.

We met one evening in her apartment on Riverside Drive amid a clutter of books and papers and cartons of more books and papers, some of which she moved away to make room for my tape recorder on the coffee table. A handsome, auburn-haired, voluble woman in her late forties, Edith Gold could hardly wait to start the story that came tumbling out and to give her thoughts about the failure of the system she worked in, trying to come to grips with the problems presented by the Wayne M.'s.

"The reason I wanted so much to talk with you is that when I learned what had happened to a child I had tried to work with within the system, I felt I had to do something, because this situation is repeating itself over and over. I'm not interested in trying to help this particular child because it's too late now."

She had written out by hand from various records available to her a summary of Wayne's school history, which she gave me. When I read it over later I learned that he had been identified as a child with problems as early as second grade. He couldn't read, he couldn't sit still, he was "a very disruptive force" in the classroom. As time passed, referrals, reports, evaluations began to fill a file, but not much happened to Wayne. A lot of testing, summarized in a lot of jargon ("perceptual motor functioning below age-expectation, impaired controls in emotionally charged situations . . . uses bravado to compensate for feelings of inadequacy and displays extreme preoccupation with bodily harm and violence . . .").

And there were some biographical facts. Wayne's mother was fifteen when he was born. Wayne's father had disappeared before his birth and he never saw him. When Wayne was five, he saw his mother killed "by a gunshot to the head fired by one of mother's boyfriends." He knows that no one was ever convicted for her murder. For a while after his mother's death, he lived with a great-uncle until the uncle, too, was murdered. After some shuffling around among relatives, he came to live with his great-grandmother, a woman in her seventies. It is not surprising that no one bothered to register Wayne for pre-kindergarten (for which he would have been eligible at four) or even kindergarten at five.

He was entered in school at six as required by law and was placed in an EH (emotionally handicapped) class at age seven, in second grade, when it was recommended that he also receive counseling and tutoring. He failed to appear for most appointments, and as for school, the record indicated "he is most of the time suspended as a result of violent conduct . . . is most of the time involved in fights with other students . . . disrupts the class so that effective teaching would be impossible." Still, in the course of time he was "articulated," as the records put it, to the junior high school level; again, as in grade school, he was placed in an EH class. It was then that he came to Edith Gold's attention.

In order to explain to me how it had happened that she had a letter in her hand authorizing an alternative program to the regular school for Wayne at the time he was arrested, Edith Gold had to tell me a little about Wayne in addition to the facts in his records. She had learned when she interviewed him that Wayne had been arrested for a mugging. He'd been brought to Family Court, where, in his words, "they didn't do nothing." Edith also needed to tell me something about the system in which she tried to deal with the many Waynes who came her way. As a matter of fact, she had quite a lot to say about the New York City public school system.

What she describes is a once-proud system in disarray,

attacked by special-interest groups without and beset by bureaucratic paralysis within, and the increasing frustration of
all her efforts to make something happen in the lives of the
children she is supposed to be helping.

"I'm supposed to be writing my dissertation, but I somehow reached the point where my rage at the nonsense that
was getting heaped on us, more demands to do more crazy
things, was getting to me and I began to think about what's
wrong. So I spent New Year's Day writing a voluntary piece
of testimony for the State Assembly Education Committee.
What I was trying to show was what's happened and what
the educational system is today. Until the New York City fiscal crisis, even despite the battles over integration and community control, it was still an affluent system. We had
guidance counselors and support services. And we didn't yet
have the flood of problem students we have now. What you
might call the population ecology is getting very scary—the
proliferation of the incompetent, the damaged, and the dam-
aging, while those who are more competent flee if they can
or get submerged by it all.

"But what I wrote didn't so much address the demographics as the educational system itself and how two movements
had coalesced. One was the fiscal crisis of the mid-1970s,
which led to a real stripping of services in the city agencies.
Vast numbers of support people were taken away from the
school system—psychologists, social workers, guidance counselors. They're the ones who used to be there in the schools
day in, day out, somebody who really knows the school,
available for consultation with the teacher on a problem
child. And at the same time that you had this cutting of services, the other movement coming along was the parents of
the handicapped saying, 'Our children have been excluded
from public schools.'

"Up to then the attitude of school boards all over the

country had been, 'If your child can't make it physically or emotionally, behaviorally or in learning—*out!* We may have a class for the retarded, but other than that, go find them something on your own or keep them home. It's not our problem.' Well, they organized parent groups around the country and a very heavy law was passed in 1974—Public Law 94–142—guaranteeing a free and appropriate public education to *every* child. It doesn't have to be optimal, it has to be appropriate.

"Now this has created a fantastic change in the schools. In many places the requirements of the handicapped, the damaged, the disabled have taken priority over regular education. The parents of the handicapped demanding their rights have a stranglehold over the Board of Education. You wouldn't believe the number of parents coming along and saying, 'I have my rights because I have a handicapped child'—when between you and me some of them may have contributed significantly to the 'handicap.'

"There are eleven categories of 'handicapped,' some of which are physical, but the two categories I'm talking about here are 'learning disabled' and 'emotionally handicapped.' Now this is a tricky distinction at best. Many kids have difficulty *learning* because they're *emotionally* disturbed. I'm not sure there's such a thing as a learning disability, with the possible exception of a delay in perceptual motor functioning.

"But what are we going to do with all these children who can't function in school? You take a lot of do-gooders like me, and what we do when we get the next kid who's way behind is, we call it a learning disability—because what else are we going to say? There are times when we've all done it in order to get a kid help.

"So you have these hordes of children referred to as handicapped, because you have nothing else. And no support personnel to deal with them, no guidance counselor to even make a referral."

She stopped, as though momentarily weighted down by what she had just heard herself say. After a moment she went on.

"Now when you think about it, this is a very expensive way of doing business. You see, when you say a child is handicapped, action must be taken. Whether it's a parent, or a teacher, or a kitchen worker—if anybody refers a kid for evaluation as handicapped, that child must receive psychological testing, a social history must be done and an educational evaluation completed within sixty days. This is the federal law and the *José P.* court decision.* Nothing says it has to be a good evaluation, it just has to be a fast one. This is part of what gets me. They don't give a goddamn if it's valid, they only care if it's fast. 'How many children did you do today?' So we're spending a fortune on putting numbers to the simple fact that these kids can't function in a school with the expectations that we would probably agree should be the expectations of society.

"I'm still on my way to talking about Wayne," she said, as though apologizing. "But I want to emphasize some of the differences from when I came into the system. How many fifteen-year-olds had babies then? Now I don't think the life on welfare is great and I don't think women have babies to

---

José P. v. *Ambach* was a class action suit brought in 1979 on behalf of a group of handicapped children by United Cerebral Palsy of New York against the New York State Commissioner of Education and the Board of Education of New York City alleging that handicapped children were being deprived of the free and appropriate public education to which they were entitled by federal and New York State law. The *José P.* decision mandated timely evaluation and placement as well as the right to all related services necessary to implement a program based on an individual educational program for each child in the least restrictive environment. In a related 1979 case, *Dyrcia S.* v. *Board of Education*, handicapped Hispanic children with limited English proficiency were guaranteed a bilingual-bicultural special education.

get that subsidy, but what we have here is an underclass that's perpetuating itself and where the value system has changed. It's really not just the lack of thought about tomorrow. There's a conscious, deliberate decision in a lot of cases—I'll have a baby and then the world has to treat me nice for a day or two. *Then* comes not thinking about tomorrow. There's no sense of reality. And often the mothers who are now the young grandmothers encourage it. They really feel differently about this baby—they've gotten a little older now—than they felt about their own daughter. So they don't mind so much. Others encourage the girl to have the baby in order to teach her a lesson. 'We're tired of you getting pregnant and helping you get an abortion. You have this baby!' Isn't that a wonderful punishment? What a way for a baby to come into the world. I have plenty of kids like that. So this is one piece of it.

"But, you know, when I talk about the learning disabled and the vast amount of paperwork and the vast expense because so many of them are dulled who might not have been with more early stimulation, that's one thing. But the behavior problems are something else to my mind. Not that we can always tell them apart, because a behavior problem can often start from frustration or low self-esteem of the 'I can't keep up with the other guys' kind. And I think that may be what happened with Wayne. Nevertheless, once the kid is the mocked, angry, sociopathic kid, to say that this is a handicapped child and have somebody fill up lots of pages of paper about him—well, it doesn't begin to make a dent in the problem.

"If you have ten angry boys and you put them in a room together, what are they going to do? They're going to sit around saying, 'Motherfucker, motherfucker' all day long. There's nothing about that grouping that's going to increase the likelihood of learning. Sure, it gets them out of the way of the other kids and presumably it enables the teacher to go on teaching the regular kids—but the poor teacher who's sentenced to this other group! If ever a class needed a talented teacher, it's those ten awful boys. But, of course, who goes into that classroom? Our most junior person, because—you know—who wants it? I wouldn't want it. My hat's off to the ones who do it, but nobody lasts very long at it.

"Look, we have a program for kids like Wayne called day treatment. What do you think we mean by that? Do you think there's any treatment? A half hour a week with a guidance counselor is what we're talking about, and now the pressure is on to see them in groups so we can get more numbers in. And if there's a psychologist in the picture we're told the testing comes first. Every child must be reevaluated every three years. What does the testing and the evaluation lead to? It leads to the fulfilling of the paper requirements. Sound like Kafka? Sometimes I think he's running it all.

"What it comes down to is this: so that the State Ed Department can keep track of the few dollars it gives us, a lot of papers are filled out. And there is nothing less helpful to a kid who's emotionally disturbed. You wouldn't believe the forms. They're called Individual Educational Programs, IEPs. You check off a few categories, make a recommendation . . . 'needs constant supervision.' It's about as helpful as astrology."

She poured some coffee into the cups in front of us and stirred hers absently.

"And that finally brings me to Wayne. One of the schools I've been assigned to is a junior high and in junior high, 'emotionally handicapped' means the bad kids. Now one of the EH teachers grabbed me when I appeared last fall and said, 'You've got to help me. There are three kids in my class who've got to go.' Now these kids are already in EH class, not regular ed, so I was reluctant to jump to the conclusion that they really had to go, but I have to admit that in the light of later events, although she may not have been the greatest teacher, she was right about those three kids. And one of them was Wayne.

"Well, I went to the social worker on our team and I asked her—now this isn't the way I wrote it up officially, because I covered for people. I wasn't going to criticize the teacher or the social worker. Anyway, I asked her to get the parent in. It's the social worker's job to have a discussion with the parent about a more restrictive placement. She kept claiming she'd sent letters and more letters but never got an answer. Wayne's grandmother never came. Meanwhile I kept getting reports of trouble with him. So when I saw there was a form on him that was incomplete, I knew that would be more important in this system than the fact that the teacher was having trouble with him.

"The paper—which is what counts, not the kid or the teacher—is not complete. He's had a psychological, he's had an educational, but he hasn't had a social. So that's a more compelling reason—isn't it disgusting?—to get the grand-mother in than that he's throwing things around the room and not paying any attention to the work. As a matter of fact, he's on informal suspension. Of course, you can't suspend a kid anymore without a full legal hearing, so you don't call it suspension. 'Informal' means you do something illegal and you don't call it that. We really have no other recourse, they make it so difficult to get a legal suspension, no matter how violent the kid.

"Meanwhile Wayne is out on the street because we can't handle him in school and nobody's making any other arrange-ments for him. I keep after my social worker to call the grandmother and she keeps telling me she tried and got no answer, so finally I look in the file and find the number and I call myself and I get the grandmother and she comes in.

Right there I have to ask myself why we missed a few months on this, but anyway, when the grandmother finally comes in—she's very old, she's actually the great-grandmother, I think—she says she isn't aware of any problems with Wayne. And she misses a lot of appointments we make for her to come back. She's something like seventy-six and it's hard for her to get around, and to keep coming in to hear how much of a trouble the kid is . . .

"So we finally sent the case up to the Committee on the Handicapped. There's the School Base Support Team, that's me and my partners, and the next level up is the COH. According to the law, the recommendation for a child to be placed in a more restrictive school program has to come from the COH. And who is the COH? There aren't any special qualifications, it's whoever the chairperson decides will be the committee on that particular day—that's the COH. Sometimes it's the most experienced people, sometimes the least—because they'll do what they're told. Sometimes it's the same people every day, sometimes it's a rotating job. Anyway, we sent up the case. We're not supposed to make a recommendation, because legally only the COH can make a recommendation. But we made it very clear that what we thought Wayne should have was a treatment setting.

"Looking back," she observed, "I'm not sure there was much basis to think he was treatable. But in the Board of Ed you never wash your hands of a child.

"If you can't deal with him in regular day school you can't just say, 'This is a lousy rotten kid.' At one time we used to have only what are now called day schools, the old 600 schools, for incorrigible kids. And then there was a lawsuit— the *Lora* decision—that said there were too many minority kids in the 600 schools, and if the numbers are disproportionate it must be prejudice and discrimination and we must be doing something wrong at the Board of Ed. Well, how about saying they're sick? So we tried day *treatment* schools and found we had the same ethnic problem. Kafka again. I mean, there's no real logic to it.

"First we try EH classes in the regular school. Then you take them out and put them in special schools we call day treatment schools, where there's an underlying assumption there'll be more policing, or at least people in sufficient numbers to deal with these kids. Not to treat them, really, just to deal with them. I keep writing letters to the administrators: 'Can we please have treatment in the day treatment schools?' and I don't even know that you can treat these kids in any thorough way, but there should be a team of social workers and psychologists on-site, and there isn't. Just two days a week. Mostly they do testing. And you can't send a troubled kid to them when they're testing. So they might as well not be there at all in terms of being accessible to the troubled kids. So why do we call it a day *treatment* school?"

She paused, as though half expecting an answer, then, pushing a strand of reddish hair off her forehead, went on.

"Anyway, the COH overruled us on day treatment for Wayne. They said, 'Put him in an NIEH class.' Now that's NI, neurologically impaired, combined with EH, and it's supposed to be for the emotionally handicapped who also have a lot of learning disabilities. Still no treatment, though. Well, we said no way. We didn't go through this whole thing for that, and we appealed it. But you see, there was no procedure to let us know what the decision was. Is this ridiculous? I want to know what happened, but they're too busy to tell me. Then when I finally hear what the decision is and appeal it, more time has gone by—most of the year, in fact.

"Meanwhile, a social worker from an outside agency had talked to Wayne, unbeknownst to me because I was overwhelmed with other pieces of paper, and he told her he would agree to go to a residential facility run by the Bureau of Child Welfare [now Special Services for Children, or SSC]. A parent can request placement and Welfare will pay the child allotment to the school. A lot of these parents fight us all the way. 'My kid doesn't need to be in special ed. It's the teacher. She's prejudiced against my child,' and so on. This goes on from age seven to about fourteen or fifteen, when the mother walks in and says, 'Take him away, I can't do anything with him, I can't stand another minute.' First they fight the system and then they dump the kid on the system—it's really hard to deal with.

"You see, we were recommending day treatment because although it's possible to place a kid in a residential facility through the Board of Ed, it's very expensive and you have to show that it's educationally necessary. Well, by the time we met Wayne we weren't going to be able to educate him no matter where he was living. I wanted him in some kind of detention—out of the school and away from semi-normal kids. A BCW residential placement would have been just fine.

"As far as we knew, Wayne hadn't hurt anybody yet, he was just impossible to have in school, and there were these two separate attempts going on at the same time, the social worker from the outside agency who was functioning as his counselor, and my team, both trying to get Wayne into some kind of program outside the regular school and the grandmother is saying he's getting too difficult for her to handle, she wants him to go, and he's saying he wants to go—and *nobody was hurt yet*.

"But we couldn't get any answer from BCW. In June they told us they'd been inundated with cases of kids who were physically abused and that took priority. And let me tell you, BCW does *nothing* about any kid unless you can show them the wounds and a photograph of the person inflicting them. You know, some of our teenage mothers are very cruel; some of them are pretty sick themselves, and they have no empathy with the baby. What Wayne experienced as a baby we don't know. What he did to that woman we do know, and it makes you sick to think about, but it's not really surprising what some of these kids can do when you know what's been done to them."

The room was hot and seemed to get more close and confining as Edith Gold talked, perhaps a measure of the discouragement we both felt. She went on.

"Anyway, BCW has its priorities, and they never took action. Meanwhile, summer came, and the COH finally agreed Wayne should be in day treatment. We got an option letter from the Board of Ed offering the great-grandmother a place in a day treatment school for September. Now the culmination of a COH procedure is you send a letter to the parent and you document, to cover your ass, that you did all the things you have to do, and the Board of Ed did all the things it has to, to offer the parents their rights. If the parents are ignorant or non-responsive, that's not supposed to be our problem because the people who are after the Board of Ed are only interested in 'Did you give the parents their *rights?* Did the children have their *rights?*' They don't give a *shit* about *children*.

"Therefore, if the parent doesn't answer but you can show that you've made a couple of attempts to contact them, it's finished. That's where it ends.

"Well, nobody's going to tell *me* there's no procedure, it would be too expensive to assign some clerk to let me know whether the option letter came back. I kept coming back, asking about it. They kept telling me, 'Go away, we've got to count, we've got to post.' They've got to figure how many days since the first option letter went out before they can send another option letter. But whether any answer ever comes back or not is irrelevant.

"And then came that morning in August. I was reading the *Post* on the subway going out to visit a friend in Brooklyn and the name just stopped me. I kept reading it over and over again, Wayne M———, Wayne M———. I just couldn't take it in. I couldn't process it. And I haven't got a learning disability. It was like I was in shock. Finally, on the fifth try, I got it."

There was a pause as she seemed to relive that moment of recognition on the train. Then she shook her head and went on.

"There was one more thing I did. I did not want this child walking into my school in September. So I asked my boss to find out whether or not we'd ever gotten the option letter back. I knew even though Wayne had been arrested and scheduled for a hearing, he could be released. Do you think they send them all away? I said just this one time I would appreciate having an outreach worker sent to the home to have the great-grandmother sign this letter. My boss did it, and we got the signed letter back.

"Now I know this sounds ridiculous at this stage of things, but knowing the legal system, it is entirely possible that if there was a hearing and the finding was that for some procedural reason—they asked him at the wrong time or in the wrong place—his statement was inadmissible, he would be released. And a child always has the right to go to his last school until his parents have agreed to something else. Wayne would have had the absolute right to come back to our EH class and if we had not had the signed option letter we would have had to let him enter the school in the fall and I'd have had to go to the principal to set up an administrative hearing. When we showed the newspaper clippings, they'd have agreed. The great-grandmother would probably have agreed when she got the legal papers asking her to come to a hearing. But that would have been the cumbersome way to do it. So I made sure there was a signed option letter, just in case."

Whose responsibility are the Waynes? Who will *take* responsibility for them?

"In Wayne's case," says Edith Gold, "we couldn't get anywhere with BCW because there wasn't any documented violence yet, so we were dependent on the educational system—which means on the rights of the parents. The educational system is there, a giant apparatus, to do what the parents want. That's what the courts ask: Were the parents given their rights? The principal has no rights. The system has no rights. You know, in a mixed district like this one, principals don't want to be known as having gone against a parent. I don't blame them. The local school board takes the position that parents are always right, minorities are always right, wiping out any sense people might have that these are *children* who are in the public schools.

"As far as Wayne is concerned, I think that the gigantic craziness, his being an educational problem, begins from day one. When you think that his mother was fifteen when he was born, that she was shot to death before his eyes when he was five . . . I don't bleed for Wayne now, but I bleed for that five-year-old, and when I'm told that when he was six and went to school he had trouble learning to read—can you imagine what his life was like? At that time, he was living with a great-aunt who was all of about thirty, because in that family everyone has a baby at fourteen or fifteen. She already had four children of her own, and then Wayne. Imagine how much nurturing he was getting! So when he comes to school, if he's a problem, they put him in the resource room. That's really going to get to the heart of this—one period a day in a group of five! I'm not saying, 'Poor Wayne.' Not now. What

I'm saying is how inappropriate is the way our society is addressing this whole problem."

Given the increasing number of teenage mothers, many of whom are inadequate parents, some of whose children are neglected and abused, the number of children entering the public school system with serious emotional/educational deficits is also bound to increase. What can be done with them?

"Well," says Edith Gold, "I don't know what Wayne was like at six. Maybe he was a hard case even then. But if you're going to get through to them at all, it's got to begin early.

"I think if they're young enough and you have enough individual attention—without the label of 'special education' and all the paperwork that comes with it—you can free up human beings to have more contact with them. I think people could make some difference, but not paper. I never saw a child helped by a piece of paper."

She leaned forward and said with a new burst of energy, "There are kids all over the neighborhood who've worked with me and with whom I didn't do near enough and who look to you and me on the street like tough, angry kids, but they recognize me—'Oh, hello, Mrs. Gold, how are you?' and they stop and talk—you know? Something got through to them of my impossible, nutty concern for them, together with a certain toughness they respect. I'm always saying, 'No, you don't get what you want first, and then you'll produce. First you produce and then you get what you want.' One of the things that's wrong for these kids is that in their life experience so far nothing has had a consistent and predictable consequence. I think it's terribly helpful to them to let them know that if you tell them, 'You do this and that will happen to you,' it does. That's a brand-new experience for them."

One day in late winter I rode the dismal BMT to Brooklyn to visit a non-secure detention facility where up to twelve boys (there were seven the day of my visit) live in an old but comfortable house on a tree-lined residential street. Pius XII is a facility for fourteen-to-sixteen-year-old boys the Family Court thinks should not be paroled to their families while waiting for their scheduled dispositional hearings but should not be locked up in a place like Spofford. No one stays there very long, but very often it represents the first taste of rehabilitation in the juvenile justice system. It's a kind of transit station for a handful of boys at a time, a "group home" that isn't anyone's home, for a family that is only temporary, with a schoolroom where no one stays long enough to learn anything much. It is also the pleasantest and most peaceful place many of these boys have ever lived in. The outer doors are not locked during the day and the boys are free to walk out. Some of them do, occasionally making for the subway station and home. It is not unheard of for one to try to pick up some easy pocket money on the way and find himself back in court.

Pius XII is in a recently gentrified section of Brooklyn, in a house that has seen better days and worse ones. The house was built around the turn of the century for a large, prospering bourgeois family with several servants. The family and the servants and the way of life lived there have all disappeared without trace, the graceful mantelpieces, moldings, and architectural details of the house painted over and many of the once graciously proportioned rooms partitioned into smaller and more efficient spaces. If the ghosts of another kind of family life linger on, they give no sign, and if any of the boys the court sends here miss such a life, they give no sign either.

This visit had been arranged by the head of the Corporation Counsel office of Queens County Family Court for members of his staff and included one of the judges as well as myself. I was the first to arrive and as I was shown into the head counselor's office she was ending a conversation with a boy who had come to her to complain because his girlfriend wasn't allowed to visit. Frances Anastasi explained to him patiently—not, I gathered, for the first time—that only relatives over eighteen were allowed to visit. The boy left, righteously indignant. His parting protest: "It's not fair."

Fran and I talked while we waited for the others. She explained that if the boys behaved they were given cigarettes, money, and weekend passes to go home. The cigarettes surprised me. "You have to compromise," she said. "We only have token discipline here. And they have total freedom over the weekend. A lot is given but a lot is not demanded of them. This is a temporary holding system. You have no lever if the kid doesn't shape up."

The others arrived and we were shown around the house— simple but comfortable bedrooms, classrooms that were unused now in the late afternoon, with a few beginner readers and workbooks lying around, a large kitchen downstairs with a round table, a dozen chairs and a couch on which several teenage boys sat smoking and watching TV. They waved to us as we went by. One of them recognized and greeted the prosecutor and judge he'd been before a few days earlier.

Afterward, drinking coffee out of Styrofoam cups in what had once been the library, Fran said, "They're really wise. They know all the ins and outs. The Legal Aid lawyers explain it all to them. They really hurt our cause by educating the kid to what's not helpful to him and undermining our program for him.

"One assaultive kid can wreck the program. We know all the signs of provocative behavior and sometimes we can see it coming, like sitting on a time bomb. But if we take him back to court to ask for a more restrictive placement, the judge says, 'Take him back and try again.' Can you imagine what it feels like coming back on the subway with that kid? He knows you lost. 'I got juice,' is what he tells the other kids. 'See, I came back, they couldn't do nothing to me.' These kids are not defenseless. But the kid in the courtroom looks like a doll. He'd be a fool not to. So the judge is reluctant to send him to Spofford."

The judge interrupts her. "Spofford is a bad place for a kid. I'd rather take a chance with the kid in NSD [non-secure detention group homes] than have him raped in Spofford. You know," he adds, "the court system can't resolve all the problems of society. More stuff is coming into court than ever before, things that never would have been seen in a courtroom ten, twenty years ago, things that would have been settled in the family, in the community, in the school, by the minister."

It's a slushy day and some of the boys have been asked to shovel the remains of snow on the front steps. One of them appears at the door of the library, complaining that Daryl took his hat. Daryl is right behind him, denying it. They sound like any two kids in a family—except that they are twice the age and twice the size for this kind of thing. It seems like play therapy, making up for times they never had. The matter gets settled, they leave, and Fran talks about her frustrations. There is no way to enforce rules, no sanctions, and, she has found, no therapeutic possibilities, especially in the short time these boys are here.

"They don't see being here as a consequence of their own behavior. If you ask them they'll tell you it's the rotten cop or the horrible judge that got them here. They operate out of a different value system: 'I'm poor, I got a raw deal, so I'm entitled to take what others have.' Counseling just isn't possible. I feel like I'm talking Chinese and they're talking Swahili."

Leonard Blake is the director of Pius XII. The room in which he talks with visitors, now an office, had been a parlor or perhaps a formal dining room. There is a bay window with a built-in window seat overlooking what was once a garden. No one sits there now, but the room seems less removed from its past than the rest of the house, perhaps because of the atmosphere created by so many books and papers, perhaps because of the manner of the man who sits behind the large desk that occupies the spot where a table must have once stood.

Leonard Blake comes from a West Indian family and like many people of similar background seems to have softer edges than most blacks who would describe themselves as Afro-Americans. Some of the members of his staff who work with the boys day in and day out, talking their language—street black or Spanish—seem harder. Perhaps they have to be. An appearance of hardness is about all that's permitted them in dealing with youngsters who are nothing if not tough. There's usually not enough time to develop the kind of relationship that would promote identification with a counselor's or teacher's finer qualities.

"In the last ten years more than three thousand boys have passed through here. Most of them come from single-parent families. Some of those mothers are strong, some just cop out. The only constants in many of these kids' lives have been television and drugs."

Like many others, Leonard Blake thinks the breakdown of the family is the pivotal issue today. "Until the war"—he means World War II—"there was a culture, shared values, respect for older people, relatives to guide kids to maturity.

Then American blacks came north and what family culture there was was destroyed by the social services—public aid for everything. The Sixties carried that attitude even further—rely on the system, expect it and exploit it.

"And then the drug scene came along as a livelihood. Drugs had been out there before, but only a few were involved. Now there's big money to be made. Kids get turned on, they get hurt, and there's no family, no one to care anymore."

Leonard Blake's background lends what he has to say about the boys who come to Pius XII a unique kind of authority. As a child, Lenny Blake spent several years in an institution himself.

"It was the kind of orphanage for homeless boys who got in trouble with the law that was established during the Depression," he says. "The idea was to provide a caring atmosphere for waifs. It was supported by voluntary contributions. It wasn't until after the war that the city got involved.

"I was there for five and a half years in the early Fifties. My mother just couldn't manage to take care of all five of her kids. In those days, social services were provided mainly by charities in the private sector, some religious, some secular. Once the city got involved there was a change in the child-care business. But it wasn't only the public funding that made a difference. When I was there, such places were not for delinquents, they were for boys with family problems. Then the values changed. Everyone began to look for a way to beat the system. If you said you were in need, they doled out maintenance. The system made it easy to rely on public aid and people found ways to cheat.

"Our kids here all have lawyers and the lawyers are good at bargaining for their clients. But are they bargaining for the right things for them? These are kids who can't get along with authorities. Their value system is in disarray. They're aggressive and they often carry weapons. They have no discipline. They're slick. They like to think they can beat the system, go you one better.

"Yet they often respond to understanding and structure together, to a nurturing contact. We try to help them through the anger stage, help them learn to control their behavior, teach them to trust adults.

"They ought to have a longer term here. Even when they leave to go to another program they lose momentum. The work we've done is undone." He pauses for a moment, as though looking for the right word. Then he says, "Lost."

10

The Least Restrictive Alternative

The Court shall order the least restrictive available alternative . . . which is consistent with the needs and best interests of the respondent and the need for protection of the community.

—Family Court Act (1983), Article 3, Part 5, Section 352.2

The gray and bustle of the city give way to the rolling hills of Westchester as one travels up the Saw Mill River Parkway to the village of Lincolndale, past leafy verdure and, in springtime, blossoming white dogwood and pink and red azaleas glimpsed through the trees that line the parkway. Turning off the highway onto smaller roads one passes the stone entrances to mansions built in grander days, many of them still maintained in style as corporate headquarters, schools, or religious institutions. Beyond one of those imposing entranceways is Lincoln Hall, a "private non-secure non-sectarian residential treatment facility" affiliated with the Archdiocese of New York, which contracts with the New York State Division for Youth and the Commissioner of Social Services of the City of New York for the placement of boys aged eleven to sixteen who have been judged by the Family Courts to be delinquents or PINS, persons in need of supervision.

The visitor to Lincoln Hall turns into a driveway surrounded by lawns and landscaped vistas, dotted with handsome and well-maintained brick buildings that house administrative offices, schoolrooms and library and laboratory facilities, building, drafting and auto mechanics shops, as well as leathercraft, woodworking, and art workshops, TV and photography studios, a cafeteria and, visible across the lawns and up the hills, eleven cottages resembling ranch-style suburban family homes in which the boys live in groups of up to twenty-two (twelve in each of two dormitory bedrooms) with counselors who function as house parents. There are kennels for puppies, a barn with half a dozen horses kept well groomed and ready for the boys to ride, and up one of the hills a rope-tow used for winter skiing practice. There is a swimming pool and a running track, athletic fields and, extending from each cottage, a gym with basketball court and athletic equipment. The buildings and surroundings compare favorably with those of any of the preparatory schools in the Northeast. The staff members one meets are personable, attractive, articulate, not unlike the staff of any private school. Only the youthful population strikes a different note. Most of them are black, many from the inner city, and they have a street-smart manner, a vocabulary, and a set of habits that serve to remind the visitor that this isn't, despite appearances, a prestigious prep school, a summer resort, or a country inn. Nor is it a health spa, although the first thing the visitor is shown is the impressively equipped infirmary, where many of these boys receive the first medical and dental care they've ever had. They also receive psychiatric care and counseling when needed.

Eating lunch in the cafeteria at the same time they do, it's hard to talk because of the noise level. But it's the noise of lively adolescents, and there's an underlying orderliness, neither the chaos of the out-of-control nor the regimented passivity of a place like Spofford. Of course, the population is different. The boys here have been carefully chosen as those most likely to succeed—to benefit from the opportunities a place like this can offer them. None of them has been found to have committed an act of violence—armed robbery, for instance, or sexual abuse or arson. They rob, for the most part. They truant, and they're hard to handle. This is what the law calls the petty stuff. They are not considered dangerous. And the idea is, after a year (the average stay) here, to return them to society better able to get along with their families, in their schools, and on the streets where they live. In 1985, it cost about $38,000 a year to keep a boy at Lincoln Hall. Almost all of it is paid by the State of New York and the federal government's contribution to Medicaid. A large private endowment is used for capital improvements on the very valuable property and to make up temporary deficits, which occur as the number of boys in residence (and thus the public funding) fluctuates with the school year. The questions everyone asks are how much can you do in a year and what good will it do to send them back into the same world they came from?

The staff members at Lincoln Hall do not seem to have any great illusions about the answers to either of these questions. What they do seem to have is a commitment to trying and a realistic good humor in the face of heavy odds, which may augur better for success than starry-eyed idealism. They know what they're up against. Perhaps it's the Catholic orientation—original sin is probably a more useful view of human nature than the we-are-all-victims sentiment of the Legal Aiders. And it tempers the psychiatric social work orientation. The Church has always understood the uses of being tough with kids, and since there are plenty of built-in safeguards against cruelty in the system of which Lincoln Hall is a part, it remains a benign toughness.

Father Patrick Jordan makes a jovial and informative guide as he answers visitors' questions and volunteers information about what we're seeing. He plays the perfect host as we tour the grounds, peek into a math class and a leathercraft workshop, follow the boys into the computer room and the library. A fourteen-year-old is playing a video game on one of the dozen computers. In the library three boys are lounging on a couch watching a videotaped lecture-demonstration on chemistry. Another is consulting the librarian about an assignment. (I wonder which of these big, mean-looking inner-city black boys has been reading A. A. Milne. A copy of *When We Were Very Young* is lying on one of the tables next to an announcement of an essay contest on "My Favorite Person in Black History." Were any of these kids ever very young? What do they make of the nanny and the menagerie in the nursery? One wonders.)

Father Jordan is a tall, barrel-chested man with graying hair and a florid face over his clerical collar. He has an easy manner as he leads us up a gentle green slope into Falahee Cottage. The twenty boys who live here are in class now, so we're free to walk around their living area. On the wall-to-wall carpet stands handsome, very heavy wooden furniture, its practical sturdiness offset by the bright patterned tweed upholstery. Through the red-curtained windows one sees trees and the hills beyond them. In one corner of the room there's a large color TV and a VCR. There's an open kitchen for evening snacks and weekend breakfasts; the bathrooms are attractively tiled and have clean new fixtures. Down the hall is the dormitory bedroom where each boy has a bed covered with a bright red bedspread and, at the head of the bed, a locker. Most of the lockers have posters taped on them. Rock stars and nubile, teasing semi-clothed girls face the doorway, over which hangs a portrait of the Virgin, blue-cloaked, gazing heavenward, eyes averted from the company she keeps.

Father Jordan says there are plans under way to construct smaller bedrooms so the boys will have more privacy.

One of the visitors, a social worker at a small Brooklyn group detention home, asks how the boys readjust to urban poverty and ugliness after experiencing "all this richness." Father Jordan smiles ruefully, tells her that actually the boys don't experience it as richness. "They just think of it as doing time." Of all the varied privileges they can earn here, he tells us, the most jealously guarded is the weekend pass. Once a month a bus takes the boys home to their various towns and cities throughout the state. Those who come from New York City are taken to Fifty-ninth Street in Manhattan, where they're given a subway token for the trip uptown to Harlem or the Bronx or down to Brooklyn or over to Queens and told to be back Sunday at 5:00 P.M. for the return trip to Westchester County.

Father Jordan is clearly not happy about the weekend pass, which he says is "not beneficial. For many of them it's just a weekend of booze, sex and drugs." Some of them will never leave the midtown area; they'll just hang out all weekend around Times Square. Some are met by friends—or enemies—in some cases former residents who know when the bus arrives, and they take off together. And some of them don't show up for a day or two after the weekend. Not long ago, Father Jordan says, a bunch of eleven- and twelve-year-olds came to him and asked him indignantly if he realized that the rule requiring them not to be high when they returned at 9:00 P.M. on Sunday evening meant they couldn't use anything after two that afternoon.

"When the bus rounds the last corner before entering the grounds on Sunday night, there's a flurry of stuff thrown out the window. They probably figure they'll come back the next day and find it, but we're on to that," says Father Jordan, "so there's someone waiting to collect it all and destroy it."

But it's not uncommon for parents who come up on the bus dispatched for them every Sunday, which is visiting day, to bring their children drugs.

"Hard drugs?" someone asks. "No," Father Jordan says, "usually it's just grass."

Why send the boys back to the city to take two steps backward when so much time, energy, money is being spent to move them three steps forward? It's the state's decision, Father Jordan explains. The New York State Department of Social Services mandates home visits and to deny them is a violation of the child's rights. "So if we think a boy shouldn't leave for the weekend we can't call it a punishment. We have to put it in therapeutic terms—'He can't handle it at present.'

"Most of these boys have never had the things they get here—three square meals a day, a bed of their own, a doctor on call all the time just for them. Surrounded by caring people, on beautiful grounds. A swimming pool, a ski tow . . ." Father Jordan digresses to tell us that a wealthy donor has contributed an ice rink, which will be completed by next winter.

"They've never experienced the feeling of success. They think of themselves as born losers or as Mr. Con. What they have a chance to experience here for the first time is a positive attitude about themselves. The born loser can learn what it feels like to do well, the con man learns something about rules and responsibility."

If you're old enough, Father Jordan reminds you a little of Spencer Tracy as Father Flanagan in *Boys Town*. But these boys don't live the lives of Mickey Rooney ("He ain't heavy, Father, he's me brother") and the other MGM delinquents. Father Jordan tells about being asked by one sixteen-year-old if he would baptize his second child. He says he draws the line only at "their five-percent stuff—they can't have any of that here," referring to a subgroup of the Black Muslim movement that preaches black racism and black violence.

He's had calls in the middle of the night, like the one from a boy asking for a worker who is no longer there but who is remembered tearfully, on a midnight jag, as "the only person who ever cared about me." And there are also occasional daytime callers, quite sober, who want to keep in touch, let the staff know how they're doing, say they remember how "somebody did something for me"—which Father Jordan defines as giving them "a sense of accountability, and a sense that they could be the opposite of what they were when they came here."

A sign at the entrance to the grounds reads "Lincoln Hall: Guiding Boys to Useful Manhood Since 1863." If one is inclined to eye it somewhat cynically on entering, one leaves with a certain respect for the no-nonsense attitude displayed here, despite the luxury, the permissiveness about such things as smoking and street language, the absurdly short tenure of a boy's stay here. You may have to turn away to hide your reaction when one of the earnest social workers asks a boy, "What would you say was the one most important thing you learned here?" and he responds smoothly, without a moment's hesitation, "The difference between right and wrong." You know one of the boys sitting on a stone wall in front of the schoolroom having a smoke break went AWOL from here a couple of weeks ago and while he was out stole a car. You don't know how many of the two hundred or so boys here now—or the thousands who have been here over the years—will do better for having been here. There are no reliable follow-up figures. You just feel that if effort, intentions, and atmosphere can make a difference, the people at Lincoln Hall have a shot at it. And, as a visiting assistant Corporation Counsel put it on the way out, "As long as the law mandates some form of non-secure detention for these kids, you might as well give it the best shot you can."

One tends to begin the tour of Lincoln Hall feeling a little like Dickens's Mr. Bounderby in *Hard Times:* "that these people were a bad lot altogether, gentlemen; that do what you would for them they were never thankful for it, gentlemen; that they were restless, gentlemen; that they never knew what they wanted; that they lived upon the best . . . and yet were eternally dissatisfied and unmanageable." There seems something inappropriate about providing wrongdoers with what Mr. Bounderby calls "the lap of luxury," with "turtle soup and venison, with a gold spoon." They seem to be reaping the rewards rather than the penalty of doing wrong, and one tends to resent it, thinking if not of one's self and what a summer week in a place like this would cost (a lot of joking about this among the visitors, under their breath), then certainly of the many kids in Harlem, in the East Bronx, in Bed-Stuy, who resisted the impulse to steal and are stuck there in the dirt and heat and crowding even as the boys who gave in to their urges to take what they wanted compete at games here on the playing fields of Lincolndale.

Spring had given way to summer on the Saw Mill River Parkway and although I'd left Family Court, Probation, and detention facilities behind me for the weekend, I found myself thinking of Lincoln Hall as I traveled in the same direction again but this time with a very different destination.

The setting was a manicured estate in Katonah, about an hour north of the Harlem slums but a world away. It was a hot June Sunday afternoon, but here the sky was blue, the grass was green, the flowers profuse and scented, the box hedges trimmed, the pool inviting and the white wine chilled. We'd driven up from the city, glad to get away from the steaming asphalt and the crowds and radios that took over the park on weekends. A few of the other guests had driven up from the city, others had come over from their own places nearby. Among them were a publisher, a couple of lawyers, a member of an important newspaper's editorial board, a psychoanalyst. There were a few people I'd never met before, and we did the little pas de deux of introductions, establishing what everyone did and thus who and what they were—how interesting, how formidable. Our hostess mentioned that I was a writer.

Helping herself to a slice of iced melon from the tray that was being handed around, the woman next to me asked perfunctorily, "Oh? And what do you write?" I mentioned a previous book and told her I was presently working on one about the juvenile justice system. She raised her eyebrows, smiled. "Really?" she said. "That's my field."

"Oh, are you a lawyer too?" I asked. Her husband, I'd already learned, was a rich and politically well-connected former labor lawyer, now working for management. I'd already decided I didn't like him. He was loud, not in the way of people who want to be heard but in the way of those who are used to being listened to. His voice simply overrode everyone else's, emphatic in a way that didn't seem to go with the graceful afternoon, the pleasant scene. It was more suited to an office, along with the cigar he was smoking.

Both husband and wife were constantly dropping names of the rich and famous. "Actually, we only know one person in Australia," the wife had said when someone had mentioned that country. "Rupert Murdoch. He's a good friend of ours." Other good friends among the international power-broking set were mentioned in connection with whatever places or events came up in the general conversation. A Baron Rothschild, a former labor minister of Britain, a one-time French president now dead, the owners of theaters and builders of buildings that bore their very droppable names—all of them were "good friends of ours." It must be nice, I thought, to have so many good friends.

And it turned out that knowing a lot of the right people—not being a lawyer or, as a matter of fact, having any other kind of related training or special knowledge or experience—was what had made the lawyer's wife an important influence in "her field"—juvenile justice. She had been active on citizens' committees and on boards, where she'd contributed money of her own and raised more from her many good friends and her husband's business associates and wealthy clients, and with a little help from her friends, had been appointed to commissions, been granted federal funds for pilot projects she'd administered, and now had been appointed by the governor to head an important state advisory commission that would have considerable input in forthcoming deliberations having to do with criminal legislation. And it was her firm conviction, formed somewhere between Park Avenue and Cap d'Antibes, that even murderers, if they were twelve or thirteen years old, were *children*, and to be treated as such. The juvenile offender law (which had moved particularly vicious young criminals into the adult courts to be tried there) was a disgrace, and publicly funded one-on-one therapy the most promising approach to juvenile crime, caused as it was by social injustice. She was elegantly coiffed and dressed, and—a touch I would have rejected as too much if I'd been inventing the scene—carried the tiniest of miniature poodles, whose occasional yaps she quieted with long, carefully polished red-tipped fingers as she chatted casually about how honored she was by her appointment and how pleased she was to feel she'd been able to "educate" the legislators when she'd gone up to Albany the previous week to be confirmed in her new position. She'd made them understand, she felt, that they had to think of *all* children—no matter what they'd done—as just children.

Her generous, charitable point of view contrasted strikingly with what I'd heard from some other members of the governor's constituency just the day before. I'd been on jury duty, and my fellow grand jurors included a number of working- and middle-class blacks—bus drivers, teachers, data processors, a cashier, a couple of retired civil servants. They didn't think of children who killed as just children. They didn't think of them as needing help. They thought *they* needed help—protection from the marauders who preyed on the community where they lived and walked the streets and brought up their own children, or waited for the grown-up ones to come back and visit them. They were similarly unsympathetic to rapists, robbers, burglars, and drug dealers of whatever age and not very sentimental about the children whose recreation took such forms. But then they couldn't afford the rich white liberals' pieties any more than their creature comforts. They had nothing to feel guilty about, or even to justify, and a lot to be angry about in their own daily lives as they encountered the predators it was so easy—and so satisfying—to think of as unfortunate children as one lounged in the sun chaise sipping one's drink, petting one's poodle, and dropping the names of people who, while perhaps better known, could certainly not be said to be doing anything more important—more worthy of attention—than one's self.

About a month after I'd moved on from sitting in with Pat Brennan in Probation, I'd found myself in the building again and stopped by her office to see her. I was lucky. She was there and no one was with her at the moment. Pat was on the phone but gestured for me to come in and sit down and when she hung up, she favored me with her beaming smile and, in answer to my questions, began to fill me in on the subsequent developments in some of the cases I was familiar with. What about Neal, the boy I'd been so charmed by, the one who was interested in new words—"Ad-vance"—and knew how to be polite to a stranger?

Pat made a little face, lifting her shoulders and drawing her brows together as she gave a kind of half-smile. "I don't know how to tell you this," she said ruefully. Neal had been arrested again only a few days after we'd met. He'd gone downtown to do some shopping, but found himself a little short of cash. This time he decided to advance it to himself from a middle-aged woman's purse. Later, Neal claimed she dropped the purse outside the subway station from which they both just happened to have exited at the same time, that he had picked it up intending to return it to her and that she, turning around and seeing him holding it, misunderstood. He was loudly accusing her of having attacked him when they were brought into the precinct station. The woman, gray-haired and stocky, said he grabbed her bag from under her arm and that she turned and grasped his jacket as he tried to run away. She held on, sustaining bruises and lacerations as he hit at her and tried to pry loose, and she made so much noise and created such a commotion that a couple of onlookers among the normally phlegmatic and laissez-faire New Yorkers came to her aid and a policeman appeared on the scene to find the woman hanging on to Neal as he dragged her along, with Neal still holding on to her bag. So much for the manners that had so impressed me, although in the matter of verbal skills, Neal did demonstrate a certain ingenuity in demanding to press charges for the damage that had been done to a fairly new and impressive jacket emblazoned with an alligator.

Neal, it turned out, had a record of twelve prior arrests in New Jersey, a record of which the New York Family Court, the Probation Department, and Pat Brennan were all unaware. It had been assumed that Neal's first contact with Family Court in New York was his first court contact. However, Neal's family had recently moved to New York from across the Hudson, and the sovereign state of New Jersey, or at least its juvenile justice system, had evidently been glad to wash its hands of Neal, who was on probation there at the time, and let him become New York's problem.

Neal's New Jersey record came to light because a reference in the probation officer's report to some problems Neal mentioned having had in New Jersey led someone in the Corporation Counsel's office to call the New Jersey probation office. A clerk there, against regulations, obligingly came up with the information. She may have been unaware of the regulations. Perhaps no one had ever asked before. In any case, what she had to report was a record of eleven cases, ranging from misdemeanors to felonies and including robberies and assaults. Neal had done a lot of stealing. In fact, one is tempted to call him a habitual criminal. At the time I met him, he was on probation in connection with an assault charge.

When Neal was arrested for the attempted purse snatching, he was remanded to Spofford until the fact-finding hearing, at which time the judge agreed to parole him. "He's very personable," said Peter Reinharz, "and personality gets you a lot in this court. This kid is a perfect example of one who looks like an angel sitting in the courtroom—but not if you meet him on the street or in the subway. He can be charming, but Mr. Hyde is always around the corner. He gets enraged, and then he attacks other people violently."

At the dispositional hearing, the Corporation Counsel asked for authorization for Neal to be placed in a locked facility if, any time in the first sixty days of his placement in an unlocked facility, that did not work out satisfactorily. After sixty days, a special hearing would have to be held in order to move him from a limited-secure to a secure facility, from one relying on rural isolation to keep the boys from running away and on structure and supervision to keep them behaving, to one with "hardware"—locks on the doors.

The judge was reluctant to grant authorization at first, but the recommendation was seconded by the court psychologist and the probation officer as well. In the face of the unanimous position taken by everyone but Neal's lawyer, "the judge," as Peter Reinharz put it, "finally got the idea."

After stating that Neal would be remanded to Spofford while DFY found a place for him, the judge said to him, "I want you to understand that we don't want to punish you. Everyone here thinks this is the best thing for you. The experts say you need to learn to handle your aggression."

I saw Frances Anastasi a few days after I found out about Neal, and when I told her the story, commenting with some chagrin on my ability to judge character (early admission to Harvard indeed), she didn't seem particularly surprised. In fact, she seemed more surprised at my disappointment—at my expectations, really—than at the outcome, which it was obvious she had anticipated almost as soon as I had begun my tale. Fran had been there before.

"Look," she said, "kids like Neal are very manipulative. They know how to act in whatever way will do them the most good at the time. The same kid can be darling one minute and a bastard the next. They know how to go for what they want when they get a chance at it."

We were talking in her office at the Pius XII home in Brooklyn. We could hear a noisy game at the pool table in the next room and the sounds of footsteps and lively voices on the stairway.

"It's all a question of values," she went on. "Lying and stealing are the way they've learned to operate. It's perfectly logical, it makes sense in their community. They're normal kids in a sick value system. In their world, everyone uses drugs, pot at the very least. Some use coke. They get the money for it by ripping off old ladies. This kid doesn't have any feelings for the old lady, he just thinks, 'She's got, I haven't.' This is what they're taught as they're growing up. Survival is the only thing.

"In the six weeks that's the average stay with us—some of them we have only two weeks, three months is the longest anyone stays—we try to confront them with the consequences of their behavior. They have to be shown that one kind of act will lead to freedom, another to losing their freedom. Forget right and wrong; it's too late for developing a conscience. The only thing that works is a strict behavior-modification program, with no room for manipulative behavior on their part. But Legal Aid works against us. They get the kid off through some lie and just reinforce his old value system.

"From the point of view of what we're trying to do, Legal Aid is a destructive influence. It's just an extension of the kid's system—you lie, cheat, steal to get off. Take Rafael." And she told me about a twelve-year-old who was being transferred to another facility because the staff here could no longer work with him. He'd been lying to the social workers and then lying to the teachers, playing them off against one another, until they finally figured out what was going on and why everyone was at cross-purposes about him.

"Rafael needs to learn how to deal with people by means of other strategies. But with his Legal Aid lawyer in the picture, not a chance. The lawyer 'care'? Listen, the ones that tell me, 'I don't care about the kid, I'm here to defend his legal rights according to the system'—I can deal with that. But the ones that say they have sympathy for the kid, for poor little Rafael—they don't even know him! If they took the trouble to get to know him, they'd understand that what he needs is security, structure. He doesn't run away from us only because he has no place to go. He's abused at home. And we tell him the court will be harder on him if he does run. Rafael has enough control to stay. But not all of them do. All we can do is try to work with them; it's their choice whether to stay or not. Under the present system we have no way to restrain them, no way to impose external controls until they can develop some internal ones. That would interfere with their 'rights.' But what they need more than legal rights is parenting: consistent care and discipline. What they need, what they've never had, is to be taken care of.

"Unfortunately, a lot of the child-care people are only one step above the kids. Maybe if we paid them more money we could get better people. Maybe if we had time-out facilities, a place for these kids to quiet down and where they could feel someone is in control . . . Would these things work? No one knows for sure. But we owe them a try.

"Instead, the kids are laughing at us. They have no personal appreciation for what the Legal Aid lawyers do for them. They just use them to get off. One kid said, 'I got me a white racist—she's buying my act.' Liberals believe these poor kids can't be expected to function like others, like their own." Then, scornfully, "They'd never let their own kids get away with doing these things." I thought of the newly appointed official I'd met at the house in Katonah, of the private schools and Ivy League colleges she boasted of her children having attended and done so well at, of the high standards they'd been expected to meet, and doubted if she'd have been so tolerant, so forgiving, so unconcerned if her own children had jeopardized their future by getting into any serious trouble. Or if she expected as little in the way of attention to discipline, conformity to social standards, from those she paid to look after her own children as she did from those she was content to have in charge of the less favored.

"As for keeping the family together," Fran was saying, referring to another of the social work pieties that inform a good deal of the system's decision making, "what it means for many of these kids is just back to the scene of the crime—to Mommy and Daddy, who did it to them to begin with."

Fran had walked me to the door and out onto the front porch. As we stood outside talking, a head appeared at a second-story window. A curly-haired cherub. Rafael, Fran told me softly.

"Hey," he called out to her, "didja call my lawyer?"

I learned more about Lincoln Hall ("the best shot . . .") in the months that followed as I began to look into various books and articles that dealt with juvenile crime and the network of institutions that had been set up to deal with it. Lincoln Hall, I learned, was the place from which a fifteen-year-old boy who had been rehabilitated there walked out in the spring of 1980 a few nights before his transfer to a halfway house back in the city, ran down the road intending to rob a house nearby, and ended up brutally murdering the elderly woman who lived in it. Having smashed the head of her invalid husband upstairs in bed, he turned—whether in frustration, anger, or panic is not clear—on the wife and savaged her with a piece of firewood. Afterward, he claimed to have sodomized her broken body before leaving with a few dollars and a watch and returning to Lincoln Hall, where a number of his fellow rehabilitees who knew about his plans ahead of time and about the outcome afterward kept quiet about it. As did a social worker who had been told ahead of time that something was being planned.

How could this be? Going somewhat deeper into the world of Lincoln Hall than a cursory visit and guided tour and the official printed information revealed some interesting facts about the subculture of the boys living there and the staff responsible for them.

The boy who committed the murder had committed a

string of robberies in his upstate home community. Nothing that had happened to him at Lincoln Hall had soured him on robbery as a way of making money; what he had learned was the importance of leaving no witnesses.

He knew about the house he made plans to rob because of a Lincoln Hall companion of his who had been working there for several months doing chores for pay, an arrangement brought about by the desire of the family—and in particular the murdered woman—to help troubled adolescents find their way, presumably by showing them how the other half lives. They had talked with him about his plans for the future, tried to make him feel, they said, "like one of the family."

But the family he belonged to at Lincoln Hall, the boys grouped together in the twelve cottages headed by "prefects," had other values and made other kinds of plans. The pecking order in the cottages depended on who was stronger, tougher—and meaner. Often, this meant being stronger than the prefect, in most cases someone who was waiting for a better opportunity somewhere than his present low-paid if grandiosely named position. And often the strongest and most ruthless of the boys were depended on by the prefect to keep order and enforce his rules. They had "respect." A black market of rewards and privileges, including drugs, was part of the system. And also part of the system was a taboo against "ratting" on another "dude." Not only when you knew he was planning something, but even when you knew he had done something. Even when it was what would seem to most of us like the worst kind of crime imaginable.

This is the reality lived at Lincoln Hall in what its impressive literature describes as its effort to provide a "home away from home" in which the staff "fosters a closeness with their residents and the opportunity to provide consistent, caring direction for daily living" as "surrogate parent . . . and role models for the boys" and in "guiding boys to useful manhood."

The alumni of Lincoln Hall's well-intentioned program—and of the efforts of well-meaning residents of the neighborhood like Eleanor Prouty, the murdered woman—are to be found in many of the higher institutions of the penal system, to which they graduate as adults. Many of them wind up in New York City's jails and New York State's prisons. Those who do not enter places like Lincoln Hall as already hardened criminals will probably learn much there from those who do. An agricultural school originally administered by the Catholic order of Christian Brothers to care for homeless boys in a religious atmosphere has gradually been transformed by legal requirements and social change to a place that must cope—without violating their rights—with a new breed of cynical and remorseless delinquent.

The boy who accompanied the murderer on the robbery spree that ended in the mutilation and death and violation of Mrs. Prouty was originally a PINS case. He seems to have gone along with the violence-prone killer to gain acceptance and respect in the society of Lincoln Hall in which he had been placed. In the end, the law treated him with a respect that accorded him the same sentence as the boy who had wielded the murder weapon.

There are no statistics available—from the officials of Lincoln Hall or anyone else—on just how many of the boys who pass through Lincoln Hall are changed by the experience and go on to lead honest and useful lives and how many go right back to stealing when they need money and sometimes on to killing when they need thrills or feel cornered.

Does Lincoln Hall do any good at all? Does any attempt at rehabilitation work? After all these years and the expenditure of hundreds of millions of dollars, no one really knows.

Everyone in the system can point to one or two cases in which some intervention by some individual like Pat Brennan did make a difference to some youngster, but for every story like that she herself has dozens of disappointments to tell about.

What makes it so hard to determine what kind, if any, of rehabilitation works and to what degree is the formidable set of obstacles in the way of designing valid studies because the subjects are so difficult, the legal and social constraints so complex, and the issues so politicized.

Any study worth doing would require cooperative subjects, cooperative families, cooperative lawyers, and cooperation from officials whose jobs might disappear as a result of the study as well as from community and political leaders whose constituencies might not welcome the results of such efforts.

This is a tall order, and until we can fill it, we won't really know whether the millions of dollars in state and federal tax money spent each year at the Lincoln Halls result in any lasting effect. Are 90 percent of the boys helped or 50 percent or 10 percent or only 1 percent?

And even if some good came of these millions multiplied many times by the number of publicly supported rehabilitation programs throughout the country, shouldn't we perhaps ask ourselves whether the money might be better spent by sending promising youngsters from poor but nurturing families to a place like Lincoln Hall to give them a head start?

Although there is little or no convincing evidence that programs like that of Lincoln Hall do much good, there are one or two facts that have been replicated over and over by many studies. The first is that with those few violent youngsters who commit most of the serious crimes, who start their criminal careers early, who usually come from fragmented families and are often the issue of teenage pregnancies, who have been abused as children and have grown up with psychological disabilities that are incurable with our present therapies—that with these youngsters, no rehabilitation, nothing that has been tried, really works.

The second fact that has emerged from a number of studies over the years is that although nothing really works to change the basic attitudes of such boys—influence their values or affect their lack of feeling for other human beings—the one thing that results in behavior change—controlling their impulses—is the imposition of serious sanctions that are perceived as punishment.

11

The Worst Possible
Future

*Those who become part of this small population [of serious,
violent, chronic delinquents] are well on the road to the worst
of all possible futures. . . . The best thing we can do . . . is to
decrease the probability of their spending their adult lives in
prison.*

—"Serious Juvenile Crime: A Redirected
Federal Effort." Report of the National
Advisory Committee for Juvenile Justice
and Delinquency Prevention, March 1984

Delinquency in a Birth Cohort, the study of 10,000 boys born
in Philadelphia in 1945 by Marvin E. Wolfgang, the director
of the Center for Studies in Criminology and Criminal Law
at the University of Pennsylvania, and his colleagues, revealed, as we saw in an earlier chapter, that as few as
6 percent of chronic offenders accounted for over 70 percent
of the most serious offenses—homicides, rapes, robberies, and
aggravated assaults. Follow-up studies showed that eight out
of ten of those chronic juvenile offenders had adult arrests for
serious and violent crimes, suggesting that most of those violent few who start their criminal career as boys continue this
pattern into adulthood.

A second study of chronic offenders in Philadelphia was
done in order to check the results of the previous study. This

time 27,000 children who were born in 1958 and raised during the years of protest and permissiveness in the late 1960s and early 1970s were studied.

Paul E. Tracy, a professor of criminal justice at Northeastern University who conducted the second birth-cohort study with Wolfgang and his colleague Robert M. Figlio at the University of Pennsylvania, says that the Philadelphia results are paradigmatic for large cities because the population mix, the crime rate, and the juvenile justice system are so similar. The study, the largest project of its kind ever to be carried out, was financed by the National Institute for Juvenile Justice and Delinquency Prevention. The later study found again that only a small percentage of all delinquents— 7 percent—were chronic offenders responsible for 75 percent of all serious crimes committed by their age group. While it found that roughly the same percentage of youths in each generation committed crimes, the repeat offenders of the more recent generation committed more crimes and more serious ones—more robberies, violent assaults, and rapes. And of those who committed serious crimes, nearly half were never incarcerated or even put on probation. Commenting recently in the press, Professor Tracy said, "If you let a kid do what he does with impunity, then he's going to continue doing it."

A study of criminal careers by a panel at Carnegie-Mellon University in 1986 supports the finding of previous studies that early onset of criminal behavior is one of the best predictors of later criminal behavior. The study found that while the average robber has a short career, committing about four robberies a year during his teens, a hard-core group consisting of about 5 percent commit between 180 and 400 annually during their criminal years.

Richard Garmise, a clinical psychologist, has interviewed hundreds of adolescents in the course of preparing mental health status reports for Family Court. As clinic director of Mental Health Services in New York County, he sees juveniles who have already had findings (convictions) and are awaiting dispositions (sentencing). Tall and gangly, and as youthful-looking as some of the older boys he interviews, Dr. Garmise has an engaging smile that punctuates his earnest, rapid speech. As we talked in his office in the Family Court building between his appointments, he sketched a psychological picture of some of these chronic offenders.

"One of the most significant things about the kids who come in here," he said, "is that they have no sense of the future, no plans, just a day-to-day way of thinking and functioning—even moment to moment. They often commit violent crimes for the least understandable kind of gain, for very little money and very little purpose. Theirs isn't the goal-directed activity you find in other kids.

"My contact with them is a single interview but my impression is that for an awful lot of these kids and their parents—which usually means their mothers—the court is no longer seen as an unusual kind of intervention. There's a fatalistic attitude about it, an assumption that you will get arrested sometime, you will go to court, you will be placed—maybe somewhere upstate. It's part of their expectation to go through it. It's been very rare in my experience that I've had a kid express to me that he's genuinely appalled by being here, or that he never expected to wind up in court.

"There are two things involved for a lot of these kids. One is the lack of thought or, if you want to call it that, morality—the lack of an internalized conscience when it comes to what goes on in the street. And the other thing is the acceptance of the fact that they're going to be placed sometime. There's a lot of street smarts about which places are which and who goes where. It's not an unusual thing in their world."

Dr. Garmise, in his shirtsleeves on a humid New York

summer morning, gets up and walks around the office as he talks. "Some of the kids we see are picked up for innocuous crimes like token-sucking [stealing tokens from subway turn-stiles] but when you talk with them you find they've committed absolutely horrendous crimes—designated felonies for which they weren't caught. You have to remember that the legal concept is that the child has done what he's convicted of and hasn't done what he hasn't been convicted of. That's not very helpful at the mental health level. You don't reha-bilitate an act, you treat or rehabilitate the whole person, which means all the things he's done whether he's been caught at them or not. I've seen kids come in for minor offenses who were incredibly violent, sadistic kids, and in those cases I rec-ommend the most restrictive placement there is. You may not be able to rehabilitate them but you can isolate them from the rest of society for a time.

"I am thinking of one kid who had been arrested for a minor offense but in my judgment was a very bad person. There was something very heartless and unmotivated about the act, something very blasé, extremely cold about him that made me think he was potentially very dangerous—in some ways more so than other kids who had done worse things. The trouble is, we have to operate in this system on the fiction that this is all he's done, so we should deal with him only on the basis of this one act.

"For a lot of these kids thirteen, fourteen is much too late. There's a predatory quality by that time. A meaningful in-tervention would have to be made much earlier."

Dr. Garmise is called away to testify in a hearing that lasts the rest of the morning. After lunch, I return to his office and he picks up where he left off.

"The most violent kids, potential psychopaths, are often made that way by sexual abuse by an adult; they're the most difficult group to deal with, the hardest to get in touch with, and no attempt at rehabilitation can deal with that trauma. All you can do with the really heartless is isolate them. The most violent crime is committed by a small group of kids, those who are seriously disturbed and those who just lack feeling. The first have poor reality testing; sometimes they hallucinate, sometimes not, but there's gross developmental deviation, funny use of words and thought. The other group are schizoid kids who function perfectly well except that there is some piece missing. In the middle-class culture they might be computer buffs without any social life, or work in the post office at night. A third group is from the drug culture. A lot of crime originates with three kids just standing around on the street and they want to buy ten bucks' worth of cheeba and nobody has the money, so you rip somebody off to pay for the marijuana. Or they commit crimes when they're under the influence.

"It's a miserable life they have. They have no emotional support or resources, they're really very passive and there's not enough mentation to make a mind-altering drug an issue. It's not a matter of looking for new experiences, it's just a matter of blunting what happens day by day and that's the path of drugs they follow, marijuana to drinking to heroin, the pattern that blunts the depression or, for some of these kids, an attempt to make some feeling where there isn't any, to feel alive inside instead of the chronic boredom. The drug is an attempt to stimulate some sense of self, of action, because there's such a vacuum, like a black room, no environment. And if you're in a black room with nothing to do and you have to live there, you take drugs trying to create something. . . ."

Although the Carnegie-Mellon study of criminal careers confirmed other studies that have found that young black urban males commit violent crimes more frequently than whites—

as much as five times more frequently—there is much to suggest that the racial difference is an effect rather than a cause. In fact Garmise believes that the single most important cause in the psychological development of the violent few—those capable of feckless rape and murder—is the pregnant teenage female from a fragmented underclass family.

"I think the whole issue of violent youth has to do with the increasing youth of parents," he says. "The kids are often raised with a tremendous amount of personal violence against them and without much sense of the baby as a human being. When you talk to some of these young mothers you find they don't have any goals for their kids, any ideas about shaping their lives, or even of what their needs are as infants."

A few days after I talked with Richard Garmise I came upon a document that seemed to illustrate his comments with chilling objectivity. It was the report of an investigation by a Brooklyn grand jury in 1983, and it gives some idea of the magnitude of the problems and the inadequacy of the solutions. As anyone who follows the press reports is aware (PROBLEMS BESET CHILD-CARE UNIT CHIEF, reads the headline on a typical story about SSC as I write this), there is no reason to believe that the problems or the way they are handled has changed since these findings were made.

"This grand jury," the report states, "began an investigation of several child-care agencies as the result of an incident in which a young woman (referred to in this report as Jane Doe) severely scalded her two-and-a-half-year-old daughter Tammy. Investigation disclosed that Jane Doe had killed her seven-month-old daughter Fay . . . that she had repeatedly injured her daughters Kim and Tammy . . . and that Kim and Tammy had been temporarily removed from her custody by court order. The children were subsequently returned to her custody and further injuries occurred, ultimately leading to the severe scalding of Tammy which left her permanently disfigured. Throughout this period, two child-care agencies, Special Services for Children (SSC) and a well-established voluntary agency in the city of New York (hereinafter referred to as WVANYC) had legal responsibility for supervising the care of these children, but these agencies failed to prevent this injury from occurring." (SSC may contract for some of its functions with private agencies such as WVANYC but, according to the law, it is SSC that retains ultimate responsibility, and SSC must approve major decisions such as the return of an abused child to the custody of its parents.)

How could this happen?

Of all the agencies ancillary to Family Court, the Office of Special Services for Children is the most beset with seemingly insoluble problems. The number and quality of child-care workers dwindles as the number of cases explodes along with the number of children born to young women—most of them poor and black—without husbands or stable families and without the capacity to care for their young or even, in many cases, for themselves. Caseloads of as many as fifty or sixty compete for workers' time and attention with the need to fill out hundreds of required forms for each one. The frustrations are endless, the compensation minimal, and the training all but useless. Directors of the agency come and go as scandals erupt in the press and the courts.

The SSC is the New York City agency responsible for investigating reports of child abuse and neglect, providing emergency shelter for endangered children, arranging foster care and adoption placements, and providing services for what are referred to as "troubled families," with the aim of keeping families, wherever possible, intact. The law that established SSC's investigatory responsibilities makes it responsible as well for "providing protective services to prevent further abuses or maltreatment of children and to coordinate, provide or arrange for and monitor the provision of those services necessary to safeguard and ensure the child's well-being and development and to preserve and stabilize family life whenever appropriate." There is a built-in contradiction in this mandate—the obvious paradox of trying to "preserve," presumably for the sake of the children, even a "family" in which they may be routinely mistreated and even repeatedly brutalized. In the Alice-in-Wonderland logic of the public social welfare agencies, keeping a family together can take precedence over keeping a child alive.

According to the report, Jane Doe gave birth to her first child, Fay, at the age of fifteen. When Fay was seven months old, she was admitted to a hospital with a double fracture of the left arm. X-rays revealed an older untreated fracture of the child's right arm. The hospital reported the suspected abuse to SSC and an investigation was begun. Meanwhile, Fay remained in custody at the hospital.

At that time, SSC had no formal training program, and the investigator who spoke to Jane passively accepted what the grand jury report refers to as her "farfetched explanations for the injury"—it occurred when Fay was vaccinated, or when a friend bumped into the baby's arm sticking out of the crib; Jane hadn't sought treatment because the baby hadn't cried and so she hadn't noticed the injury—even though he found them "simply unbelievable."

"The investigator apparently did not think that implausible explanations of numerous bone fractures in a seven-month-old child," states the report, "were sufficient to constitute 'some credible evidence' " of abuse. Nor did he bother to review Jane's history, which would have revealed that as a child she had been abused by her own mother, a circumstance "strongly associated with being an abusive parent." SSC's own records described Jane when she was about eight years old as having "a low frustration tolerance, poor impulse control, and a tendency to act out."

With the investigation dragging on, Jane agreed to enter a child-abuse program, and SSC, with the social worker's belief in the miraculous power of "programs" and "treatment," immediately returned Fay to her mother's care "upon the mere representation that Jane would participate in the program and before she had attended a single session. The SSC investigator appears to have been more concerned," the report notes, "with the rehabilitation of the mother than with the safety of the child." In fact, "when Jane admitted at the first program session that she had knocked over Fay's stroller and caused Fay's fracture, the SSC investigator regarded that admission not as evidence of abuse warranting the child's removal from the home . . . but as an encouraging first step toward rehabilitation."

Jane was given an appointment for another session about two weeks later. Two days before the scheduled second session, Fay was brought into the hospital by the police and pronounced dead on arrival as a result of a subdural hematoma. There were old and new bruise marks on her body. Jane's explanation was that "the child had hit herself in the head with the arm that had the cast on it." With the investigation of the first abuse report still pending, Jane admitted to the police that "she had toppled Fay's crib in a fit of anger, provoked by a fight with her husband and the baby's persistent crying." Only now were the fractures characterized as abuse by the SSC investigator. And now Jane was arrested and indicted on a homicide charge. An SSC supervisor duly wrote a memorandum to a deputy director of the agency. "He noted that the poor handling of the case demonstrated both the need for training of caseworkers and the need to have serious injury cases handled by a special unit" and "expressed concern that no mechanism existed to notify SSC if the abusive mother gave birth again because 'the potential for abuse again is high.' "

Nevertheless, "SSC did not institute a formal training program at this time, nor did SSC establish a special unit for serious injury cases . . . inexperienced caseworkers without formal training continued to be assigned cases involving allegations of serious physical injury or death to a child." Nor did SSC "establish any mechanism by which it would be alerted if a mother who killed her child gave birth again."

Ninety days later, Jane Doe's case was closed with this notation: "Child had died from injuries and case has been referred to the police. There are no other children in this home." At the time this was written, Jane was pregnant again.

There was no attempt to follow the case in any way but quite by accident some months later, a hospital social worker read a newspaper article about the criminal case against Jane and recognized her as a patient receiving prenatal care at the hospital. The social worker informed SSC that Jane was due to give birth soon and another investigation was ordered and a new investigator assigned.

The report continues, "The new investigator obtained a Family Court order placing Jane's new baby daughter, Kim, in the custody of the Commissioner of Social Services on the ground that she was in imminent danger of being abused." Kim was placed in a foster home. Meanwhile, Jane pleaded guilty to the homicide charge and was placed on probation; the condition of her probation was her participation in a residential child-abuse rehabilitation program at WVANYC. As part of the rehabilitation program, Kim was returned to her. The private agency contracted to supervise Jane and her child day-to-day, with SSC responsible for monitoring their performance.

Jane was now seventeen years old and pregnant again. Her third daughter, Tammy, began life with her mother in the residential program. There, the report states, "under constant supervision, separated from her husband, and receiving regular individual and group therapy, no abuse occurred."

So miraculous was the therapy that Jane was soon considered by the WVANYC to be "able to assume a nurturing role with both of her children" and was "no longer at great risk for abuse." Having "made substantial progress," she was sent home with her two daughters for a ninety-day trial period during which she was to attend a weekly session of the rehabilitation program as an outpatient. A WVANYC family assistance worker was to visit the home twice a week.

Family assistance workers were paraprofessionals "intended to be a source of aid and support to the parent—a 'friend' whom the mother could come to trust." There were no requirements, not even a high school diploma, only the ability to "care" and a "desire to help others." They received no formal training and, although they were given some literature dealing with the injuries and behavior characteristic of child abuse, there was no testing of their understanding of the information it contained or of their ability to apply it to particular cases. They were expected to report their observations of the parent and child to the social worker in charge of the case.

Nevertheless, the family assistance worker assigned to Jane and John Doe's home reported conflict and violence almost immediately after Jane's discharge, but her warnings went unheeded. Both agencies recorded the information in their voluminous files, but neither took any action to protect the children. Jane began to miss her rehabilitation program sessions, claiming she had court appointments or was attending school, though she was not. "Although the workers were aware she was lying to them, they did nothing. The discharge was not terminated even though by failing to attend sessions and avoiding home visits, Jane had violated the conditions of the discharge. The children," the report adds in a chillingly simple statement, "remained at home."

Six weeks later, the cycle began again. Kim had a swollen

jaw and a black eye, Jane gave implausible explanations, a report was filed, an investigation ordered, and the children remained at home "pending the outcome of the investigation." There were reports of frequent violent fights between Jane and John, after which he would leave the house and return to find the children hurt—facts duly noted in the worker's log as "serious," yet, notes the grand jury, "no action was taken."

Jane began to avoid the worker's visits and continued to miss her sessions. The papers in her file grew. So did Kim's obvious fear of her mother, reported by Jane's probation officer. Still, continues the grand jury report, "despite Jane's continuing violation of the discharge conditions and the obvious danger to the children inherent in the volatile home situation, neither SSC nor WVANYC took action to remove the children from the home. Instead the WVANYC caseworker 'discussed' with Jane her feeling that it was bad for the children to be exposed to so much violence."

Things continued to get worse—the parents fighting, Kim bruised and swollen, Jane lying about her missed appointments and canceled home visits. Finally, in a struggle with Jane, John twisted Kim's arm and another abuse report was filed. The earlier one was still pending.

Finally, "the children were removed from the home by court order, not at the request of the child-care agencies but because Jane's probation officer had gone to court alleging Jane had violated the terms of her probation." In short, the children were placed in foster care not because they had the marks of beatings on them but because their mother had been missing her rehabilitation program sessions and visits to her probation officer.

According to the grand jury, no one had acted earlier to take the children into protective custody because no one had assumed responsibility for their safety. "The family assistance

worker believed she had fulfilled her responsibilities by reporting her observations to the WVANYC caseworker, who
believed she had fulfilled her responsibilities by filing a child-
abuse report with the state and SSC. SSC took no action, and
has no explanation for its failure."

When a doctor examined Kim after the children had been
taken into custody, he found welts on her abdomen and buttocks apparently made by a strap. They could not have been
observed during home visits since unclothed examinations of
children are not routinely conducted in the home by child-
care workers "because they might interfere with the relationship of trust being established between the mother and the
family assistance worker and because they might anger the
mother and provoke violence against the family assistance
worker or the child."

A neglect petition was filed by SSC in Family Court and
Tammy and Kim, both of whom had physical injuries inflicted by their parents, were placed in foster care, where
they remained for a year and three months, at which time
the WVANYC staff concluded that Jane and John had made
such significant progress as outpatients in its rehabilitation
program that plans should be made to return the children to
them. Home visits were begun.

Jane was nineteen now. According to an SSC psychiatrist,
she remained "immature and inadequate for the care of young
children" and her visits with the children should at all times
be supervised. SSC, on the basis of this report, filed for an
extension of the children's placements, but "at the same time
SSC was requesting that the placement orders be extended,
WVANYC was actively planning for the release of the children to their mother." A trial discharge was suggested, but
although SSC said no to the discharge and to unsupervised
home visits, unsupervised home visits continued and a formal
request for a trial discharge was drafted by WVANYC and

transmitted to SSC. The request referred to "significant improvements in her lifestyle" made by Jane Doe and stated the opinion that she was now able to care for her children. This opinion was written by the foster-care worker, who was later to explain that "she had no personal knowledge about the case after discharge and did not have access to the [outpatient rehabilitation program] files," which foster-care workers (in the same agency) were prohibited from reading "on the ground that the files are 'confidential.' "

The discharge request, which contradicted everything in the agency's files, was nevertheless submitted to SSC, where a new caseworker, totally unfamiliar with Jane's history, and without consulting the prior worker or reading the case records, signed it and passed it on to her supervisor. She said it was "not her job to consult others or read records," but just to look at the form and "if it looks normal," process it.

By this time Jane was pregnant again. Her husband had been arrested on a rape charge and she had begun an affair with a married man. She was not keeping her therapy appointments and was saying to anyone who would listen that she could not tolerate the children's crying. All of this was information readily available to anyone who had bothered to review the records. No one at either agency did, and the children were discharged to Jane again.

The family assistance worker's visits were sporadic, but before the third month of the trial discharge was up, she had seen injuries on both Kim and Tammy. She accepted Jane's explanation of the injuries as accidental although she noted that Kim "seemed to be getting hurt a lot," and a request was made for an extension of the trial discharge. A treatment conference was held at WVANYC and in spite of the fact that Kim's "accident proneness" occurred only when she was in Jane's care and not in foster care and in spite of the fact that Jane and the two children were now sharing a couch with

Jane's sister in her mother's apartment, and in spite of new injuries to Kim, the caseworker failed to follow up a medical report about Kim or to consider the fact that Jane had killed one of her children and frequently abused the remaining two.

At this point the children were finally discharged to their mother by WVANYC. Later, no one was able to remember or find any record of exactly who had authorized the discharge. Within weeks, both children were injured again but although the family assistance worker reported these injuries and Jane's various explanations to the caseworker, the caseworker did not file a report or take any other action.

The next time the family assistance worker showed up, Jane refused to let her in. The following time, Kim was not home when the worker visited. Meanwhile, the caseworker left the agency for a new job and the case was reassigned.

A month after the final discharge, two-and-a-half-year-old Tammy was brought to the hospital by her grandmother. She was severely scalded. According to the grand jury report, "She had second- and third-degree burns on her feet, left hand, and buttocks. Fifteen percent of her body was burned. As a result of her burns, several of Tammy's toes on both feet had to be amputated. She began to lose the nerves in her hand. She had to have several skin graft operations and plastic surgery. She began seeing a psychiatrist." The hospital filed a child-abuse report and notified the police.

"Nonetheless," the report continues, "the WVANYC records consistently refer to the scalding as an accident. The family assistance worker told the grand jury about the reluctance to characterize the injury as abuse: 'After you have worked with a woman for so long, you say, dear God, did this mother do such an awful thing? After all, the skin was coming off this baby.'

"WVANYC made no attempt to insure Kim's safety or remove Kim from Jane's custody after the scalding. Instead, after viewing and reporting Tammy's injuries, the family assistance worker went home. She told the grand jury: 'It was a very bad experience really. So, I called my supervisor, whatever, and I went home. I was taken [sic] care of me at that particular time. To see a child with the feet all burned up to the ankle, the stomach, you know, the hands and whatever, you needed to have some kind of care for yourself at that particular time.' "

She felt that she had fulfilled her responsibilities by reporting to the supervisor. In her monthly progress report to the agency, she described the general physical health of the family as "fair," adding that Tammy "got scaled [sic] this month." She described the burning as a "bad accident."

A new caseworker—the sixth—was assigned on an emergency basis and allowed Kim to remain at the grandparents' apartment after talking with them over the phone. A seventh worker took over two days later and "SSC took no further action to remove Kim from her mother's reach, relying on the grandmother's representations that the child was well and safe."

The police finally removed Kim from her grandparents' house to ensure her safety after criminal charges were filed against Jane as a result of the hospital report on Tammy. When the police brought Kim to a hospital for examination, the doctor found rope marks on her wrist and ankle and scars on her lower back. Kim was sent to a foster home and Jane was prosecuted and convicted of assault on Tammy and sentenced to a prison term. Meanwhile, she had given birth to her fourth child. It was a boy.

The grand jury noted that the child protective agencies involved had failed to protect the children and, in a fragmented system staffed by inadequately trained people, no one had followed through or assumed responsibility, and it found that "the child protective system emphasizes rehabilitation of the parent to an extent that is inconsistent with the safety of the child." It raised the question of whether the statutory mandates to protect an abused child from further abuse and maltreatment could be fulfilled simultaneously with the requirement to "preserve and stabilize family life" by "help[ing] the family with services to prevent its breakup or to reunite it," and it suggested a number of reforms it was hoped might improve the system.

How realistic are such hopes? How many Jane Does are there among the growing number of teenage girls having babies? And who is there available to do the kind of work required to look after them? Even if we design a better system and manage to prevent the kind of ultimate horrors that were the fate of Jane Doe's children, what is the best the children of such mothers can hope for? What will their earliest experiences be, and how will that affect the kind of people they grow into? Just how much can we expect of "rehabilitation"?

"The basic problem is clearly too many kids, too young," Richard Garmise says, tossing his pencil onto the pile of folders on his desk. "Children having children, without any thought about having them or any ability to nurture them."

I've come back to talk with Garmise again in his office in the Mental Health Services department in the Family Court Building.

"Sixteen- and seventeen-year-olds having their own children already have two strikes against them." He pauses. "Why not have some real financial incentives not to have children? Target a population of adolescent girls and say, 'We're going to give you X number of dollars a month but if you become pregnant before a stated age, you're going to lose that stipend. After that, if you have a kid or two, you get a certain stipend but if you have more, you lose it.' I don't know what else we can do, except try to raise the female education rate, which is historically associated with the birth rate going down." He pauses again and this time adds with a tired shrug, "But what do you do with people who have educational facilities available and don't take advantage of them, because they don't really see education as a value?"

Dr. Garmise is not alone in his views. Commenting on a murderous attack by two teenagers on five neighborhood children they left for dead, Richard J. Herrnstein, a Harvard professor of psychology, suggests that "shallow emotional attachments first to their parents and then to society in general" are the cause of much of the random violence by adolescents. His Harvard colleague, James Q. Wilson, adds, "Very few people are driven to violent crime by poverty. The crucial test . . . is how they are raised and the presence or absence of character and conscience."

Again and again as we talked Garmise came back to this theme. "There's no question in my mind that a lot of kids are carrying out the ethos of the family. The offense is not an offense in the context of their community. It doesn't present a conflict for the kid, so how do you treat him? From his point of view a lot of the violence is adaptive for the kid. They weren't brought up not to be violent. And treatment is done by talking, and words and language often don't have the same meaning to these kids that they do to other groups of people. Many of them have reading scores that are even poorer than their IQ would lead you to expect. It's a matter of both individual development and social milieu. Their language is very primitive, as is their way of thinking about other people and about antecedents and consequences. They don't conceptualize, don't distinguish between petty theft and bopping someone on the head. Verbal skills, as middle-class people define them, aren't valued. And you talk about putting kids with that orientation in treatment?" He shook his head hopelessly, and I thought of a story I had heard earlier that day.

Over lunch in one of the Chinese restaurants that prolif-erate in the courthouse neighborhood, a young lawyer who was then an assistant Corporation Counsel told me about a case she'd handled recently, which she couldn't quite shake loose from. It was a case in which a ten-year-old boy had sexually assaulted a two-year-old girl who had been left in his care by the baby's mother, a neighbor in the welfare hotel where he lived with his grandparents. The boy had told how he had rammed a plumber's plunger in the little girl's vagina when he saw her bare from the waist down with her legs in the air. He was still angry at the baby's mother for taking some money from him a month before when she was high on drugs. He had been charged with aggravated sexual abuse and assault in the first and second degree. His court-appointed Legal Aid defense lawyer was attempting to have the case dismissed on the grounds that the boy's rights had been violated during the police questioning. He had told his story voluntarily when asked—but the Legal Aid lawyer al-leged that he had not been formally apprised of his rights and neither of his grandparents had been present. In case of dis-missal, the boy would be returned to the welfare hotel and his grandparents, and it was unlikely that he would receive any kind of treatment or any effective help at all.

"The people in this case all live in a welfare hotel," the young lawyer said, moving the noodles around on her plate with a chopstick but not eating. "It's like a zoo. The mother of the victim is totally inept, inarticulate, saw the blood on the baby's diaper when she got back from wherever she'd spent most of the night after leaving this kid with her baby, but had no idea of what happened or how, so the detective assigned from the sex crimes unit interviewed all the people coming and going in this completely disorganized place, trying to see who was in the apartment, who had been with the baby. He got all kinds of rambling stories, a big jumble— you've got not very great historians relating the event—until he finally got to the kid, who told various stories before he finally told what had happened."

What the ten-year-old told the detective was, "I wanted to hit her in the head [because, he explains, of her mother's having taken his money the month before]. Instead of hitting her in the head I jammed the plunger handle into her pussy. I pushed it in hard. She screamed and cried. I put the plunger handle back on the plunger . . . When I came out of the bathroom I saw a trail of blood from the bedroom to the living room. I picked up a rag and wiped up the blood, then I grabbed the baby and wiped her with the same rag. Then I put a new Pamper on her. I hid the rag in a hole in the bathroom behind a pipe." The rag was found where he said he had put it.

As she looked across the table at me, the lawyer said, "What is incomprehensible is that this boy, regardless of what he did—and I can hate this act he committed until the day I die—but what is incomprehensible is that this kid could have seen so much and could have been brought up in an environment so tainted and so disgusting that he could even conceive of doing an act like this."

What, she seemed to be asking—and the question lay there, unspoken, between us—are we going to do with the children in all the rooms in all the buildings like that one?

If the number of black adolescent boys growing up on the streets and turning to crime is growing, it is not because they are poor but because they are fatherless and without families. So says Thomas Sowell, an economist and social philosopher now at the Hoover Institution in Stanford, California. Sowell himself is black and comes from a poor but solid family. An

intense and articulate scholar, Sowell maintains that what
has characterized every other racial or ethnic group in America that has climbed out of poverty is strong families sticking
together while working and saving for their children's future.
Immigrant groups have developed networks in specific occu-
pations, like the Korean produce-store owners in present-day
New York, and put the whole family to work financing the
education of the young. He suggests that this pattern was
derailed for black families when they became the recipients
of federal largesse in the form of Aid to Families with Dependent Children. The burden of responsibility was shifted
from the head of the family to the government, with the results we see in the inner cities today.

Much of the evidence seems to indicate that it is emotional
deprivation early in life rather than economic deprivation that
is at the source of the high rate of violent criminal activity
among a small number of poor black adolescents. It is a cliché
by now to point to the many intact black families—black and
white alike—that have raised law-abiding citizens and eventually made good through education and effort. Growth
without guidance is the most common denominator among
the children who grow up to be robbers, rapists, and killers—
not poverty per se but family instability and emotional im-
poverishment.

In a sense, a tendency toward criminal behavior is inherited. That is not to say that it is genetic, like skin color. It is
more like the family jewels, passed on from one generation
to another, not biologically inherited but a social inheritance.
The origins of crime are not economic but personal, to be
found in the patterns of child-rearing that foster such traits
as resentment and impulsivity. Those patterns, while they
may characterize many who live in poverty, are not caused
by their poverty but by the chain of erratic, neglectful, sometimes abusive parenting transmitted from generation to gen-

eration in unstable families. While we know this to be so, we do not know of any way to generate those emotional bonds with others once they fail to take root in early family experience.

What we do know about the importance of early nurture from a half century of maternal deprivation studies was summed up by Selma Fraiberg more than twenty years ago. No one has put it better since.

"These bondless men, women, and children," wrote Fraiberg, "constitute one of the largest aberrant populations in the world today, contributing far beyond their numbers to social disease and disorder. These are the people who are unable to fulfill the most ordinary human obligations in work, in friendship, in marriage, and in child-rearing. The condition of non-attachment leaves a void in the personality where conscience should be. Where there are no human attachments, there can be no conscience. As a consequence, the hollow men and women contribute very largely to the criminal population. It is this group, too, that produces a particular kind of criminal, whose crimes, whether they be petty or atrocious, are always characterized by indifference. The potential for violence and destructive acts is far greater among these bondless men and women; the absence of human bonds leaves a free 'unbound' aggression to pursue its erratic course."

The cure for the "diseases of non-attachment"? "Ensuring stable human partnerships for every baby." How to do this? Perhaps one small step would be to do as much as we possibly can to discourage births to girls who are by virtue of their age, their own inadequate development, and their psychological problems unready to nurture a child adequately.

Most evenings when I left Family Court I took the A train to Columbus Circle, where I transferred to the local before the A went on past the Manhattan stops along Central Park West up to Harlem. On one of those evenings when I was lucky enough to get a seat, I sat mulling over the day's scenes, reviewing the cast of characters.

I thought of the neglect hearing I had attended that day. A mother had appeared with two teenage daughters, one of them visibly pregnant. She had failed to appear for an earlier court appearance to explain why she had not taken one of her children to the hospital clinic where school officials had made an appointment when he had an epileptic seizure in a classroom. This time, a warrant had been issued and she had come with her two oldest children, leaving three younger ones at home. She was thirty-four but looked much older, faded, shapeless, beaten down. Like her older daughter, she was pregnant. There was no husband/father living at home. The family lived in subsidized public housing and received welfare, Aid to Families with Dependent Children, food stamps, Medicaid, and free breakfast and lunch programs in public school. A Legal Aid lawyer requesting that the warrant be vacated before the proceedings began approached the bench to explain the woman's failure to appear for the previous court date.

"Your honor," she said, "my client didn't come to court because she distrusts the system."

The next case is that of Johnson AKA Jackson AKA . . . There's been a warrant outstanding on him for a year, which comes to light only now that he's been picked up on a robbery charge. No parents have appeared. No one seems to know where he is or cares. He gives an aunt's telephone number. No answer there. He is assigned a lawyer as guardian, a surrogate parent to discuss non-legal matters with him in place of the parent who has failed to appear. "Congratulate me," he says to the lawyer. "I just had a son."

I wondered whether it would be safe to reserve a place

here for that child in fourteen or fifteen years, the way prep school places are reserved for infants of another class. What future for the child of a parentless delinquent, born to an unmarried teenager while his father is in a facility upstate?

Still later, a grandmother brought a PINS petition against her granddaughter, whom she said she could no longer control. She wanted her out of the house. She wanted her "put somewhere she couldn't get into trouble." The girl was thirteen and she was pregnant. She wanted to have her baby and keep it. Placement in a group home would be explored. Counting attorneys, caseworkers, and court personnel, there were nine people involved in the proceedings.

Although I am here to observe the proceedings in delinquency cases, what I find is that a neglect case precedes the delinquency case—in every sense. In the last case of the day, an elderly couple petition the court for the right to adopt six children of their unmarried daughter by two different men. One of the children had been sexually abused by her father. The other father is serving a twenty-year prison sentence. There are so many representatives of various social agencies involved that the judge has trouble getting them all sorted out. The petitioners had been assigned their lawyer only that morning. The bureaucratic tangle seems hopeless, but the judge will try to cut through it. Having natural relatives who want the children is an unusual advantage.

As the train pulled out of the Times Square station I looked up and an advertising placard caught my eye. Between an ad for Roach Motels and one in Spanish for Preparation H for hemorrhoids, partially decorated by a scroll of graffiti initials, was a picture of a pretty black girl holding a telephone. She looked about fourteen. The message next to the picture read:

"You're not alone! If you're a teenager and think you may be pregnant you can get help with—" and then it went on to list "pregnancy testing, medical care, nutrition, housing, financial aid, legal services, job training, day care," and ended with the invitation to "Call the Teen Pregnancy Hotline," giving an 800 toll-free number. You wouldn't even have to pay for the telephone call.

I made some bitter little jokes to myself. If I were a young girl whose family had never talked about college, who had no particular job prospects or vision of the future, I'd get off the train at the next stop and get laid so I could start collecting on the promise of housing, financial aid, and legal services, to say nothing of day care. It was quite an offer. An appealing package. The ad was signed by the New York State Health Department.

That day I had read that more than half of the black children born in the United States are born to unmarried women. Half of those, a quarter of all black children, are born to unmarried teenagers, and three-quarters of *poor* black children grow up in a "family" without a resident husband and father and find their only models for what it is to be a man on the streets. In New York's central Harlem in the mid-Eighties, the percentage of babies born out of wedlock was almost 80 percent.

12

The Object of Concern

Serious crime should be treated seriously regardless of the offender's age. . . . Humanity, not juveniles or adults, should be the object of concern.

—dissent by Marvin E. Wolfgang in *Confronting Youth Crime: Report of the Twentieth Century Fund Task Force on Sentencing Policy Toward Young Offenders* (New York: Holmes & Meier, 1978)

If most violent juvenile crime is committed by that hard core of repeat offenders whose psychological makeup seems devoid of ordinary human feeling and conscience, boys from fractured families with parents who can provide few opportunities for normal developmental experiences, and if this pattern has been reinforced by some of the social legislation of the last half century, the problem of juvenile crime has been even further complicated by recent legislation affecting the practice and philosophy of juvenile legal proceedings.

Astonishing as it may seem, there is no way to know the exact number of violent crimes committed by the under-sixteens in New York or in a number of other states. The experience of everyone in the system indicates that the number is high, but all we have to rely on is anecdotal evidence. Statistics are kept by the State of New York only for those who are fingerprinted and photographed, and these include only thirteen-, fourteen- and fifteen-year-olds who commit A, B, and C felonies (murder, armed robbery, rape, assault with a deadly weapon) and twelve-year-olds who commit A and B felonies. There are no figures for one-on-one robbery on the street without a deadly weapon, or for second-degree assault, in which a weapon is used and physical injury is inflicted but the gunshot wound or the stabbing is not considered serious enough, or for third-degree assault, in which someone is injured but there is no deadly weapon involved—some of the most brutal crimes occur in this class—or for possession of a loaded gun, or for cases adjusted, which are always sealed. Even the Probation Department doesn't have access to data about the adjusted cases for purposes of its investigation and reports. As a probation officer puts it, "If we have to do an I and R, *we* don't even know if the kid has any previous history in the court because his records have been sealed if the case was adjusted."

"There's no doubt that there's lax tracking of what goes on in Family Court," says an attorney in the Bronx office of the Corporation Counsel. "There's no reason to keep track of what goes on in Family Court because the court is closed. Those who are responsible for the policy say they don't want to track because they want to avoid stigmatizing the youths. That may be appropriate for some of the 'youths,' but none of the bleeding hearts in organizations like the Citizens' Committee for Children or the Vera Institute of Justice want to face the hard truth that some of these kids are animals. So they pick and choose and put out their own figures on how well kids are doing in their various facilities."

Despite the fact that career criminals start early and stay late, with 80 percent of chronic juvenile offenders becoming chronic adult offenders ("We know who he is by the time he is thirteen or fourteen," says Paul Tracy, one of the authors of *Delinquency in Two Birth Cohorts*, of the chronic offender), more than half the states keep no record of juvenile offenses. As of the end of 1986, the Justice Department's Bureau of Statistics revealed that twenty-six states had "no juvenile records or that records pertaining to juveniles are not retained," and that among those which kept juvenile statistics on file the data was very incomplete and hard to come by, even for officials of the legal system.

Since the juvenile delinquent is "not criminally responsible for [his] conduct by reason of infancy," as New York's Family Court Act puts it, New York law and that of many other states requires that juvenile records be kept confidential to avoid stigmatizing the young. Today we know enough about the violent few who commit the worst crimes—and commit them over and over with impunity—to see this belief in the prospects for rehabilitation of the habitually violent as misplaced optimism. Opening the court to public scrutiny, identifying the repeat violent criminals, and making their records available to an adult system that functions in continuity with the family court or juvenile court would provide a more effective means of prevention of violent crime, control of the criminal, and protection of the community.

In 1986, Merril Sobie characterized the closed-door policy that excludes press, public, and officials, as well as researchers and attorneys not connected with the case, from Family Court proceedings, as "built upon an extremely shaky statutory foundation."

Mr. Sobie, a professor at Pace University School of Law, ought to know. He was the principal author of Article Three, the section pertaining to juvenile delinquency, of New York's Family Court Act. He is also the chief legal consultant for the New York State Bar Association study of the Family Court law guardian system and was executive officer of the Family Court from 1971 to 1975.

The statute, as originally written, presumes Family Court proceedings to be open, but gives the court discretion to exclude in particular cases. Mr. Sobie, a man of intelligence as well as legal expertise, sees that there may be more reason to close the courtroom in some cases than others—say, those involving psychiatric testimony in a dispositional hearing more than those involving publicly committed acts of delinquency in a fact-finding hearing. According to him, although the practice of conducting hearings behind closed doors has become a hallmark of juvenile justice, the present provisions "are incomplete and far from desirable. A new approach is needed, one which considers carefully the competing interests, rights, desires and expectations of the bench, the bar, the parties, the news media and the public at large."

At the time of the Shavod Jones shooting of the policeman in Central Park, former Family Court judge Nanette Dembitz raised the question of "when a boy like Shavod should be treated like a misguided child and when he should be treated like an adult criminal." Judge Dembitz, one of the better people to have sat on the Family Court bench, noted that, at the time of the shooting, fifteen-year-old Shavod was free after a conviction of robbery, awaiting sentencing at a later date. He had a long history of prior arrests. That record had, according to the provisions of a 1982 New York law, been sealed, unavailable even to the judge hearing the case of his latest crime.

Judge Dembitz has no argument with the position that an employer should not be able to refuse to hire a young person simply because he has an arrest record. She knows that many young people are involved in petty crimes they don't repeat. And she knows that a poor child is more likely to be arrested for shoplifting than a middle-class child because police and shopowner will perceive the middle-class parents as more likely to make restitution as well as to keep their child in line in the future. She knows an arrest record can thus be an unfair disadvantage to an underprivileged youngster looking for a job.

However, she also knows that in the case of a serious criminal charge, "there is no more reason for blinding justice in regard to a juvenile's arrest record than to an adult's."

And, in a burst of common sense as rare as virtuous defendants, she adds, "When the police take a loaded gun or cocaine from a youth's pocket, the boy is, in fact, guilty even if the charge is dismissed because the police lacked a warrant. That type of arrest means as much in the case of a youth as it means in the case of an adult.

"To fulfill his or her obligation to protect the community from crime, a judge must have full knowledge of what a defendant has done. Helping an underprivileged youth means satisfying his emotional, social and educational needs at the earliest possible time. Compassion does not call for sealing records to limit a court's information, or permitting the youth to victimize others though he has himself been victimized, sometimes even before birth."

The policy that bars juveniles' criminal proceedings from public scrutiny and results in their criminal records being sealed and expunged from the public record may have made more sense in the past, when juveniles committed delinquencies rather than felonies, when the community was capable of invoking meaningful sanctions, and when shame and remorse could be an expectable reaction on the part of a youngster. Today many of the teenagers arrested actually flaunt their criminal acts in their communities. Arraignment in Family Court becomes a rite of passage, a sign of having arrived as a leader among peers. So the only people who are denied knowledge of the criminal acts are those who need the knowledge most in order to make reasonable assessments based on fact.

This aspect of the infancy defense, like the infancy defense in general, founders on a fact of contemporary life—that 70 to 80 percent of violent crime by juveniles is committed by a small number of detached, hardened young criminals who are chronic offenders by the time they are twelve. They are neither innocent nor tenderhearted, nor do they seem to be changeable by any means that society has at its disposal at the present time.

Marvin E. Wolfgang, one of the authors of *Delinquency in Two Birth Cohorts*, thinks it is the seriousness of the crime, not the age of the criminal, that should be considered when a crime of violence is committed against a person, and he opposes special treatment for youthful offenders who commit serious and violent crimes. "A murder by a sixteen-year-old," he says, "produces a dead victim just as surely as a murder by a thirty-five-year-old."

Wolfgang says that trying to deal with adult career criminals is starting "at the tail end of a much larger animal." Closing juvenile court records to the criminal court, "permitting serious recidivists to be reborn with virginal records" at a later age, says Wolfgang, "is failing to protect society from persons who have already established a criminal career by that age." For the chronic violent few, he suggests that there should be a continuity between juvenile court and the adult criminal system that would provide the accused with all of the constitutional protections while at the same time affording society a better measure of protection than it now enjoys.

Since the present juvenile court system fails either to rehabilitate or to deter young criminals—and, in fact, by failing to punish them may actually seduce them into continuing and even escalating their criminal careers, to their own disadvantage as much as to society's—many observers think it should be abolished altogether.

Ernst van den Haag, professor of jurisprudence and public policy at Fordham University, would have everyone over thirteen dealt with by the adult court system (although of course imprisoned separately from adults). Lawyers would still be there to argue for the young offender's incompetence, "but," says van den Haag, "incompetence should no longer be assumed automatically on the basis of age."

At the present time, as he points out, "the first crime is on the house," since probation will in most cases be its most serious consequence. Not only does this do little to discourage first offenses, it may even be the consequence not of a first offense at all, but only of a first conviction.

"A second conviction, at any rate, demonstrates that the first did not discourage the offender," says van den Haag, adding that since most crimes are committed by young males who enter crime early and stay late, "punishment for young second offenders should be harsh enough to deter them and their peers from pursuing criminal careers. For second offenses, youth should be a reason for severity rather than a ground for leniency."

Some also believe that the non-punitive manner of familiarity in Family Court breeds nothing more than contempt, serving as a misleading signal to prospective young criminals, ultimately leading to betrayal and adult incarceration. Andrew Oldenquist, a professor of philosophy at Ohio State University, argues that "a symptom of the de-moralization of juvenile justice is informality. A judge who sits in black robes, in a setting that is dignified, solemn, and formal, is universally understood to speak for the moral will of a community. The delinquent knows it is serious and that *he* is taken seriously. A judge or hearing officer who abandons formal ritual and 'raps' with a delinquent, trying to be his buddy, is likely to be viewed with contempt. Juvenile justice officials who think informality and de-ritualization better enable them to 'reach' delinquents probably accomplish the opposite of what they intend."

"It's no longer a defensible position that children cannot do bad things, cannot be bad people." This is Philip Dobbs talking—the probation officer who was one of the most thoughtful and experienced men I met in the juvenile justice system. "We have seen the escalation of crimes of violence among the young, of assaults on teachers and group robberies and rapes, with kids coming back to the court over and over, surely an indication that something isn't working. If they are not punished—and immediately after the 'incident' in question—if they don't learn their conduct is unacceptable, they conclude that the court is a charade and that nothing will ever happen to them—or at least that they have a pretty good chance of not having to suffer any consequences for what they do. If, after the first serious crime, there was a serious consequence, it's a pretty good bet there would be fewer repeaters."

One factor that is constantly cited as a reason why the system doesn't work is inadequate training of personnel, who are often not the most talented or the most dedicated to begin with—from the paraprofessional family assistance worker employed by SSC through the social worker who supervises cases for the Department of Probation right up to the judge who is appointed to sit on the Family Court bench. But while there is no question that the system, with rare exceptions, fails to attract or keep many of the best and brightest, Phil Dobbs is surely one of those exceptions. And what he has to say as he reflects on his long experience in the system raises interesting questions about the very premise on which the juvenile justice system is based—and about the inherent limitations of efforts to change people.

A compact man, graying at the temples, he enters the courtroom with an air of quiet authority and usually leaves it with a dry comment. His wit is as welcome in the atmosphere of the court as it is rare. Everyone seems to like him, whether on the Legal Aid or the Corporation Counsel side, and to respect him. Consequently, he is listened to more carefully than most of those who speak before the court, where he serves as probation liaison officer, presenting the department's recommendations to the judge hearing a case.

In his own office, he is surrounded by posters depicting endangered animals in the wild, scenes of unspoiled nature, and some of the memorabilia of more than two decades serving in various positions in Probation. As he talks, leaning forward over his desk, he seems to have a baby seal over one shoulder, a metal filing cabinet on his other side.

"Most of the kids in this place," he says, "in my opinion—this is obviously not official policy, but in my opinion—are going to get relatively little in terms of rehabilitative value out of what we do—for a number of reasons. One is that there has to be personal involvement of somebody in the system with a kid in order to effect any kind of meaningful change in his behavior. I worked for a special unit in probation that was designed to provide the maximal possible involvement.

"When I was in college back in the Sixties I was trying to find something that was meaningful. You know, that was activist time. And just as I graduated and got married, the Department of Welfare opened up a number of jobs. They were saying, 'Come help the poor of New York.'

"At that time, I was a B.A. I went to school for a lot of years during the Vietnam era and I ended up with some horrendous number of credits, with majors in English literature,

German, psychology, biology, and philosophy. So naturally," he adds with his lopsided grin, "I became a probation officer." The crooked grin is a result of a serious car accident some years ago, but it seems so integral a part of Dobbs's style that it is hard to imagine him ever without it, even when he was young and before a philosophical attitude replaced an idealistic one. It is not that he is a cynic. He clearly believes in doing the best job he can of the work he is doing. But it is just as clear that he does not suffer fools, or what he considers foolish ideas, gladly.

"The disaffected of that period, the overeducated and overqualified, tended to end up in Welfare. There were a lot of people who were just kind of aimlessly drifting, uncertain about what they wanted to do for the future. The certain ones became engineers. The uncertain ones became welfare investigators. And after two or three years of doing welfare investigations on addicts and alcoholics and families in the South Bronx, I was sufficiently jaded so that when an opening came up in Probation, I applied for it—and came to Family Court.

"Now I understood that courts are, by definition, coercive agencies. If people could be relied upon to do what was best for themselves all of the time and each so-called bad action or crime was a mistake, then there would be no need for courts. The premise that courts are founded on is that people are not able to take corrective actions for themselves. Therefore, the courts are there to force that action on them, to compel them to do what is necessary, and also to protect the community. And then there's also the whole codicil about how it's important to protect their rights while this process is going on. 'Well,' I said, 'at last, some firm authority to make people do what's best for them.' And I hopped the fence. I came over to Family Court Probation and since then I've done everything here—investigations, supervision, intake—and now liaison.

"In those years—the early Seventies—the department had an extremely social-work-oriented commissioner who tried a lot of special programs. That's how differential treatment, that intensive intervention unit that I was in, got started. We were taken off staff for eight months and trained in diagnostic interviewing to be able to pick out what kind of a kid we were talking about so that we could match him with a person who would work best with him."

This sounded like the model program for intervention with delinquents, or indeed for anything—selecting and training the best people for the job—and I asked Dobbs how it had worked out.

"It worked out super as far as ending recidivism was concerned," he said, pausing for emphasis before adding, "for as long as the unit was functioning. But it was, I believe, deemed to be rather cost-ineffective since our caseload was five, and the other probation officers were carrying a load of ninety to a hundred cases. Now, granted, these were five kids who were slated to go to training school—that would have been Goshen nowadays—and instead we kept them in the community.

"One of the kids I had had twenty-four petitions at the time that I got him. I mean, he was gone. One of the petitions was for burning a six-year-old all over his body with a cigarette. These were not nice boys we're talking about. One had ten petitions of armed robbery of taxicabs. And I would say that after the first three months I did not have any repetitions of this behavior.

"We worked with them intensely. We saw each one of them a minimum of twenty hours a week. They all had our home phone numbers. They all had been to my house, either in groups or singly. We went on trips out to the beach every summer and around to the museums and the zoos. The youngest of the ones I had was fourteen, and the oldest was just shy of sixteen. All of them stayed with me for the better part of two years, and while they were with me, there was no recidivism."

How, I wondered, could such a success rate be questioned?

"It always depends," Dobbs said, "on what perspective you're looking at it from. The union was screaming that we were a privileged group—they called us 'the elite'—because the other probation officers were carrying a load of a hundred and we were carrying five."

"What," I wanted to know, "were you doing with these kids? I know you were taking them places, but what was happening?"

"Well," he said, "the basic concept was that you would be able to serve as a role model for them; they would begin adopting your ways of doing things and your mannerisms, just as a small child does with a parent. In effect, we would be acting in loco parentis for their social development, which was severely retarded for a whole panoply of reasons, most of these having to do with emotional deprivation as they were growing up.

"My personal belief is that if there is sufficient personal, one-on-one involvement with any individual, you can effect meaningful changes in their behavior and in their level of perceptual maturity. If you've read Piaget, you know he has a whole sequence of perceptual development that children go through. Well, most of these near-adults that we were dealing with were at relatively low stages of that sequence of development, having been stunted there. And the idea was to try to give them tools where possible to raise their level of perceptual maturity.

"I'll give you some for-instances. The levels that I worked

with were the third and fourth levels. The third level is a kid who does not see anyone in the world as a discrete individual. These kids see only types of people. They stereotype outrageously. And they have no ability to empathize. They can't project their feelings. Everybody feels the way they do about things. They're very concrete in their thinking. If you ask them standard open-ended interview questions—like, 'What kind of a person is your mother? What is she like?'—she is invariably fat, thin; the most abstract that we got was 'nice': 'My mother's good to me.' That's the kind of person she is.

"Within each of these levels of perceptual development there were behavior subtypes, based on how they responded to their perceptions. The kind I worked with were the manipulators, the kids who used muscle. They were very unsubtle manipulations. We're not talking calm here. But their idea was to manipulate types of people through what they thought were the rules. 'If you're a cop and I say such-and-such, you'll let me go.' That's the way they functioned, just on that level. And what you had to do with that kind of person was never be what they expected, not be punitive, but not be overly stroking either. And what you had to wait for, the cue for when they were going to begin trying to change was when they gave up on trying to manipulate you according to their own ideas and asked, 'What do you want?' That was when you began to see that they were breaking out of the mold and moving. They were starting to see you as something different from anything that had ever happened to them before.

"As for the level fours, well, there are an enormous number of perfectly functional level fours in our society. The problem is in the behavioral subtypes that result from it. Neurotic acting out was the chief one that I dealt with. They were very challenging people. They generally subscribed to the broader terms of societal values, but they found reason within themselves to justify everybody's bad expectations of them. They had bad expectations of themselves. And they were horribly, horribly difficult to work with. The best form of treatment that I found was in techniques of conjoint family therapy where you act as a translator to them and to meaningful people in their environment, from whom they initially got the bad sense of self, and translate what the other people are saying into straight terms—no hidden messages, no hidden agendas. And after you did that a sufficient number of times over a sufficient period of time, they both began to hear what was being said and it relieved the pressure. Unfortunately, most of the people that we dealt with were not sufficiently sophisticated to be able to internalize this and once the person they leaned on, their crutch, was out of the picture they fell right back into it again." He paused, as though remembering.

"What happened to them?" I asked.

"What happened to them? Four of them are in jail and one of them's dead.

"The one that's dead was a manipulator. Boomer had an IQ of about 60. He was a huge, hulking, incredibly ugly black kid and his thing was panhandling. His mother was schizophrenic and mildly retarded and his father had worked as a brush dyer in Brooklyn for the last thirty years trying to hold the family together. Boomer had an older brother who was smarter and who was always getting arrested and winding up in criminal court.

"Boomer would go out on the street and try to panhandle, but he was a huge ugly kid with such bad manners—'I want money!'—that people would get scared. They'd run away. They'd yell for a cop and he'd get frightened and he'd beat on them, so he'd come in on these attempted murder and assault charges. During the first month that I had this kid he threw an IBM typewriter at one of the teachers in the school-room in the Department of Probation offices. She responded negatively to him when he asked for some crayons and he got mad and threw a typewriter. It didn't hit her, fortunately. But that's the kind of thing he did. And there was no way this kid had the equipment ever to advance beyond the level three that I was amazed he had arrived at.

"So what I had to do with him was just teach him how people would respond to different kinds of approaches. I demonstrated. And you have to give positive reinforcement in order to get any kind of meaningful change. So what I taught him to do essentially was how to panhandle effec-tively, how to be nice, how to approach people, how to mod-ulate his voice. 'Do it the way I do it, Boomer, do it like this.' And he would do it. And after about five or six months he got very good at it. He really did. He made a sufficient living panhandling to help at home."

"Vocational training," I suggested.

"In a manner of speaking," Phil Dobbs said, smiling. "This kid was never going to have a job.

"I worked on it for a year and a half but I never could get him to stop drinking. And what eventually happened— this was after the program had been phased out—was that he got rearrested and ended up in Criminal Court. And that's how I found out about him. He hadn't appeared for a hear-ing. He'd died in the hospital, of cirrhosis of the liver. He was sixteen and a half years old."

Dobbs was silent for a minute and then he looked up and said, "Once I took a vacation—I hadn't had one in four years—and I'd prepared them all for a good month in ad-vance. The unit was set up so that it was like a family and everybody knew everybody else's cases, so that if there was an emergency and one of us wasn't there, the others could handle it, and I told the kids if they had any problems to talk to Chuck about them and I'd be back in two weeks and we could deal with anything then that wasn't heavy and meanwhile I didn't want them getting into trouble. And on the day I was due to leave, old Boomer came walking into the office and stuck out his hand and I thought he was going to shake. So I walked around the desk and I put my hand out and he grabbed me and picked me up off the ground. He's hugging me, crying on my shoulder, saying that he didn't want me to go. I mean, oh, Jesus Christ, good and bad, you know?

"But that's what I mean, to get back to your original question. Yes, you can do something if you're going to put in sufficient effort. But it's almost impossible to put in that kind of effort. I mean, I tell you honestly I was glad when they folded the unit. I would never have asked for it, but most of us were burning out at that point. We were trying to handle these incredibly complicated problems with five different kids. You had to know everyone in their families. And you had to know all of their teachers. You had to know all of their friends, and everybody in all the community agencies they were involved with, and talk with these people and check with them to make sure the kid was—I mean, just the logistics of the thing were overwhelming. Never mind the emotional drain of maintaining a relationship like that. It can be done, but it calls for a commitment that goes far beyond that. What would have to be done is to change the general level of education and the general economics of the areas we're dealing with, the high-crime areas. And where is that effort going to come from?

"Emotional commitment is fine and dandy. However, it doesn't last forever. It burns out and you have to keep hiring to replace people, and you have to offer salaries commensurate with the kind of involvement and effort that's required. Believe me, I know, having been there. The training would have to be enormously detailed. And even then, if all you're doing is putting people—however well trained, however involved—in there to deal with stunted kids without changing the conditions that stunt them, what you do is, you mask the symptom, but the disease remains. We'll go on breeding kids like this."

It is not the laws alone that are at fault for the present mess that is the juvenile justice system, but the perversion of the laws by ideological zealots. What the Supreme Court did in the *Gault* decision was to define minimum due process rights for juveniles. The lower courts, including Family Court, then went about making their own interpretations, adopting those minimum standards for procedural rights or extending them. The problem has not been the *Gault* decision but the extremes to which it has been taken under the aegis of the Legal Aid philosophy, which has pushed for granting juveniles all of the rights of adults with none of the sanctions.

In a number of cases, the Supreme Court has made clear its intention to distinguish between the rights of children and adults, holding that we deal with children differently in such matters as jury trial and reasonable doubt, because while punishment is the purpose of adult incarceration, children are presumably being placed for the purposes of reform and rehabilitation. *Gault* was one such case, a landmark decision that reformed a system that had been in disarray. Until then, there had been no uniformity in juvenile courts; judges enjoyed powers they administered haphazardly at best. *Gault* laid out guidelines constituting a minimum framework for the court system, bringing order and rules to a chaotic situation.

In the years since, the law guardians have used arguments relying on *Gault* to extend due process rights for juveniles, making them equal to adult criminal due process rights. By thus "criminalizing" the juvenile system, they have in one sense moved away from the traditional emphasis on rehabilitation and reform. According to Assistant Corporation Counsel Peter Reinharz, "They have transformed the juvenile justice system into a miniature criminal system minus only the jury trial.

"What the law guardians are doing," Reinharz contends, "is trying to have the best of both worlds. In effect they wear two hats, practice two kinds of advocacy. When it suits them, in fact-finding hearings, they act as criminal defense lawyers. Then at disposition, they act as social workers, asking for what's best for the kid, which they interpret as asking for what he wants, for sending him home.

"This situation has hardened the prosecutors," Reinharz says with some indignation. "They see the inconsistency of saying on the one hand that the home environment causes delinquency, while on the other hand maintaining a presumption against placement. It's the realists versus the theorists."

One example he points to is the law guardians' position that a juvenile suspect cannot be arrested in his own home. In the adult criminal system an arrest warrant alleging probable cause is issued by the court prior to proceedings. But juvenile delinquents—as distinct from juvenile offenders—are not "arrested," they are "taken into custody."

"If a kid is picked up at home," Reinharz says, "all the fruits of the investigation can be thrown out, but there's no such thing as an arrest warrant for a kid. So you can't pick up kids without a warrant but you can't get warrants for kids. And then," he adds, sitting back in his chair with a look of disgust, "Legal Aid tells them that if they're asked in a job interview if they were ever arrested, they don't have to say yes because the euphemism is that they were taken into custody, not arrested."

One of the most significant recent cases in which the lines were drawn between what Peter Reinharz calls the realists and the theorists was *Schall* v. *Martin*, which the Supreme Court heard in 1984. At issue was a challenge by the Legal Aid Society to the New York State Family Court Act's authorization of the use of pretrial detention for juveniles deemed to pose a serious risk of committing a crime prior to their court appearance. The facts as described by the court were these:

"Appellee Gregory Martin was arrested on December 13, 1977, and charged with first-degree robbery, second-degree assault, and criminal possession of a weapon based on an incident in which he, with two others, allegedly hit a youth on the head with a loaded gun and stole his jacket and sneakers. Martin had possession of the gun when he was arrested. He was fourteen years old at the time and, therefore, came within the jurisdiction of New York's Family Court. The incident occurred at 11:30 at night, and Martin lied to the police about where and with whom he lived. He was consequently detained overnight.

"A petition of delinquency was filed, and Martin made his 'initial appearance' in Family Court on December 14, accompanied by his grandmother. The Family Court judge, citing the possession of the loaded weapon, the false address given to the police, and the lateness of the hour, as evidencing a lack of supervision, ordered Martin detained. . . . A probable cause hearing was held five days later, on December 19, and probable cause was found to exist for all the crimes charged. At the fact-finding hearing held December 27–29, Martin was found guilty on the robbery and criminal possession charges. He was adjudicated a delinquent and placed on two years' probation. He had been detained between the initial appearance and the completion of the fact-finding hearing, for a total of fifteen days."

Schall* v. *Martin* was an appeal to reverse the decision in a class-action suit that had been brought on behalf of thirty-one juveniles who, like Gregory Martin, were detained for a week or two prior to a court hearing and then released or placed on probation.

The first question that might occur to one innocent of the byzantine workings of the juvenile justice system is why these boys were sent home *after* the hearings. The legal question, however, was why they were not sent home *before* the hearings—whether preventive detention serves a legitimate function and whether the New York Family Court Act, in allowing it, meets the "fundamental fairness" standard of due process required by the Fourteenth Amendment.

The Supreme Court took the position that "the needs and best interests of the juveniles" had to be balanced against "the need for the protection of the community" and that preventive detention was intended "to protect the child and society from the potential consequences of his criminal acts." It also pointed out that in weighing the state's interest in protecting the community from crime against "the juvenile's countervailing interest in freedom from institutional restraints, even for the brief time involved here," it was appropriate to recognize that "juveniles, unlike adults, are always in some form of custody." Children are taken care of by their parents, are subject to the control of their parents, and, when their parents fail to take care of them, are subject to the control of the state as *parens patriae*. The state thus has the right "in appropriate circumstances" to control the child.

The court went on to affirm the adequacy of existing procedural safeguards to protect the juvenile and agreed with the argument presented by the Corporation Counsel's office that preventive detention was not "used or intended as pun-

*Schall was the name of the commissioner of juvenile justice at the time.

ishment." It pointed out that the statute set a strict limit—
fourteen days—on the period of time a juvenile could remain
in detention and found no justification for the Legal Aid position that detention was being used as "a punitive rather
than a regulatory measure." In conclusion, the court ruled
that New York Family Court's use of preventive detention
was not invalid under the due process clause of the Fourteenth Amendment.

Schall v. *Martin* had an interesting sequel. In the bitter aftermath of the case—Legal Aid deploring the decision, Corporation Counsel applauding it—James Payne, then chief of the
Corporation Counsel's Family Court Division, decided to take
advantage of the information the brief provided to test a theory about preventive detention. Corporation Counsel had
maintained in its arguments before the court that the defendants had been remanded to detention facilities prior to trial
because their previous records suggested that they might not
appear in court or might commit further crimes before their
cases were scheduled to be heard. Lenore Gittis, attorney-in-
charge of the Juvenile Rights Division of the Legal Aid Society, maintained that detention was being used to punish those
who had not been found to have committed any crime.

Referring to the constitutional rights of juveniles, she said,
"Nor can a juvenile legally be detained as punishment—to
teach him a lesson—before he has been proven to have committed an illegal act, although Mr. Payne by his own statements obviously encourages such illegal detention, even for
those arrested for the first time."

It all seemed to hinge on the presumption of innocence
and Jim Payne set out, during his tenure at Corporation Counsel, to discover just how on target or wide of the mark was
the decision to remand Gregory Martin and his co-defendants

on the assumption that they were likely to commit other crimes. As it turned out, it was a bull's-eye.

What the class-action lawsuit made it possible for him to do was track the subsequent criminal careers of the thirty-one defendants. The names of respondents are kept secret and records are sealed in Family Court, but when the Legal Aid Society instituted its suit in 1978 it did so in the name of thirty-one juveniles. Once those names had been made public by the suit, it was possible for Payne to run a computer check on them.

Thirty-one "Request for Records Checks" turned up twenty-four adult "Criminal Record and Arrest Reports"— usually referred to as "rap sheets." There were records on the other seven as well but not every detail of what is referred to as the "pedigree information" matched—sometimes an address was different, sometimes there was a discrepancy in the spelling of a mother's maiden name—and these were discarded. Of the original defendants, then, a minimum of twenty-four of the thirty-one continued their criminal activities into adulthood. Some used as many as eight or ten aliases. Most were versatile, trying robbery, assault, grand larceny, reckless endangerment, narcotics, attempted murder. No one seemed to specialize, although all remained in the crime field, in which they'd gotten such an early start as youngsters. Some of the rap sheets are as long as sixteen pages, with three to five arrests on every page. The shortest one is that of Gregory Martin, whose propensity to commit forcible theft with a deadly weapon—loaded—seems to have been abruptly curbed after only two pages, whether by death or removal to another jurisdiction is impossible to say. The legal system has lost track of him, although he remains immortalized in its terminology.

The fact that so many of these juveniles wound up in prison as adults seems to add some credibility at the very least to the decision to detain them in custody prior to court appearances when they were younger. It also raises the disturbing question of why they were so often released after those appearances. The presumption of innocence seems to have worked against them, robbing them of whatever chance they once had to be changed. Their law guardians had won for them their right to go on being criminals, to wind up in jail, and sometimes to die before their time.

13

In a Later Decade

When and how fifteen-year-old violent offenders are handled in one decade can have an effect on how fifteen-year-olds behave in a later decade.

    —Tracy, et al., *Delinquency in Two Birth Cohorts*

When I set out to write this book, my aim was to provide the reader with a hitherto unavailable view of the juvenile justice system—from the inside; to show how it really works and doesn't work; to expose the internal paradoxes of the system, and the existential corruptions and follies that have eroded the standards and practices of the court, until it hardly serves the community at all and only at great cost in dollars and in human pain.

This chapter, a kind of epilogue, is an attempt to go beyond that view of present problems and describe some possible avenues of remediation that have been proposed by various experts, in an attempt to approach a few of the complicated issues involved. Since really effective solutions can only emerge out of changes in a whole network of social institutions—political, legal, educational, economic, cultural, moral—it is unlikely that any of these piecemeal proposals will have much real effect in themselves. But the reader should be informed about them in any case.

It became clear to me as I gathered the material for this book that one of the catastrophes of modern urban life is the birth of increasing numbers of children to unready, unwed, teenage girls. Almost every case I saw and heard about was a catastrophe sooner or later—multiplied thousands of times, an epidemic of catastrophes resulting in a cohort of psychologically damaged boys, the worst of whom make up the violent few young criminals, and psychologically damaged girls who make up the next generation of teenage mothers.

As yet there are no real solutions, only compromises. Prevention is the only real solution.

Since there is no way we can pass laws regulating pregnancy and childbirth and still remain a free society, we have few options for dealing with teenage pregnancy. How can we influence such basic matters of pleasure and denial in these adolescent girls from fragmented families, many of whom are psychologically disturbed or emotionally immature?

In the past, religious and moral sanctions worked wonderfully well in keeping powerful feelings in check. In retrospect, we can see how effective shame and remorse were as regulators of behavior and inhibitors of social problems. But, whether we like it or not, modern urban America has done away with remorse and shame. And going back is not the answer, even if it were possible.

Religion has lost its hold on the imagination of the urban underclass. Today, for a large class of children, the sources of moral values are TV and films; parental authority is nonexistent, and leadership and developmental models are sought and found in street heroes and among peers.

Given this state of affairs, where can the power to influence come from? Only from a mixed bag of social and economic rewards and punishments—the right combination of

carrots and sticks, beginning as early as possible, oriented toward discouraging early pregnancy and encouraging more
schooling, vocational and career goals, and ethical values that
combine to provide alternative ways of growing up.

The National Urban League's publication *The State of Black
America, 1986* attributes at least part of the discrepancy between black and white income levels to the lack of family
structure, and gives a high priority to reducing the rapid rise
in teenage pregnancy brought about by the climate of greater
sexual permissiveness and the influence of the mass media—
but in particular by the erosion of traditional values that accompany the crumbling of the black family structure. What
is needed are programs "designed to influence behavior by
changing values and enhancing the ability to resist peer pressure." One such is "Teaching Teens to Say No" in the Atlanta
schools, which takes the position that youngsters should not
be having sex rather than teaching them how to use contra-
ceptives. Another is the Male Responsibility Campaign
launched by the NUL in the spring of 1985 to reach young
black males through the media with the message that being
a teenage father is not the equivalent of being a man and that
if they do father children, they must assume responsibility for
those children. How much effect programs like these can
have remains to be seen. It will take a lot to reverse the trends
set in motion by the sexual revolutions of the past quarter
century.

When I asked Richard Garmise for his ideas about solutions,
the Family Court psychologist had a ready enough answer
for what we *ought* to do. "Parents have to somehow be made
accountable for their children—in the schools for instance.
Better than expelling a kid from school—the parent may not
even be home—we ought to bring the parent into the school,

into the classroom, impress them with their own complicity, inconvenience them and maybe even embarrass the kid rather than making him a hero. It would force the parents to pay attention to what the kid is up to, and he'd get a lot more flack from a parent who had to lose time from work. School hours might be longer and vacations shorter, since there's very little of value going on at home and their only organizing experience is in school.

"Television is also critical in these kids' lives. The less intelligent, the more troubled, the more influenced they are, particularly by the dehumanizing aspect of violence in the cartoons, the magical sense that these things can happen and nobody gets hurt. There's no sense of the pain, the actual sequelae for the person who was hurt. The person just disappears." Yes, I nodded in agreement. "But how do we do it? How do we get those parents to be accountable, responsible, involved?" He smiled a wry smile and shrugged his shoulders.

But Dr. Garmise is not alone, even though he may feel that way at times, situated as he is in the front lines of the struggle. In recent years, social determinism has been giving way to the assertion of individual free will among those who think about crime and criminals. Whether or not we can turn around the violent few among the young, and until we learn how, there is a growing consensus among researchers and policy makers in the field of juvenile justice (although not, of course, among legal defense lawyers) that we should reorient our focus to the victim and the community. In a 1981 report of the National Institute for Juvenile Justice and Delinquency Prevention, the authors summarize the findings to date on serious juvenile crime in general and the dangerous few in particular, and make a number of recommendations. They suggest attacking what are understood to be the causes of serious delinquency by strengthening the socializing institutions of the community, starting with the family. At the same time, they suggest targeting high-risk individuals and groups for community-based intervention, stressing that "participation of community residents and utilization of community resources should be maximized. . . . Primary responsibility for preventing its youths from engaging in delinquency should rest with the community." The role of professional and governmental agencies should consist of funding, research and development, and technical and organizational assistance.

As in the case of Head Start, the report suggests that we might find that encouraging community response to community problems solves many more of those problems than are specifically being addressed. The bonds created by mutual responsibility are what is most missing in the communities where youth crime is highest. Efforts directed at the crime problem by families, neighbors, local teachers, businesspeople, and ministers might just connect them with the young and with one another in ways that would in themselves remove part of the problem.

These suggestions call for efforts to bring about far-reaching changes in the communities in question. While we are trying to bring them about, and while we are trying to understand more about the problem of the criminal young, what do we do? How do we stop the violent few? What works? Does anything work?

It is not easy to answer such questions. But present laws make it almost impossible even to study the questions and collect the facts. In 1980, Congress funded the Violent Juvenile Offender Program, and the Office of Juvenile Justice and Delinquency Prevention undertook research projects in five areas with high rates of violent youth crime—Phoenix, Denver, Boston, Newark, and Memphis—to see what could be learned about dealing with the target population of chronic violent juvenile offenders, a definition that had to be expanded to serious offenders when selection criteria failed to provide a large enough sample of violent young criminals: For most of the eligible young, prior records were not available, making it difficult to pinpoint the chronically violent.

It was not that there were not enough violent juveniles around, but that juvenile court policies—such as those of New York's Family Court among others—make it impossible to distinguish them from other delinquents. The lack of records and the sealing of cases prevents researchers, as well as those responsible for the public safety, from identifying the really dangerous criminals among the young—thus explaining the low number of individuals identified, the slow intake, and the necessity of expanding the criteria for inclusion in the study.

We know that a history of violence—early onset and frequency of violent acts—is the best available predictor of subsequent violence, but without access to an individual's history, it is not possible to identify him as a suitable candidate for an experimental program dealing with chronically violent juvenile offenders. It seems then only common sense to open the courtroom to the public and press so that more is understood about its workings. Public awareness is what drives legislation, and an informed community is in a better position to protect the interests of the many as well as the few. The more open the discussion of issues, the better the likelihood of making reasonable policy choices.

Doing away with the secrecy of the closed courtroom should also mean doing away with restrictions on the relevant information available to judges about an individual whose case they are considering. And there is apparently nothing more relevant than the prior record, the criminal history of the youth who commits a brutal crime, as the work of a number of researchers has clearly shown.

We know now from the findings of *Delinquency in a Birth Cohort* and *The Violent Few*, the Columbus, Ohio, study confirming the findings of the earlier Philadelphia longitudinal studies, that violent juvenile offenders are a very small fraction of youth—even a very small fraction of those youth who break the law—and that these juveniles do not typically progress from less serious to more serious crimes. They start out committing serious crimes. Furthermore, for this violent group, "the impact of institutional treatment was basically negative. Time on the streets between arrests diminished dramatically after each institutional commitment." At best, there seems to be no correlation between recidivism and attempts at rehabilitation of the most dangerous violent offenders; at worst, institutionalization may increase the likelihood of future criminality.

The initial study, *The Violent Few*, was followed by *The Young Criminal Years of the Violent Few*, which continued the analysis of the violent young into early adulthood, looking for patterns that might reveal something more about different types of criminals and the crimes they commit and offer some clues for controlling them. Is it possible to identify the most dangerous juvenile delinquents early in their criminal careers? And, if so, once having identified them, what is the most effective way of dealing with them?

Analysis of the Columbus study data revealed no way of predicting individual violent behavior, no consistent pattern of escalating violence in individual juvenile criminal careers that would make it possible to predict who will commit violent crimes and who will not. There is no group of juveniles out there committing only violent offenses. Violence occurs in connection with robberies and other offenses, and appears to be random. It's the chronic character of the juvenile's criminal behavior that is the predictor for the worst offenders. Committing a single crime of violence does not necessarily predict a further career of violent crime; but committing repeated offenses of any kind does, since many of those crimes eventually involve assaults on other people. Therefore, the study suggests, it is the *chronic* offenders who should be the focus of federal, state, and local efforts, from the funding of various attempts to design preventive projects in the community to programs within the existing justice system. These chronic offenders are the boys who start early, go on interrupted only by time spent locked up, and wind up in the adult criminal system.

These findings also call into question the logic of the sharp break that now exists between the juvenile and the adult systems, where, in New York, for instance, a boy may commit an act with relative impunity a day before his sixteenth birthday for which he can be severely punished the day after it. Instead of a "juvenile" system that treats a delinquent boy with leniency and then suddenly closes its books on him when he reaches the arbitrary age of sixteen, seventeen, or eighteen, turning him over to a new "adult" system, we should consider ways of integrating the two systems. Since we know there is a continuity between the chronic youthful offender and the adult criminal, we ought to change the courts, the correctional facilities, and the non-institutional programs so that there is a continuity in them as well. A unified system would create some sense of accountability in the juvenile programs, the results of which could be clearly tracked as individuals grow up and either continue to appear in the court system or stop their criminal activities. This accountability would create some pressure to do things right—to show some results for public money in terms of public good. That means improving the public safety, but it also means improving the chances of some young men growing up to lead useful lives who now grow up to be criminals—or don't grow up at all.

We know what they are like, these violent few, and even something about how they got that way.

We know that these children who are not children, those with an early history of serious criminal and deviant behavior, who attack, rape, rob, sometimes kill, are alienated and hostile, with anti-social values and attitudes, unable or unwilling to control themselves. We know they often come from backgrounds that seem to support their criminal behavior; that they have had inadequate parenting; that the only models they have had for what it is to be a man are those they have found on the street; that they feel no connection with family, school, church, or other socializing institutions of society and have no sense of a stake in the system; that their impulsiveness and poor judgment reflect their failure to grow up. They remain infants in a child's and then a grown-up's body. Missing from their development from the very beginning have been those identifications that define character, create conscience, and organize the mature personality in stable family relationships. Language and thought development have lagged, too, in their chaotic worlds, and, without insight, empathy, or verbal skills, they are not reachable through psychotherapy.

I asked Dr. Garmise what he thought works best with such kids.

"What I think might help," he said, "is a behavioral approach. Any punishment, any attempt at rehabilitation, has to happen very quickly after the act you want to correct, but our system of law is that of due process and what might work from a behavioral point of view is inconceivable legally. It might help if we could pursue all first offenses, not just adjusting them at the intake level. If we had a different kind of system we might say when someone commits a criminal act we are going to pick them up that day, the day we find them, and dispose of the whole thing within twenty-four hours. There would be some sense that something happens as a consequence of the criminal act, not the magical thinking that maybe I won't get caught, maybe it'll get adjourned two or three times. From a behavioral standpoint, it might be more effective to take kids off the street for two weeks at a time right away, immediately, than to futz around for six months and then remove them for six months.

"I think any deterrent impact is completely vitiated by that waiting period. Because what they find is that they can live with this cloud hanging over their heads—I might go or I might not go—and if they get off, it has that much less reality the next time. And not just for them. They tell their friends, 'Look, I made it, it went six months and I was sweating it out, but it's okay. Nothing happened.' I would opt for putting less emphasis on the amount of time you send them away for; I think instead it's the time that lapses between the act for which someone was arrested and the consequence of that arrest that counts.

"Of course, from the standpoint of society, length of placement may count. There are some kids who are going to be criminals no matter what you do, and the longer you keep them in, the safer it is for the rest of us. These are kids who are major delinquents and for them I think there should obviously be longer and more intensive placement. But I've seen kids sent to private placements who continually run away and, for whatever reason, the people in charge feel a loyalty to the kid and not to the society or to the court. They don't really deal with the kid at all and in those cases, I think tougher would be better, for everyone involved."

Garmise may be right. There is some evidence that incapacitation—the euphemism in juvenile justice literature for imprisonment—works. Punishment does indeed seem to be the best deterrent we have found so far for the persistently dangerous delinquent. The Chicago Unified Delinquency Intervention Services project of the mid-1970s studied juveniles sentenced to training schools who had an average of over thirteen arrests with more than eight of them for the most serious and violent offenses. Their later arrest records were compared with those of "reasonably comparable" juveniles who received educational and vocational training in the community or were placed in group homes where they received counseling. The authors of the study found that both kinds of intervention worked. All kinds of placements and sentences, according to the authors of the study, influenced delinquents' perceptions of the consequences of continued delinquency. Prior to placement in one program or another, they had been in and out of juvenile court repeatedly, often for violent offenses, but nothing had ever happened to them. At worst they were expected to show up for a weekly appointment with an overburdened probation officer. They might have had to listen to a lecture from a judge. Not infrequently they may even have been encouraged to "beat the system" by a lawyer committed to their defense and more concerned with their legal rights than with their futures.

Those who were given the less drastic placements were put on notice that the next step for them was the training school. And those sent to the training school were subject to the regimentation and other indignities and pains of incarceration, not the least of which is the inevitable victimization of the weak inmates by the strong. This aspect of institutionalization is not planned, but neither should it be a reason for not using incarceration as a last resort for dealing with those who, as one sociologist puts it, "will have killed, raped, robbed or beat their way into" such places.

The Chicago study found that both the juveniles sentenced to the training schools and those receiving less drastic alternative treatment showed "reasonably comparable" results as measured by number of arrests before and after intervention. In both cases the researchers found a decline in the number of arrests afterward, the so-called suppression effect being 53 percent in the case of the alternative placements and 68 percent for the training school subjects. Their conclusion, which is supported by studies of other programs in California and Utah, is that many kinds of intervention tend to suppress delinquency. Incarceration seems to have the strongest effect, but less drastic residential placement and community-based training programs have an effect too. No one can say for certain to what extent the deterrent effect is a result of the education or training offered in these programs and to what extent it results from the fear of being locked up once all the pains and humiliations of that situation become clear. The authors of the Chicago study concluded that awareness of the possibility of being sent to a locked institution has a deterrent effect both on those who have experienced it and those who have heard about it from others.

So incarceration and the fear of punishment do appear to reduce crime in that chronic group of repeaters from whom the violent few emerge. And while it obviously does not deter that hard-core few, who go on behaving violently no matter what, there seems to be reason to believe it keeps some youngsters from becoming part of their number. Institutionalization takes the worst criminals out of circulation, and the available evidence indicates that it deters some of them and some others as well by showing them that society means business and their criminal acts are likely to have painful consequences.

Deterrence, however, depends on the perception of risk. The penalties have to be severe enough to be taken seriously, but the harshness of the possible penalty is not enough. It is the certainty of the penalty that is most important in deterrence. A documentary film entitled *Scared Straight* was shown on national television in 1979 and again in 1987. It showed the confrontation between a group of adult inmates sentenced to long or life terms in Rahway State Prison in New Jersey, and a group of juveniles brought to the prison in an effort to turn them away from further involvement in crime. In the film, the inmates do indeed paint a frightening picture of the horrors of prison life, including vivid accounts of constant assault, murder, and gang rape by fellow inmates. *Scared Straight* won an Academy Award and was the model for similar programs undertaken by prison administrators in a number of other states.

The claims made by the Juvenile Awareness Project and other prison-based efforts to deter crime by confronting juveniles with adult prisoners are difficult to assess. Very little is known about the thousands of youngsters who have been brought to prisons for these sessions, and there are no controls to give meaning to whatever statistics there are—and there are few. That a taste of prison on one afternoon is enough to spoil the appetite for crime from then on remains debatable. Critics of the Rahway project have maintained that few of the juveniles taking part in it were involved in really serious delinquency. More rigorously designed attempts to measure the effects of such programs in Michigan came up with no significant differences in recidivism between youngsters who had visited the prison and those in the control group, who had not.

However horrible the fate outlined for the boys and girls visiting Rahway State and other prisons by the inmates who confront them there, they can always say to themselves, "Not me. I can beat it." And if there is one thing kids who know anything about the law know, it is that the odds on beating it are in their favor. Which may be why the *Scared Straight* project and similar attempts to impress the young with the horrors of prison life have proved relatively ineffective.

They're impressed, all right, they just don't think it will happen to them. That and the fact that, as one analysis of the project put it, most of them were straight even before they were scared. The youngsters chosen to visit the prison were not by and large those with a past record of serious delinquent acts and might very well have been among those young troublemakers who grow out of it as they grow up. Very likely, the only people who were really scared by the Rahway convicts were those who watched the documentary about the project on television—and possibly the people who made it.

Perhaps the difference between the conclusion of the Chicago researchers that the fear of being sent to an institution acts as a deterrent to some juvenile delinquents and the failure of the New Jersey or Michigan projects to demonstrate any significant effect on juveniles exposed to prison inmates simply means that these teenagers can identify with the fate of others their own age more readily than with that of adults. Few of them are encouraged to plan for their future or even to think about it seriously. To many of them, the future is simply unreal.

Because of the evidence that *certain* incapacitation has some effect on crime reduction and deterrence, in the summer of 1986 the Justice Department's Office of Juvenile Justice and Delinquency Prevention recommended to state legislatures the adoption of a system of fixed penalties for convicted juveniles. The punishment would not only fit the crime, it would be predictable—a probable deterrent factor—and fair, since it would do away with the sometimes whimsical discrepancies that result from judges' powers of discretion in disposition.

The sentencing guidelines would remove much of that discretion from judges and parole authorities. While no one can argue with the equity of the proposal, there is a good deal of objection to its probable effects, which would in all likelihood be to lock up more juveniles in already crowded facilities.

Washington State has already adopted a fixed-sentence policy, but its population and its problems are hardly those of New York or Detroit. However, legislators in both California and Pennsylvania have shown some interest in the point system by which the seriousness of a crime and the age and background of the offender would add up to determine the punishment. A robber's age (a seventeen-year-old could be held more accountable for his actions than a thirteen-year-old), the number of his previous arrests and convictions and the nature of the crimes committed, the degree of the present crime, the time elapsed between the last conviction and the present one would replace the impressionistic judgments and intuitive decisions of child psychologists and social workers that judges often rely on for guidance. And youth agency parole boards could no longer quietly release habitually violent youngsters on a staffer's whim or to free up beds for newcomers.

To the objection that imposing fixed sentences might lead to injustices in particular cases, OJJDP officials respond that judges who feel that a "manifest injustice" would result will have the option of departing from the guidelines as long as they provide a written explanation.

To the objection that incarcerating more young criminals would be expensive, there is no answer. To the familiar complaint that it costs as much to keep a kid in a training school as in a prep school, one can only answer that we hope they learn something there, because it costs much more in victims' lives and victims' suffering to leave them out on the streets.

The only arguments against a policy of fixed-sentence guidelines appear to be the ACLU–Legal Aid Society position that children should be treated differently from adults—no matter that their victims may find it hard to tell the difference—and the position that "the treatment-rehabilitation approach is the hallmark of the current juvenile justice system," as the president of New York City's Family Court Judges Association, M. Holt Meyer, puts it, and should not be abandoned in favor of a punishment–crime control approach.

Judge Meyer thinks it "foolish and socially dangerous" to discard the present juvenile system in favor of the adult criminal-justice model, "which seems neither to rehabilitate criminals nor to deter crime." Can he possibly think that the present juvenile justice system does so? It would, on the contrary, seem to be thoroughly discredited by rising juvenile crime rates, partly the result of larger social conditions—the disintegration of the family, the proliferation of drugs—but at least partly the result of the system's failure to distinguish the violent few from the rest and its inability to deal with them effectively.

As long as the "treatment-rehabilitation approach" remains in place for all juveniles regardless of the nature and number of their crimes, it seems that the violent few will go on committing crimes with impunity while the community suffers. Neither Judge Meyer nor I live in the community that suffers most from the depredations of young criminals—their own—but when I meet people who do, I find there is no question where they stand on the issue. They welcome law and order, have contempt for "the treatment-rehabilitation approach" that returns brutal young predators to their sidewalks and buildings, and pray to be saved from doctrinaire liberals out to do them good.

At the present time, the system seems to teach the violent few that there is almost no chance they will be punished for their first or second offense. Their worst punishment is likely to be having to listen to the exhortations of judges, social workers, and psychotherapists. It is no surprise that they go on doing things for which they pay no penalty and hardly even incur any disapproval. And it is an often-heard conclusion of researchers that "the rehabilitative efforts that have been reported so far had no appreciable effect on recidivism." How can we expect, as James Q. Wilson has put it, to transform the character of "unwilling subjects under conditions of duress or indifference"? All we can hope to do is deter some, remove those we can't deter from the community, and deal with those in ways that offer them a chance to change their behavior but protect the rest of us from those who cannot or will not.

But the violent few represent at most only 7 or 8 percent of all juvenile delinquents. What about the others? Does anything work for them? Can they be helped, rehabilitated, deterred from criminal activity? The evidence we have so far, from the studies discussed here and others like them, is only suggestive. What it hints at is that a small percentage can be helped a great deal and a small percentage cannot be helped at all, but for the vast majority of delinquents, rehabilitation programs have a minimal effect.

Richard Garmise's experience with rehabilitation has made him circumspect and doubtful. "I think there are cases where the rehabilitation really does work—those are the kids we don't see back here again—but there are other questions you have to ask. Suppose we put a kid away. Who's he going to be away with? Who's going to be the staff? That's the big issue. Who's going to do that kind of work? What are you going to pay them? What's the night staff going to be like, the weekend staff? These are the adult role models you're providing. And then, what's the kid going to go back to? I'm not talking about the really terrible violent kids now, but the routine offender. Let's say we rehabilitate him, whatever that means. Teach him to think before he acts. Get him to graduate from high school, give him some job skills, some self-respect, some sense of other people. Then we put him out in this environment . . ."

If, however, you limit the cases to those with the best risk probabilities—concerned parents, non-violent acts—then the evidence is that diversion, the name criminologists and sociologists give to leaving kids alone, works just as well on non-serious first-offenders as anything the system can do. With the young offender charged with truancy, running away from home, shoplifting, and other such status or minor property offenses, policemen and probation officers have been doing this all along. It was only in the 1960s that sociologists decided to find a rationale for this practice and give it a name.

California's Sacramento Diversion Project, which began in 1970, involves juveniles and their families in short-term counseling as an alternative to detention. The project has been replicated elsewhere in the country, and analysis of the data collected on those involved indicates that steering kids away from court and/or offering them some short form of family crisis intervention is just as effective as either unconditional release or going on in the system to probation, remand, or parole. There is no demonstrable evidence that it was the short-term treatment that made the difference. These are the kids who tend to be good risks (as opposed to the violent), and they may just have grown out of it. What we can conclude from the evidence, though, is that sending minor offenders—not serious or violent ones—home is at least as effective as sending them to court.

What about probation? Does intensive parole supervision by well-trained and committed parole officers work? Evidently it works as well as placement in a correctional institution—again excluding those arrested for serious and violent crimes against persons, for narcotics offenses, and the psychotic and severely retarded. Throughout the 1960s, California's Community Treatment Project tried matching young troublemakers with parole officers whose small caseload enabled them to do intensive supervision, a project similar to that described by New York probation worker Phil Dobbs earlier in this book. The results of the California Project are hard to evaluate for various reasons, but what did emerge clearly was that the subjects in the project did no worse than youngsters who spent time in a correctional facility. Community-based treatment may work just as well for nonviolent offenders as incarceration.

What all of the available evidence adds up to is a pair of seemingly contradictory statements. Everything works, and nothing works. The contradiction is only apparent, however, because the two statements apply to different groups. While many kinds of intervention may work to influence the future behavior of most youngsters in trouble with the law, nothing has been found to be effective in changing the kind who make up the small core of repeat violent offenders. The one exception to that "nothing"—and it may be one of the most potent influences on the less dangerous as well—is the certain expectation of seriously painful consequences for one's criminal acts.

My journey through the juvenile justice system led me to some unhappy conclusions. Though the situation need not be hopeless, we need to see what is wrong before we can begin to right it.

The juvenile justice system doesn't work because it is obsolete and inappropriate. The Family Court Act as written in 1962 is designed to cope with 1950s-style delinquents, youths who stole cars, picked off fruit stands, or carried zip guns. Today, confronted with teenagers who commit random killings, robberies, and rapes, beat up old people, and scoff at all authority, it is powerless. It can only find them to have committed "an act that would constitute a crime if commit-

ted by an adult" but for which they are "not criminally responsible . . . by reason of infancy" and can impose only
minimal sentences after "hearings" (not trials) that guarantee
the most minute procedural rights of the accused while ignoring the more general ones of society.

Defining them as children, it emphasizes their age and not
the nature of their acts. As Alfred S. Regnery, former Administrator of the Justice Department's Office of Juvenile Justice
and Delinquency Prevention, put it, violent sixteen-year-olds
"are criminals who happen to be young, not children who
happen to commit crimes." Ignoring the rights of their victims, the present system is based on the idea that they can be
rehabilitated and yet fails to provide the deterrents, structure, and supervision that are the only demonstrable ways to
influence their behavior and thus provide a realistic chance
for eventual rehabilitation. It ignores previous acts and is
concerned with not stigmatizing wrongdoers rather than with
changing them. And all of this goes on without press and
public attendance at the proceedings in order to protect the
confidentiality of the young accused—incidentally assuring
that the excesses and abuses of the system, the incompetence
of officials at many of its levels, and the many ways in which
it fails to work or works against the community's interests as
well as against the real interests of the youthful criminal remain hidden from public view and immune to public criticism and impulse for change.

The influence of the Legal Aid philosophy and of the decisions stemming from *Gault* have criminalized the juvenile
justice system and substituted an emphasis on the legal rights
of the young for what may be in their best interests and those
of their victims (who are often their neighbors) and the rest
of the society. Their legal rights have taken precedence over
their human needs.

But the juvenile justice system is only part of the problem

of the growing cohort of alienated violent young, mostly, although not all, teenage black males from poor and broken homes. The devaluation of traditional morality and the breakdown of respect for all authority has had its influence on other institutions as well. The schools, presented with unsocialized children unprepared for learning, cannot teach them. Given a system that guarantees them many rights but exacts few responsibilities, it cannot discipline them either. Poorly paid teachers and harassed administrators are forced to define pupils as handicapped in order to deal with them, and the dealing, despite the efforts of the dedicated few, consists of more attention to paperwork than to children.

What could we do differently? As James Payne said in a conversation quoted earlier in this book, "I have no easy answers, but I do know what we've tried hasn't worked." Here, then, are some things we might try instead.

To begin with, we should redesign the juvenile justice system so it works more effectively, with less time between arrest and disposition and more emphasis on placement that provides structure and supervision intended to modify the behavior of the violent few or, at the least, removes habitual repeat offenders from the community.

We should increase the likelihood of offenders being caught (more police in the high-risk communities, less obsessive focus on procedural technicalities at the expense of fact-finding) and the awareness that when caught they will be brought to court quickly for immediate disposition of first offenses and immediate incarceration for subsequent offenses.

The nature of the crime and the prior record, not the motivation, should be the first consideration in disposition. For first offenses, there should be penalties in the form of work or fines or restitution to the victim, administered in the community so as not to clog the court calendar. In the cases of subsequent offenses, those who are secured away from the community should also do some form of work that helps defray the cost to the public of their maintenance, not just watch TV, play video games, line up for meals, and work out in the gym. Every repeat offender should know the authorities have a record of his past activities and will use it in deciding what to do with him if he violates the law again. What to expect should be spelled out clearly to all juveniles.

No punishment means a second chance—at the same crimes. For the alienated young who grow up without an internalized code of social behavior, there is no deterrent if there is no external reason not to do anything you can get away with, and the potential criminal is less likely to think twice first. We must stop thinking about crimes of violence as though every mugger were a political prisoner for whom it is crucial to provide the benefit of every conceivable doubt and even some inconceivable ones. The idea of not stigmatizing the young criminal in practice becomes a license to rob and maim.

Family Court, like the adult criminal system, should be opened to public scrutiny, especially now that it grants all of the procedural rights of the adult system to accused youth. It should be possible to observe and report on courtroom procedures as well as on individual judges so as to determine which are incompetent, which behave inappropriately. There are those who never clear their calendar, who leave early for the weekend, who indulge their own fantasies of child rescue at the expense of future victims, or, in other cases, treat first-time young offenders as hardened young criminals. Everyone in the system acknowledges this situation; without public awareness—even public outcry—the system is not likely to change.

And there is a need for change not only in the courtroom but throughout the ancillary systems that serve the court—in

particular Special Services for Children and Probation. Both
of these agencies need to be able to attract better-trained people by paying higher salaries and offering promotions and
raises for demonstrable achievement. Both of their central-
ized bureaucracies need to be restructured into smaller groups
with more accountability, closer supervision, better training,
and less of the mountain of often meaningless paperwork that
is blamed for their high rate of staff turnover.

A committee of legal experts representing a broad spectrum of thought, not just the Legal Aid attitude, might consider ways of adapting—within our constitutional framework
and recent court decisions (not an easy matter)—aspects of
the British system of administrative rather than adversarial
procedure, in which a magistrate has access to all relevant
information and can be assumed to be both competent to
judge and unbiased. (This relates, of course, to the question
of the quality of the present judiciary in our family courts—
usually political appointees.) This approach might be applied
to first offenses and less serious cases, with chronic violent
offenders remaining in a unified juvenile-adult system moni-
tored by an ombudsman, an impartial observer there to guarantee that no one's rights are violated.

Such a suggestion raises the question of whether other
countries have better systems for dealing with juvenile crime.
The social work model directed at the salvation of the errant
child characterizes the juvenile justice system of a number of
other countries, which are sometimes suggested as possible
models for us. In Scotland, a panel of lay participants confers
on the best interests of the child to arrive at a solution based
on "not trial but treatment." In Sweden, there is no court at
all and social workers handle all cases, working with the family. The worst cases are sent to a remand house, a small closed
facility with an intensive rehabilitation program. In other
Scandinavian countries, child welfare boards have replaced

courts for children. In England and Wales, lay magistrates are given discretion over juvenile cases. In Yugoslavia, social welfare agencies do the job. Where this approach is said to be most successful, as in Scotland, the community is cohesive and most children come from intact families. In such communities, it is probably realistic to think in terms of diversion from the legal system of non-dangerous youngsters, reserving judicial alternatives for the very small number of serious repeat offenders.

In England, where social conditions since the end of World War II have been more volatile than in, say, Scandinavia, this approach has had the least demonstrable success. The 1968 government white paper "Children in Trouble" inspired the Children and Young People's Act, the liberal provisions of which reflected a breakdown of traditions and a radical outlook at the same time that—perhaps as a result of the same breakdown—there was an increase in crime by young people.

In this country today, with the high rate of serious juvenile crime found in the urban underclass, the situation is more similar to that of England than that of the Scandinavian countries. The efficacy of state and local programs for prevention and diversion of delinquency from the courts established since passage of the Juvenile Justice and Delinquency Prevention Act in 1974 is still questionable. In recent years, a number of community-based alternatives to juvenile courts and detention facilities, known as Youth Service Boards, have been established. By the early 1980s, there were some three hundred of these groups in the United States, largely supported by private-sector agencies. While so far there are no headlines to be written about their effects, the most promising thing about the Youth Service Boards and similar efforts is probably their problem-solving approach rather than efforts at reform or treatment of the individual. If the family and the neighborhood are the problem, it makes sense to organize ways for families to participate in local activities, involve children with as many adults as possible who provide positive role models in sports and other kinds of after-school programs, and above all revitalize those "mediating structures" somewhere in between individuals and government— churches and fraternal organizations are two examples—that have traditionally helped those in need of assistance to get on their feet and take on responsibility for themselves and their own children.

However, the social policy based on the idea of keeping the children at home works only where there are homes. In this country, the worst of the child criminals come from a part of the society where marriage, family, and home are disintegrating rapidly. The back-to-the-community approach can't be effective where there is no cohesive community— where in fact the lack of one is probably the root cause of the problem.

While federal, state, and local government efforts to revitalize community institutions in the service of the young cannot be abandoned, the real hope can lie only in stimulating the self-help efforts of the members of the community themselves, who are mutually concerned in a way that official agencies of the state can never be.

To call for individual accountability and community self-help efforts is not, as glib 1960s social work jargon had it, "blaming the victim." Fathers who leave their children and take no responsibility for supporting them are not society's victims; they are their own children's victimizers. And while we cannot abandon programs designed to help the too-young mothers of too many children, these are stopgaps at best. It might be possible to diminish the number of neglected and abused children by such means as providing residences for young mothers without husbands or families, halfway houses in which they could be helped toward independence with education in child care, counseling, and job training. But this is only first aid for the walking wounded. Even if these young women are trained to work and jobs are found for them, who will take care of their children? Day-care workers? Leaving other problems aside, the costs of such child-care programs would be staggering, even if private-sector funding is found for some part of them. The real need is to diminish the number of children at risk by discouraging the birth of children to children.

Meanwhile, we must make better use of the schools, the first place to reach the children of the underclass as early as possible. Four should be required and three is not too early to introduce the social skills and cognitive stimulation that not only influence the ability to learn reading and computation but also affect the attitude toward learning as a valued self-motivated activity.

We must redefine the handicapped to exclude the unsocialized who cannot be educated, and free teachers to teach. Faced with disruptive and sometimes violent children and mandated to provide them with an education, schools have used special education classes, established for the emotionally and physically handicapped, as a dumping ground for those they cannot teach, calling them "learning disabled" or "emotionally handicapped." Instead, we should reintroduce a system of non-academic training for those who cannot or will not learn so that they are equipped with some useful skills that enable them to be self-sufficient rather than dependent on or even, in too many cases, preying on society. We should raise salary levels so that the bright and the best begin to compete for teaching jobs.

Today, violent juvenile crime is not just a street problem but a school problem. Robberies and assaults are common in inner-city schools, and both teenagers and teachers are at risk for being physically attacked or having something taken away from them by force. Whenever possible, parents should be made to take responsibility for their children's behavior in school, perhaps by being required to attend for a certain period of time with the child who is a troublemaker. Bills before the Detroit City Council early in 1987 included a 7:00 P.M. curfew for those under seventeen and a proposal to fine the parents of children convicted of crimes up to $500 or impose a sixty-day jail term on them for neglecting their duties. In an age that has focused almost exclusively on individual rights, including those of the criminal, it sounds strange to hear about parental responsibilities, but if parents don't teach their children respect for the law and monitor their behavior, who can? And if a society doesn't back up its expectation that they do so with real sanctions, how long can it last?

Ultimately, we can't adjudicate everything, can't solve every social problem by passing a law. Social changes in a democratic society can only come about as a result of changes in attitudes. If it is not possible, in a free society, to prevent juvenile pregnancy, we can at least stop encouraging it. Financial incentive is one avenue to explore, encouraging young women to think of their future in terms of education and jobs—and only later, marriage and family—instead of premature motherhood. One approach might be to provide young unmarried women with stipends for schooling or job training if they do not have children until a certain age, and providing group residential facilities rather than individual cash payments to those who do. When they do have children, the young men or their families might be held as legally responsible for their own families as adult males are. Reforms of the welfare structure might move in this direction by providing temporary child allowances to two-parent families rather than disproportionately benefiting single mothers, a policy that seems to have unintentionally contributed to the breakup of the family.

It may be possible to change the character of young men with anti-social impulses and no conscience, self-control, or empathy with other human beings. Given what we know about human nature, though, it seems unlikely. And human beings deprived of consistent, responsive care in infancy, neglected and abused, often sexually, in childhood, seem to be devoid of qualities that cannot be provided later. We may wish it were not so, but the evidence is there. To ignore it in favor of moral romanticization of the violent criminal is to degrade his victims, past and future.

APPENDIX

Readers might be interested to know what has happened in the professional lives of some of the men and women who figure in this book since I talked with them:

Frances Anastasi has left Pius XII–NSD and is now with the Victim Services Agency as project director in the Queens Family Court.

Pat Brennan is now executive officer to the Deputy Commissioner for Operations in the New York City Department of Probation.

Phil Dobbs has moved from Manhattan to Bronx Family Court, where he is court liaison officer.

Dr. Richard Garmise has left Mental Health Services and is currently attending law school.

Father Patrick Jordan is no longer at Lincoln Hall. The Archdiocese relieved him of his duties as chaplain and administrator there and transferred him to a nearby church in Westchester, where he serves as parish priest.

Judge Kathryn A. McDonald, after a long career in Family Court, first with Legal Aid and then on the bench, is now administrative judge of Family Court of the City of New York, with authority over the entire Family Court system in the five boroughs of New York City. Judge McDonald was sixty-eight at the time of her appointment to head Family Court and will have to retire at seventy.

James A. Payne left his position as head of the Corporation Counsel's office in Family Court to become commissioner of New York City's Department of Probation. His appointment to oversee Probation's 1,400 employees and its $40 million budget was announced in February 1987. Even before he was sworn in on April 20 of that year, he was making plans to decentralize the system. His first priorities were defined as identifying high-risk areas, deploying field service people in the communities with the greatest problem populations, providing a law-enforcement presence in those neighborhoods, and coordinating community-based services. One of his assistants described the department as "in shock." "There hasn't been so much activity around here," said another, "in the last two years as there's been in the last two weeks." In a system in which skeptics abound, and for good reason, there were those who thought Payne would make a difference and others who thought no one could. Time, it was agreed, would tell. Meanwhile, there was an energy discernible in the department that felt something like a breath of fresh air.

No one—with the possible exception of the enemies that some suggest were created among bureaucrats in a department swept by the new commissioner's broom—would have predicted that in less than four months Payne would be asked to resign and his career in city government effectively ended.

The city's Department of Investigation had found that Payne failed to file both city and state income tax returns for 1983, 1984, and 1985 until after his appointment as Probation commissioner, and then had given incorrect dates for the filings on a financial disclosure statement. For two of those years, he was owed money; for the other, he owed an amount that, with interest and penalties, came to about $150. More serious was the disclosure that he had defaulted on the student loans that had financed his law studies and on which, with interest, he now owed around $10,000. His explanation was sloppiness, a characteristic he admitted to in his personal affairs, though in his professional matters he was meticulous. "I've been professionally responsible my entire career, but my personal life has always been second to my professional life," he said. "That's one of my problems." As difficult as it was to understand a degree of sloppiness that involved "forgetting" a five-figure debt, insiders in city government suggested the facts of the case did not in themselves warrant dismissal. The matter might have been dealt with behind the scenes unless someone insisted on making an issue of it at a moment when the city administration was particularly vulnerable.

It was, everyone agreed, a matter of timing. The offenses were not so serious or even so unusual that they could not have been expected to be overlooked in another time, certainly not made public, leaked to the press, and made the occasion of a request for an immediate resignation. But the administration of Mayor Edward Koch had been rocked for the past year and a half by a series of scandals involving corruption on the part of a number of his appointees to various high city positions, and the mayor could not afford another hint of scandal. Koch had stood by some of his former friends and associates even when they were under indictment, but Payne was a man with few friends in high places, and he probably made some enemies with his blunt ways and his new broom. In any case, there was no one to make a public case for the weight of his value to the department and the city when balanced against his transgressions. He was informed on Friday, July 31, that his resignation would be expected the following Monday, effective at the end of that week, August 7, 1987. Supporters in the department met over the weekend to urge him to fight—to offer a public explanation and an apology for his mistakes and try to muster press and public support for his plans and his programs, some of them already under way. They pointed out that Koch aides had described the discrepancies involved as reflecting a lack of compliance with standards but violating no legal or ethical codes. It was clear, however, that he could not function effectively without the support of the city administration, and Payne decided that he had no choice but to resign. His successor had already been selected.

Referring to him as "first-rate," Mayor Koch accepted Payne's resignation with the comment, "It might have been forgiven in other years, but it couldn't be now."

The only thing that remained to be seen was whether the outcome was more of a tragedy for Payne personally, ending a successful career of more than a decade in city government, or for the city that had lost a leader with the energy and imagination to make a stab at turning around one of its least effective institutions. An aide who had given up a successful private practice to join him only two months before said it best: "He lost, we lost, and all those kids lost."

Peter Reinharz replaced James Payne as chief of the Corporation Counsel's Family Court Division, in charge of all five boroughs of New York City.

Judge Judith Sheindlin has moved from the Bronx Family Court to Manhattan's Family Court, where she is supervising judge of New York County. Many people hope to see her succeed to the position of administrative judge when Judge McDonald retires.

NOTES

INTRODUCTION

Recent trends in juvenile crime across the nation were summarized in an article in *The New York Times* on January 15, 1987. Official figures on crime compiled by the U.S. Department of Justice's Bureau of Justice Statistics and the Federal Bureau of Investigation in Washington, D.C., and information provided by the National Center for Juvenile Justice, a private research organization in Pittsburgh, all indicate a trend toward more serious offenses being committed by younger offenders.

CHAPTER 1

The statistics on juvenile crime in this and later chapters are drawn from a number of studies, many of them undertaken and published with the support of the U.S. Department of Justice's Office of Juvenile Justice and Delinquency Prevention (OJJDP).

One of the most significant studies of juvenile delinquents in this country, and the source of many of the figures on juvenile crime and juvenile criminals in this chapter is *Delinquency in a Birth Cohort*, by Marvin E. Wolfgang, Robert M. Figlio, and Thorsten Sellin (Chicago: University of Chicago Press, 1972). Cohort studies identify a group of juveniles by reference to birth in a specific year or years and residence in the same place during their adolescent years. Once the cohort has been defined, official records, such as police arrest records, are used to establish the delinquent acts committed by members of the cohort. In *Delinquency in a Birth Cohort*, Professor Wolfgang and his colleagues at the University of Pennsylvania used the police reports of delinquent acts committed by the almost 10,000 males born in 1945 who lived in Philadelphia between their tenth and eighteenth birthdays. They found that 35 percent of the cohort had at least one reported contact with the police. The 3,475 juveniles with at least one police contact that resulted in a written report had a total of 10,214 such contacts. Of that total number of offenses, 1,613 (15.8 percent) were committed by one-time offenders; 3,296 (32.3 percent) were committed by 1,234 recidivists (two to four offenses); and 5,305 (51.9 percent) were committed by 627 chronic offenders, juveniles with five or more offenses. A small group of chronic offenders (6 percent of the entire cohort and 18 percent of those with a record of at least one offense) was found to be responsible for a disproportionate amount (52 percent) of all reported delinquency. This same 6 percent was responsible for over two-thirds of all violent crimes and over 70 percent of all robberies.

Although they had collected extensive information on the subjects of the study, analysis of the data did not reveal any reliable predictors of the type of offense a boy was likely to commit next. The researchers concluded that "to prevent the occurrence of serious crimes in a delinquent boy's future, efforts should be made to prevent all forms of recidivism." Of the delinquent members of the cohort (committing at least one offense), only 11 percent served any time in an institution; the average amount of time served was nine months.

Another cohort study that confirmed the Wolfgang study's finding that a small group of chronic offenders committed a disproportionate amount of delinquency was reported in *The Violent Few: A Study of Dangerous Juvenile Offenders*, by Donna Martin Hamparian and her colleagues (Lexington, Mass.: Lexington Books, 1972). Their cohort consisted of 811 boys and girls born between 1956 and 1958 with at least one arrest for a major violent crime in Columbus, Ohio, prior to their eighteenth birthday. In this case, 7 percent of the arrests were accounted for by 239 one-time offenders, 25 percent by the 300 with two to four arrests, and 68 percent by the 272 juveniles with five or more arrests. Hamparian and her colleagues also collected extensive background data on their subjects but were unable to predict which of them would commit further violent offenses. "Our research," they concluded, "is only one of many studies leading to the same conclusion . . . the power to predict is too weak a basis for decision-making." Since there is no way of knowing who will commit violent crimes in the future, the study concludes, there is no way to target a group for incarceration or other attempts at deterrence until they have already committed a certain number of violent crimes. (Criminologists variously suggest that number is anywhere from three to five.) The alternatives are either locking up too many offenders or waiting until they have qualified, so to speak, as chronic offenders. Researchers are currently attempting to devise reliable means of predicting chronicity. Meanwhile, what we do know from Hamparian's study is that a substantial proportion of the small group of serious, chronic offenders continue to commit crimes as adults. Of her sample, those arrested as adults were likely to have committed major violent offenses as juveniles and to have been first arrested at age twelve or younger.

Further confirmation of the original cohort results was provided by follow-up studies which found that a small group of violent offenders was still responsible for most major crimes by the young. Wolfgang and his colleagues studied over 13,000 males born in Philadelphia in 1958 and found that roughly 7 percent of the cohort were responsible for the majority of juvenile crime committed in the years 1969 through 1975. For a detailed description of this study, see Paul E. Tracy, Marvin E. Wolfgang, and Robert M. Figlio, *Delinquency in Two Birth Cohorts: Executive Summary* (Washington, D.C.: OJJDP, 1985). Also see Robert M. Figlio and Paul E. Tracy, *Chronic Recidivism in the 1958 Birth Cohort* (Washington, D.C.: OJJDP, 1983).

In *The Young Criminal Years of the Violent Few*, a report by the Federation for Community Planning in Cleveland, Ohio, for the Office of Juvenile Justice and Delinquency Prevention published in 1985, Hamparian and her colleagues demonstrated the continuity between the chronic violent juvenile offenders in the cohort and adult career criminals, most of whom had been arrested by age twelve and committed at least once to a state juvenile correctional facility.

The birth cohort studies by Wolfgang and Hamparian and their colleagues are recognized as definitive and are all but universally cited in the juvenile delinquency and juvenile justice literature. For a discussion of the findings of these longitudinal studies and their policy implications, as well as of the demographics of violent delinquents described in this chapter, see *Dealing with Serious, Repeat Juvenile Offenders: Report of a Conference, July 30–31, 1981* (Washington, D.C.: OJJDP, 1982).

CHAPTER 3

The five-year follow-up figures on juvenile offenders are from the New York State Division of Criminal Justice Services, "Semi-Annual Report of Juvenile Offenders in N.Y.S." (Albany, N.Y.: Division of Criminal Justice Services, 1982). For a discussion of this data, see Jay S. Albanese, *Dealing with Deliquency: An In-*

vestigation of Juvenile Justice (Lanham, Md.: University Press of America, 1985), p. 118.

CHAPTER 4

Justine Wise Polier's *Everyone's Children, Nobody's Child* (New York: Scribner's, 1941) gives an anecdotal account of young law-breakers in the years before World War II and expresses the reformist outlook of the time. The "wise parent" philosophy was expressed by Judge Julian Mack in "The Juvenile Court," an article that appeared in the *Harvard Law Review* in 1909 (Vol. 23, p. 104). The *parens patriae* doctrine was applied to delinquency cases in 1932 with the decision by the Court of Appeals in *People* v. *Lewis* (260 N.Y. 171, 183). It remained in place until it was repudiated in 1966 by the U.S. Supreme Court in *Kent* v. *U.S.* (383 U.S. 541, 556).

The changing perception of juvenile crime in the wake of the changing nature of the juvenile criminal in recent years was brought home to me during the time I spent doing background research for this book. A computerized literature search at the New York Public Library turned up 130 titles under the heading of "juvenile justice," 496 titles under the heading of "juvenile delinquency," and 135 under that of "juvenile delinquency, U.S." As I looked at the printout of the titles to select those relevant to my project, I noticed a shift from an emphasis in the 1960s and early 1970s on the juvenile delinquent to an emphasis in the late 1970s and early 1980s on juvenile justice. Typical 1960s–70s titles are *They Put Me Inside; Youth in Despair; No One Will Lissen; How Our Legal System Brutalizes the Youthful Poor; The Innocent Victims*, etc. The emphasis is on understanding the criminal in terms of his disadvantages and seeing him as a victim of society. There are many books that deal with street gangs and romanticize gang life and gang leaders. By the late 1970s, this was changing to a view of the situation tending to focus more

284 · Notes

often on the victims of crime, as well as on the problems of the community as a whole, and a concern with what legal and institutional measures to take in order to cope with them. These notes include the titles of many such works.

CHAPTER 5

Charles Schinitsky's statements are quoted in *The Child Savers* by Peter S. Prescott (New York: Knopf, 1981), pp. 65, 79. At the other end of the spectrum of views about juvenile criminals is Alice R. Kaminsky's *The Victim's Song* (Buffalo, N.Y.: Prometheus Books, 1985), a bitter, anguished document that recounts the murder of her son on a New York subway platform and its tortuous legal aftermath. The quotation from the judge in the case is one piece of her evidence for the charge that, for too many in the criminal justice system, "it is possible to care more about the murderer than the victim."

CHAPTER 10

Like many other schools, Lincoln Hall can claim to prepare its students for the next step up the educational ladder. A book about the Prouty murder that deals with the Lincoln Hall and later prison experiences of the killer and his accomplice, Lester Velie's *Murder Story: A Tragedy of Our Time* (New York: Macmillan, 1983), provides some follow-up figures. Shortly after their rehabilitation at Lincoln Hall, seven of their ten cottage mates were in trouble with the law again and runaways continued to leave the premises frequently.

CHAPTER 11

The birth cohort studies are described in the note to Chapter 1. Professor Tracy was quoted in *The New York Times*, December 8, 1985, p. 61. The results of the Carnegie-Mellon study were published by the National Research Council in *Criminal Careers and "Career Criminals"* (Washington, D.C.: National Academy Press, 1986, Vols. 1 and 2). The article about SSC appeared in *The New York Times,* July 20, 1986. Herrnstein and Wilson, a professor of government, are co-authors of *Crime and Human Nature* (New York: Simon & Schuster, 1985). Wilson's remarks here are from *The New York Times,* November 29, 1986. Thomas Sowell deals with black poverty and the black family structure in *Ethnic America: A History* (New York: Basic Books, 1983); *Civil Rights: Rhetoric or Reality* (New York: Morrow, 1984); *The Economics and Politics of Race: An International Perspective* (New York: Morrow, 1983, 1985), and other works. The passage by Selma Fraiberg is from her article "The Origins of Human Bonds," which appeared in *Commentary,* vol. 44, no. 6, December 1967. These ideas were further developed by Fraiberg in *Every Child's Birthright: In Defense of Mothering* (New York: Basic Books, 1977) and *Clinical Studies in Infant Mental Health: The First Year of Life* (New York: Basic Books, 1980).

CHAPTER 12

Merril Sobie's remarks are from an article by him in the *New York Law Journal,* June 16, 1986. Judge Dembitz's comments were contained in a letter to *The New York Times* published there on August 21, 1986. Marvin E. Wolfgang's views here were expressed in "Abolish the Juvenile Court System," an often-quoted article by him that appeared in *California Lawyer,* November 1982. Ernst van den Haag's suggestions for changes in the juvenile justice system appeared in a review entitled "Thinking About Crime Again" *(Commentary,* December 1983). Andrew Oldenquist argued "The Case for Revenge" in *The Public Interest* (No. 82, Winter 1986).

Schall, Commissioner of New York City Department of Juvenile Justice v. *Martin et al.* (467 U.S. 253) was decided in June 1984.

Lenore Gittis's remarks were contained in an angry letter to then Corporation Counsel Frederick A. O. Schwarz, Jr., in which she objected to James Payne's characterizations of the excesses of Legal Aid quoted by me in an article in the *Wall Street Journal*, June 3, 1986.

CHAPTER 13

Analysis of all the currently available data on serious juvenile crime is presented in *The Prevention of Serious Delinquency: What to Do?*, by Joseph G. Weis and J. Sederstrom (Washington, D.C.: OJJDP, 1981), together with recommendations for future policy. Joan McDermott discusses the Violent Juvenile Offender Program in "The Serious Juvenile Offender: Problems in Definition and Targeting" in James R. Kluegel, ed., *Evaluating Juvenile Justice* (Beverly Hills, Calif.: Sage, 1983). Early onset and frequency of violence as a predictor of later criminality are discussed in "Strategic Planning in Juvenile Justice—Defining the Toughest Kids," by Jeffrey A. Fagan and Eliot Hartstone in Robert A. Mathias, et al., eds., *Violent Juvenile Offenders* (San Francisco: National Council on Crime and Delinquency, 1984), p. 39. This volume is a useful anthology of articles on efforts to deal with the most dangerous young criminals and presents an overview of current ideas about therapeutic programs for treating juvenile rapists and murderers as well as accounts of community projects aimed at the prevention of delinquency. It also contains a number of case studies that give some insight into the minds of the young robbers, rapists, and killers whose acts of violence "make them feel better." Among the most dispassionate and at the same time most unsettling of these studies is "A Method for Treating the Adolescent Sex Offender," by Sandy Lane and Pablo Zamora, pp. 347ff. Another glimpse into the mental and emotional life of delinquent boys is a Ph.D. dissertation by Harrell Branche Roberts entitled "The Psychological World of Black Juvenile Delinquents: Three Case Studies" (New Brunswick,

N.J.: Rutgers, State University of New Jersey, 1983 [microform]).

An especially interesting study of violent youth—both because of its depth and its readability—is a 1977 work by Andrew H. Vachss and Yitzhak Bakal called *The Life-Style Violent Juvenile: The Secure Treatment Approach* (Lexington, Mass.: Lexington Books/D.C. Heath, 1979). Anyone who wants to understand the thinking of a young man involved in crime as a way of life and the inappropriateness of most of the strategies now in place for dealing with such youth should read this book (now unfortunately out of print but available here and there in libraries), and in particular the long interview with the boy called Pirate. His own words make unforgettably clear a way of looking at life, of taking what one wants and, "if necessary," hurting others in the process, which the comments of observers can only suggest.

The material in this chapter on the impact of institutional treatment and the correlation between institutionalization and recidivism is from *The Violent Few*, which is discussed, along with *The Young Criminal Years of the Violent Few* and the Philadelphia birth cohort studies by Wolfgang and his colleagues, in the notes to chapter 1.

I talked with Donna Hamparian in the spring of 1987 and learned from her how consistent is the disproportionately small number of dangerous boys responsible for the most serious crimes of violence by juveniles and how many of them continue their criminal careers into adulthood. Hamparian and her colleagues in Columbus had just completed a study of boys committed to Ohio juvenile correctional institutions for felonies and had found that 7 percent of them were repeat violent offenders. Of those who had been released to aftercare in 1984 and were over eighteen years old, 80 percent were arrested again and went on to the adult system.

The results of the Chicago Unified Delinquency Intervention Services project were published by Charles A. Murray and Louis

A. Cox, Jr., in *Beyond Probation: Juvenile Corrections and the Chronic Offender* (Beverly Hills, Calif.: Sage, 1979). Because the UDIS findings differ from what a number of other sociologists and criminologists have said about the effects of institutionalization, confirmation by other researchers is important. The project is too recent to have been replicated by other longitudinal studies because of the amount of time required for such projects, but the results of two earlier projects lend support to the Chicago results. Both the Provo Experiment, comparing community treatment with institutionalization in Utah County, and the Silverlake Experiment, which compared community-based group homes with Boys Republic, a correctional facility in Los Angeles, found both types of placement to act as a deterrent, reducing further delinquency. In the case of the Provo Experiment, the "suppression effect" was 61 percent, and in the Silverlake Experiment it was 72 percent, roughly comparable to the 68 percent reduction in annual arrests found in the Chicago group. A thoughtful description of these and other juvenile delinquency prevention and control projects is presented by Richard J. Lundman in *Prevention and Control of Juvenile Delinquency* (New York: Oxford University Press, 1984). Professor Lundman, a sociologist who coordinates the criminology program at Ohio State University, evaluates the experimental design and analyzes the statistical results of all of the significant current research in the field.

The Rahway Juvenile Awareness Project is analyzed by James O. Finckenauer in *Scared Straight! and the Panacea Phenomenon* (Englewood Cliffs, N.J.: Prentice-Hall, 1982). Judge Holt Meyer's views were expressed in a letter to the *Wall Street Journal* published on July 14, 1986. The letter was a response to the comments by James Payne in my article in the *Journal* dated June 3. Alfred Regnery's discussion of the juvenile justice system appeared in *Policy Review* (No. 34, Fall 1985).

Jackson Toby provides a useful discussion of "Violence in School" in *Crime and Justice: An Annual Review of Research*,

Vol. 4, edited by Michael Tonry and Norval Morris (Chicago: University of Chicago Press, 1983). Special education is roundly attacked by Lori and Bill Granger in *The Magic Feather: The Truth About "Special Education"* (New York: Dutton, 1986). While the Grangers' interpretations of them may not all stand up to scrutiny, the facts and figures they present are informative. The Detroit sentencing was reported in *The New York Times* of January 15, 1987.

BIBLIOGRAPHY

Note: Information on obtaining publications of the Office of Juvenile Justice and Delinquency Prevention (OJJDP) can be obtained from the Juvenile Justice Clearing House, Box 6000, Rockville, Md., 20850.

Albanese, Jay S. *Dealing with Delinquency: An Investigation of Juvenile Justice.* Lanham, Md.: University Press of America, 1985.

Auletta, Ken. *The Underclass.* New York: Random House, 1982.

Citizens' Committee for Children. "Last Chance: Juveniles Behind Bars; a Survey of the New York State Division for Youth's Secure Facilities." New York: Citizens' Committee for Children of New York, 1982.

———. "Lost Opportunities: A Study of the Promise and Practices of the Department of Probation's Family Court Services in New York City." New York: Citizens' Committee for Children of New York, 1982. (Note: The Citizens' Committee for

Children of New York, Inc., is a privately funded, non-profit advocacy group for children who are in some form of publicly funded programs.)

Cohen, Ronald E. "Family Court Advocacy." New York: Office of Projects Development, Supreme Court of the State of New York, Appellate Division, First Department, 1980.

Family Court Act, Articles 1 to 3. *McKinney's Consolidated Laws of New York, Book 29A, Part 1.* St. Paul, Minn.: West Publishing Co., 1983.

Fraiberg, Selma. *Every Child's Birthright: In Defense of Mothering.* New York: Basic Books, 1977.

Gale, Michael R., ed. "Practice Manual for Law Guardians in the Family Court of the State of New York" (formerly "Manual for New Attorneys"). Brooklyn, N.Y.: Juvenile Rights Division, Legal Aid Society, 1976.

Glazer, Nathan, and Daniel Patrick Moynihan. *Beyond the Melting Pot: the Negroes, Puerto Ricans, Jews, Italians, and Irish of New York City.* Second Edition. Cambridge, Mass.: M.I.T. Press, 1970.

Granger, Lori and Bill. *The Magic Feather: The Truth About "Special Education."* New York: Dutton, 1986.

Greenwood, Peter. "Juvenile Offenders," in *Crime File.* Washington, D.C.: OJJDP, n.d.

Hamparian, Donna M., et al. *The Violent Few: A Study of Dangerous Juvenile Offenders.* Lexington, Mass.: Lexington Books, 1978.

———. *The Young Criminal Years of the Violent Few: Executive Summary.* Washington, D.C.: OJJDP, 1985.

Herrnstein, Richard. "Biology and Crime," in *Crime File.* Washington, D.C.: OJJDP, n.d.

Kaminsky, Alice R. *The Victim's Song.* Buffalo, N.Y.: Prometheus Books, 1985.

Kleugel, James R., ed. *Evaluating Juvenile Justice.* Beverly Hills, Calif.: Sage Publications, 1983.

Legal Aid Society. *1986 Annual Report.*

Lundman, Richard J. *Prevention and Control of Juvenile Delinquency.* New York: Oxford University Press, 1984.

McDermott, M. Joan, and Michael J. Hindelang. "Analysis of National Crime Victimization Survey Data to Study Serious Delinquent Behavior. Monograph One: Juvenile Criminal Behavior in the United States: Its Trends and Patterns." Albany, N.Y.: Criminal Justice Research Center, 1981.

Mathias, Robert A., et al., eds. *Violent Juvenile Offenders: An Anthology.* San Francisco: National Council on Crime and Delinquency, 1984.

Miller, Frank W., et al. *The Juvenile Justice Process.* Mineola, N.Y.: Foundation Press, 1976.

Moynihan, Daniel Patrick. *Maximum Feasible Misunderstanding: Community Action in the War on Poverty.* New York: Free Press, 1969.

Murray, Charles A. *Losing Ground: American Social Policy, 1950–1980.* New York: Basic Books, 1984.

———, and Louis A. Cox, Jr. *Beyond Probation: Juvenile Corrections and the Chronic Delinquent.* Beverly Hills, Calif.: Sage Publications, 1979.

National Research Council. *Criminal Careers and "Career Criminals."* Washington, D.C.: National Academy Press, 1986, Vols. 1 and 2.

National Urban League. *The State of Black America, 1986.* New York: National Urban League, 1986.

New York City Law Department, Office of the Corporation Counsel. *Annual Report, 1986.*

Platt, Anthony M. *The Child Savers: The Invention of Delinquency.* Second Edition. Chicago: The University of Chicago Press, 1977.

Polier, Justine Wise. *Everyone's Children, Nobody's Child.* New York: Scribner's, 1941.

Prescott, Peter S. *The Child Savers: Juvenile Justice Observed.* New York: Knopf, 1981.

Sampson, Robert J., et al. *Juvenile Criminal Behavior and Its*

294 · Bibliography

Relation to Neighborhood Characteristics, Analysis of National Crime Victimization Survey Data to Study Serious Delinquent Behavior, Monograph Five. Albany, N.Y.: Criminal Justice Research Center, 1981.

Shannon, L. W. *Assessing the Relationship of Adult Criminal Careers to Juvenile Careers: A Summary.* Washington, D.C.: National Institute for Juvenile Justice and Delinquency Prevention, 1982.

Shireman, Charles H., and Frederic G. Reamer, *Rehabilitating Juvenile Justice.* New York: Columbia University Press, 1986.

Sowell, Thomas. *Civil Rights: Rhetoric or Reality?* New York: Morrow, 1984.

———. *The Economics and Politics of Race: An International Perspective.* New York: Morrow, 1983; 1985.

———. *Ethnic America: A History.* New York: Basic Books, 1983.

Springer, Charles E. *Justice for Juveniles.* Washington, D.C.: OJJDP, 1986.

Stewart, V. Lorne, ed. *The Changing Faces of Juvenile Justice.* New York: New York University Press, 1978.

Toby, Jackson. "Violence in School," in Michael Tonry and Norval Morris, eds. *Crime and Justice: An Annual Review of Research,* Vol. 4. Chicago: University of Chicago Press, 1983.

Tracy, Paul E., Marvin E. Wolfgang, and Robert M. Figlio. *Delinquency in Two Birth Cohorts: Executive Summary.* Washington, D.C.: OJJDP, 1985.

Twentieth Century Fund. *Confronting Youth Crime: Report of the Twentieth Century Fund Task Force on Sentencing Policy Toward Young Offenders.* New York: Holmes & Meier, 1978.

U.S. Department of Justice. "Children in Custody: 1982/83 Census of Juvenile Detention and Correctional Facilities." Washington, D.C.: Bureau of Justice Statistics, 1986.

———. *Dealing with Serious, Repeat Juvenile Offenders: Report of a Conference, July 30–31, 1981.* Washington, D.C.: OJJDP, 1982.

————. *The Impact of Deinstitutionalization on Recidivism and Secure Confinement of Status Offenders: Reports of the National Juvenile Justice Assessment Centers.* Washington, D.C.: OJJDP, 1985.

————. *Juvenile Court Statistics, 1982.* Washington, D.C.: OJJDP, 1985.

————. *Serious Juvenile Crime—A Redirected Federal Effort: Report of the National Advisory Committee for Juvenile Justice and Delinquency Prevention.* Washington, D.C.: OJJDP, 1984.

————. Federal Bureau of Investigation. *Uniform Crime Reports,* 1970 through 1986. Washington, D.C.: U.S. Government Printing Office.

Vachss, Andrew H., and Yitzhak Bakal. *The Life-Style Violent Juvenile: The Secure Treatment Approach.* Lexington, Mass.: Lexington Books/D.C. Heath, 1979.

Velie, Lester. *Murder Story: A Tragedy of Our Time.* New York: Macmillan, 1983.

Weis, Joseph C., and John Sederstrom. "The Prevention of Serious Delinquency: What to Do?" Washington, D.C.: OJJDP, 1981.

Wilson, James Q. *Thinking About Crime.* Revised Edition. New York: Basic Books, 1983.

————, and Richard J. Herrnstein. *Crime and Human Nature.* New York: Simon and Schuster, 1985.

Wolfgang, Marvin, Robert Figlio, and Thorsten Sellin. *Delinquency in a Birth Cohort.* Chicago: University of Chicago Press, 1972.

INDEX